HEALING HANDS OF *Jesus*

WITH LOVE FROM JESUS:
BOOK 1

REKHA VIDYARTHI

Editor: Faye Levow

Order this book online at www.trafford.com
or email orders@trafford.com

Most Trafford titles are also available at major online book retailers.

Printed in the United States of America.

ISBN: 978-1-4669-1430-8 (sc)
ISBN: 978-1-4669-1431-5 (hc)
ISBN: 978-1-4669-1432-2 (e)

Library of Congress Control Number: 2012904990

Trafford rev. 03/15/2012

 www.trafford.com

North America & International
toll-free: 1 888 232 4444 (USA & Canada)
phone: 250 383 6864 ♦ fax: 812 355 4082

CONTENTS

DEDICATION

To God, Jesus, Collective Consciousness and Rainbow Angels—
Thank you for your messages, Answers, teachings, healing prayer and the
process that changes the past lives and shorten incarnations.

PREFACE

"In Jesus' holy name I request protection, clearing, and blessings for the knowledge, wisdom, teaching, and healing provided throughout this entire book. Amen."

My first book, *Emotional Healing with Angels,* is based on the ten year period from 1994 to 2005, during which I was taught how to remove the separation between my inner child and myself, enabling me to create oneness with God, and align my will with God's will. During the past six-plus years since, I have continued to learn under Jesus' guidance by applying spiritual laws throughout my life's experiences and healing of past lives. This book shares the details of my next level of learning and healing at deeper levels. Jesus loves us unconditionally and heals us all if we are willing to learn about ourselves. Jesus and His Angels are teaching and healing us on a daily basis. All we have to do is recognize their presence. They are lovingly guiding us through our own path of growth so we can clear all of our negative emotions.

In order for humanity to heal, be taught, and guided towards attaining Self mastery, many Archangels will occupy chosen human bodies as souls leave this planet, which was agreed upon before birth. Many souls from angelic realms are born as Rainbow and Crystal children to raise human consciousness, which helps to raise the planet's vibrations for the next set of souls, arriving through collective consciousness as Diamond children. They will maintain a higher vibrational pattern for the planet until greater energy arrives, as we transition into the Golden Age.

In order to properly understand the various lessons this book will offer, it is necessary to define certain terms. "Collective Consciousness" refers to a group of souls that have successfully mastered the lessons of each lifetime, having become completely enlightened. "Collective Consciousness" is an entity that has become one with God.

We can choose what we want. If we choose to learn, accept, and heal our karmic debts, then we will be on a path toward Self-awareness. We may have chosen different paths, but our destination is the same because we are all eventually going to end up at ONE place: home with God. We are on a return journey to God. The journey is one of learning, growth, ascension, and Self-mastery that continues infinitely.

Archangel Michael said, *"You are energy, and being energy, you are here, there, and everywhere at the same time. All is happening right now. Some of this life's experiences are definitely destiny. The key thing to know is that you will always be the same energy—your soul will always vibrate the same energy. Karmic things and past lives are happening right now, in this moment. You can choose to change them. It is a misconception of time to call them past lives. Time organizes to have a human existence."*

Healing sessions of many people will be described in this book. All names have been changed to protect their privacy.

CHAPTER 1

NEW COMERS' TEACHING & HEALING WITH JESUS

As I am guided by God, Jesus, Collective Consciousness, and Archangels to convey their wisdom, messages, and healing, these books are born.

This interactive method of healing enables individuals to recognize answers from within themselves, to address their present challenges, issues of anger, guilt, fear, learned behavior, parental imprinting, childhood trauma, relationship issues, etc. The Angels help to awaken the soul's memory through our inner child, where all issues are stored as unconscious memories. When we identify the connection between our outer condition and inner feelings, we are able to realize that we are the creators of our experiences. Once we do that, it will become easy to accept each experience, ask for forgiveness, heal, create Self-love, and make different choices in order to move forward. Our inner feelings may be from our childhood, parental imprinting, or a past life.

Gold Angel: *Angels' healing comes from such a high and pure dimension that it cannot be performed or duplicated by humans. Angels are the healers, not humans. This type of healing shortens incarnations because you are healing many lives by healing one personality, and integrating one fragment of your soul at a time. This is going to be a way of life until all souls on earth rise in consciousness to a point where no one kills any living being, including animals. This will be the path for souls to evolve towards to create a new world of peace.*

The Rainbow Angels are Newcomers to the world. People don't recognize Angels as teachers, ascended masters, sources of infinite wisdom, and way showers whom are assisting and helping all of you in your soul's growth. While Angels are known mostly as messengers, protectors, and healers, society often looks upon Angels as beautiful spirits that save us from harm, but not as Spiritual Teachers and Masters of personal growth.

These teachings provide the awareness needed in order to recognize the hard, analytical work that must be done on the Self to bring understanding of one's own feelings, issues, and patterns of behavior. One connects with his/her Angels, asking for answers and heals the Self through prayer. Depending upon the level of awareness and acceptance you have achieved, you will be able to release karmic debts from many incarnations of many souls through all dimensions in a single healing session. The healing process will shorten incarnations. Many souls will be ascended to higher levels of awareness. The soul will arrive in its next incarnation at that higher level of Divine connection. This is why I AM here to teach you, heal you, and assist you in your soul's ascension. You will learn a lot in one lifetime.

When I am with Rekha, while she is assisting in healing, the two of us become one in her heart. When Rekha is teaching a class, the whole room will become ONE because she will be teaching in SPIRITUAL ONENESS. This is a NEW WAY OF THINKING and UNDERSTANDING the meaning of your life's experiences. You have to create a space for NEW teachings to come in, by letting go of the old.

Life evolves in a SPIRAL, forever expanding and evolving. Every religion, every teaching, every spiritual book, every healing and channeling modality has a place in this Spiral. All that you knew prior to this point brought you here to hear these teachings about this new type of healing. In order for new to come in, you will have to make a choice and space by letting go of old beliefs, mindsets, and teachings. You can release the old by doing a simple exercise: Imagine a blackboard in your mind, write all that you have learned, and erase each thing, one by one. This will allow you to clear your mind in order to learn this new concept of teaching about your anger, fear, guilt and sadness.

Lessons and tests are given through your daily encounters and interactions with others. They are the trigger to your soul. This will make it easier to recognize, heal, and move you to the next point of evolutionary growth on the spiral. This interactive method of teaching will help you remember your soul's agenda and lessons so you can come to a paradigm shift in conscious awareness. You will be able to move beyond the illusion and duality of the physical world.

Every choice has a consequence and you have an infinite number of choices. Wheels of karma are created by a ripple effect. It affects not only your family, society, and country, but also other planets, galaxies, etc. That is why it is so important to know the LAW OF KARMA—the action of cause and effect—the action of one affects the whole and the whole affects one. Once you have paid your karmic debts, you release old energy and resurrection comes about. Resurrection equals ascension.

RAINBOW ANGELS

Each Archangel has a specific task, but they can each perform those of the others. They are interchangeable. All Archangels are healers, masters, and teachers of wisdom. They are extensions of God, and have unconditional love, compassion, and wisdom. They are extremely gentle, kind and loving teachers. When we work with one Angel, we work with all Angels, Collective Consciousness, and Jesus simultaneously because there is no separation of their energies. There are many Archangels. Here are the colors, names and descriptions of some:

Gold Angel—Jesus: God was incarnated in human body as Jesus to create Love in the human heart. Jesus is LOVE and Love is God. Jesus blesses us with Christ Consciousness, wisdom, knowledge, prophecy, healing, God's ultimate clearing and ultimate transformation for soul. He is our Father in heaven—the ultimate home for souls.

White Angel—Metatron: The guardian of Akashik Records; the Book of Life

Violet Angel—Zadkiel: Transformation, change in perceptions with new awareness

Indigo Angel—Raziel: New energy, visionary, love, passion, creative energies to bring in new

Blue Angel—Michael: Justice and truth, helps to clear negative energies

Green Angel—Raphael: Confirmation, healing, and clears confusion

Yellow Angel—Jophiel: Joy, happiness, freedom, and new beginnings

Lime Light Angel—Raziel & Raphael: Heals and clears the body's pain and suffering

Orange Angel—Gabriel: Brings information from other dimensions to humanity and announces God's coming on earth

Pink Angel—Chamuel: Love, peace, compassion, and kindness; our heart's connection to Divine love; a feminine energy

Ruby Red—Uriel: Clears hardened and dark hearts with pure love

CHAPTER 2

HEALING THROUGH
THE FIRST BOOK

HARRY AND MARIA:

Since my childhood, I have seen and conversed with Archangel Michael. Many years later, as an esthetician in a spa in downtown Ottawa, Canada, I assisted my clients in experiencing healing.

I was giving a facial to a client and noticed a tight knot of muscles on his right arm, about the size of a golf ball. When I commented on how tense his muscles were, he told me that he had had this problem for a while and that it sent a shooting pain up his arm. I asked if he was being treated and he replied that he had just received a massage to help relieve his discomfort. I then asked if he believed in God and Angels. He said he did and he was currently on a spiritual path. I asked if he would like me to say a healing prayer for him and he said yes.

I recited Angels' prayer from my soon to be released book, *Emotional Healing with Angels*. At the time, the book was scheduled to be released the next month. It took about two minutes to say the prayer in my mind. As I was praying, I felt the tension in his muscles melt away. All of a sudden, he opened his eyes in amazement and exclaimed, "My pain is gone!" I told him to thank the Angels for healing and continued his facial. He told me that he was in a state of peace like he had never known before. I knew that the peace he described was the result of having been touched by Angels and told him to enjoy it.

He excitedly told everyone at the spa about his healing, so there was much anticipation surrounding the publication of the book. In November 2005, *Emotional Healing with Angels: A spiritual guide to knowing, healing, and freeing your true Self* was published. I brought a few copies into work. As I was placing the books, Maria, the manager, walked by—A voice in my mind told me to give her a copy, so I did. She then gave me permission to sell books at work. Interestingly, two weeks earlier, I had dreamt of books being displayed at work by the girl who usually rearranges the cabinet where they were now placed.

At the spa's Christmas party, Maria was very excited to share with me how the book had impacted her life. She had wanted to wait until after a cardiologist appointment in January, but she was so happy that she couldn't wait. For the past ten years, she had a mild form of a mitral valve prolapse (MVP); a heart disorder in which one or both mitral valve flaps close incompletely when the heart contracts. She had been having yearly electrocardiograms and ultrasounds to monitor her condition and had just been to an appointment before the party.

When she was leaving for the appointment, a voice in her head told her to take the book with her. She thought she might have time to read it while in the waiting room, and put it in her purse. It turned out that she was called in immediately for her ultrasound. The technician studied the monitor, but could not find any problem. After several minutes of searching, he asked her why she was there. She told him it was her yearly MVP check up. The technician continued, and after half an hour, still could not find any problem. He finally told her to go see her doctor and not to worry about anything.

She was so happy, she felt like she was in heaven. She was also amazed because she realized that ultrasounds ordinarily take only ten minutes while this one took thirty. While she was driving home, she heard her deceased mother singing her favorite song. She had no idea how she drove home. Her mother and uncle had passed away from the same disorder. She told her husband about the experience and couldn't wait to get the final word from her cardiologist.

As I was walking to work on the first work day after the party, I heard an Angel tell me that Maria had not thanked them. I replied saying, "Yes, in her excitement and disbelief she forgot to thank you. I will remind her." But I forgot to tell her that day. The next morning I heard the reminder again and apologized, promising to do it that day. I went to see Maria but talked about other things and forgot again! On the third day, I heard them tell me again that Maria had still not thanked them. That time, I asked them to please remind me while I was with her. On that day when I saw Maria, I did remember. She said that she had not thanked them, and did not realize that she was supposed to. I explained that she must thank the Angels for healing her and she promised to do it that night.

Maria's cardiologist gave her a clean bill of health and told her that she did not have to see him anymore. Since then, Maria takes my Angels' book with her everywhere.

ABBY:

Abby came for a facial and told me that she was very confused and felt like she was living under a dark cloud. She had read my book and was aware of Angels' healing, so I told her I would say a prayer that would clear her fears, doubts, confusion, and negative energies. While I was doing her facial and saying the prayer, I discovered a hard knot on her jaw line. I asked her about it and she told me that her jaw was out of alignment because of braces wrongly placed several years prior. She had been experiencing sharp pain while eating for a long time. She was told that her jaw would have to be broken in order to fix it and she didn't want to go through that. I told her I would pray and ask the Angels to align her jaw. I finished the prayer with gratitude, as always.

After her facial, Abby reported that she was able to see and think with clarity and understood why she was wrapped up in confusion. It was her mother's imprinting. She came back a few weeks later for another facial and told me that since her last visit, her pain was gone. In response, I told her that Angels are miracle workers and we must thank them for answering our prayer.

Reiki progresses into an emotional healing.

After my first Angels' healing book was published, I began providing Reiki therapy to clients at the Spa.

LINDA:

Linda did not know anything about the healing energy of Reiki. She just wanted to experience what it was like. I explained it to her briefly and then did an Angel's prayer. I began placing my hands over the seven energy centers. After fifteen minutes, she began to cry. She told me that when she was growing up, her mother forced her to go to church against her wishes. It made her very angry and resentful. She told her mother that she would never believe in God after having beliefs forced upon her. She had a hard time believing in God ever since. I helped her realize that as a result, she was the one suffering, not her mother. She never recognized that before. I went on to explain that we can never live apart from God because our souls will bring us back to him. God is part of our souls. We needed to do further work on the issue to enable her to make peace with her mother and heal her anger. Her little girl needed to change her perspective.

I began Linda's emotional healing by requesting that the Angels bring her inner child to make peace with her mother and that she ask for forgiveness for not seeing the bigger picture. I requested clearing for Linda and her mother in all dimensions and thanked the Angels. After the session, Linda felt lighter, happier, and hopeful towards her belief in God.

This healing process is described in Chapter 6 of *Emotional Healing with Angels*.

DAVE:

Linda shared her healing experience with her friend, Dave. He booked a Reiki appointment with me a month later, saying that he wanted to clear the issues he was having with his wife. I sensed that the issues were his and that his wife's behavior was mirroring his own. He needed to recognize and accept the issues and behaviors in himself. To begin, I asked about his childhood and parental issues with anger. He said that he had been working on his anger for over five years. He believed that it was resolved. He told me that he and his brother were now able to laugh at how their mother used to treat them.

I began with a prayer to request that the Angels bring Dave's inner child. I asked Dave to tell me what the little boy was doing. He said the boy was very angry for some reason. Even though he thought he had resolved his anger, it was clear that he needed to go to a deeper level. To help him understand, I explained that we reach different levels of acceptance about our Self. Healing can only work up to that same level of acceptance. Until we reach total and absolute acceptance of ourselves, without judging others, we cannot heal completely. After that, we worked to help him ask for forgiveness from his mother in order to make peace with the anger in little boy's heart, and requested clearing with gratitude.

Next, he wanted to look at his weight issue and identify where it was coming from. An Angel brought him back to his five year old Self. He saw five year old Dave shrinking until he became two years old with a milk bottle in his mouth, drinking it to its last drop beyond being full. He remembered being praised a lot every time he ate all of his food and drank what he was given. That is the reason why, as an adult, he needed to drink something all the time.

I told him to tell his little boy that he does not have to drink any more once he feels full and that he will still receive praise. We were both surprised when the little boy then handed his half full milk bottle to adult Dave. We thanked him for understanding and changing his habit. Then I finished the session with prayer and thanked the Angels.

It takes many healing sessions and years to heal deeper levels of issues of fear, anger, guilt, and non-forgiveness. Yet sometimes, it takes only one session to release parental imprinting, or learned behavior from an environment. Angels' healing works from the inside out by releasing old energy with new understanding. Healing depends on the individual's level of awareness, self-acceptance and willingness to take responsibility of the Self.

Healing Exchanged for Angel Reading

MAYA:

In May 2006, I wrote an article that was published in a local magazine. Having read this article, Maya came to see me for a healing session. She was quite gifted with intuitive, automatic writing. We wanted to experience each other's gifts. In her healing session with me, she cleared many generations and lifetimes of familial issues and patterns that were handed down from one incarnation to the next. She filled ten extra large garbage bags with her karmic debts and past issues, making peace not only with her parents, but also clearing her ancestors. She was very pleased. Amen!

Maya wrote messages from an Angel: She needs to take it easy on herself and therefore on others. She is definitely on her path. She needs to trust to go southwest. Please release all, all, all of your past, so she can fulfill all of her master tasks. She will be surprised in years two, three, four, five, and six of her own progress. Traveling over the sea's many miles of journey; tracking must meet many, many others and join in collaboration to fulfill her spiritual journey. You must complete grieving to know great sunshine of happiness. Everything begins in love and ends in love . . . move on and love thy Self. Allow air, love, and light through, and through, to clear mind, heart, body, and sprit. You must fly a lot; be prepared for lots of flying. She will be meeting a tall, slim man in two, three, four, five or six years; unknown to her when they meet. They will work together. They are moving towards each other, but still steps yet, depending on choices. The space of time, two, three, four, or five years for the man to appear—a tall slim, very unusual, and different man.

INCREASED SELF-AWARENESS IN THREE SESSIONS—LILY:

Lily had three Angels' healing sessions showing her gradual growth and increased awareness. The first time Lily came to see me; she brought her daughter for healing because she was having a huge anger issue. I did her daughter's healing first and found that the younger generation understands faster. Her daughter accepted her anger and moved forward.

Lily reported that her daughter was happier, doing well in school and less angry after the session.

It took a while for Lily to understand that she was attracting others whose personalities were like her mother's. Her current relationships were repeating her childhood issues. Her mother treated her harshly, controlled her, made her feel guilty and as though she was not good enough for anything. She married a man who behaved like her mother, which triggered this old emotional dynamic.

At first, she was extremely confused because she was very tired from working two jobs and was experiencing a lot of emotional turmoil. I had to explain to her repeatedly that the emotional trauma was the same, but the role players were different. Then I was able to address other issues she had with her mother. She needed to work towards making peace with her mother. Her homework after the session was to write down the details of her session, so that the Angels could give her more answers. She could then continue the process of healing on her own by following the steps as written in the book. She was relaxed, but knew she had a lot of work left to do on herself.

By the time Lily came for her second session, she was already aware of the issues with her mother. She also wanted to deal with a communication issue in her new relationship. She needed to explain a situation to her boyfriend, but found it hard to speak. Her guilt and fear was holding her back. I asked her if she was always trying to please her mother or if her mother made her feel guilty if she did not do what she wanted her to do. She said, "Yes."

I began with the Angels' healing prayer. As Lily took three deep breaths, the Angels brought her to meet her five-year old, inner child. Once she connected with her inner child, I requested that the Angels show Lily where her guilt issue was coming from. Lily saw a house at the end of a long, curvy road. She entered the house and saw an old man sitting alone. He was very sad, lonely, and feeling abandoned because his entire family had left him. He was very happy to see her.

I asked if she knew who he was. She thought he might have been her father. I told her he was not and instructed her to get in touch with the old man's feelings and to tell me if she felt the same way. She agreed that he was filled with guilt, sadness and loneliness and that she felt the same. I explained to her that this was a fragment from that lifetime, still frozen in that dimension. These issues were hers before this incarnation and she chose her mother to reinforce them, so that she would remember and heal them. She understood that she created her own experiences.

I proceeded to heal the old man's issues by telling him that the Angels were going to help him make peace and heal his guilt, loneliness and abandonment. I told him that his family left him so he could accept and heal his issues by looking within to find answers. I requested that the Angels allow him to see how he created his situation by doing the same to others. He understood and was ready to ask for forgiveness from his family and chose to never abandon others or himself again. Then I requested that the Angels clear guilt, anger, sadness and abandonment from every lifetime in all dimensions, filling the core of his being with Divine light.

After that, the Angels integrated this fragment of Lily's into her higher Self and she felt a great peace within. I asked her how her little girl felt then. She said she was happy and playing with a small white dog and added that she always wanted to have a dog like the one she saw. She also said that this session was much more pleasant and joyous than her first one. I told her that awareness grows slowly. In her first session she did not know what her issues were or how to identify the connection with parental imprinting. In this session, she knew her issues so the Angels took her to the next level of awareness. Immediately after that session, Lilly called her boyfriend and said all that she had to say. She was amazed to see how easy it was to express her feelings.

Because she was having difficulty saying no to her coworkers and felt like she was being taken advantage of, Lily booked a third session. People who have issues with guilt are usually not able to say no because they always try to please others, while leaving themselves feeling empty. She hadn't totally accepted her guilt and still needed to ask her mother for forgiveness. Her little girl needed to make peace with her mother. During her first session, she received only a certain level of healing because she had only achieved a certain level of self-awareness. At this point, she was ready to go to the next level of healing and self-awareness.

I began with a prayer and the Angels brought her little girl. The Angels allowed her to put all of her mother's imprinting and mental recording in a garbage bag and told her that she no longer had to please her mother. She learned that her past life personality, which was the same as her mother's, was what brought her to this point. She spoke to her mother and thanked her for coming. Her mother gladly took the garbage bag so that they could free each other.

I requested that the Angel transmute the negative energies into love and light by asking her mother to choose differently than she had before. Lily asked for her mother's forgiveness. Her mother looked happy and very young. Lily's little girl was very happy and playing with the white dog. Together, we thanked the Angels for ending this karmic cycle for both of them.

I recommended that Lily write her sessions down to help her get in touch with her feelings and ask questions about everything that she needed to know. I told her she would be amazed to see how easily answers would come. She would learn about herself on a deeper level than just looking on the surface. Angels give us answers when we do our homework. Angels put thoughts in our minds because we all have Angels within.

CHAPTER 3

PROTECTION PRAYER FOR HEALING

The protection prayer and the process of healing were first given to me by Archangel Michael in 1995, which led to the publication of my first book. Since then, I have been saying the prayer every morning and before going to bed each night. The prayer evolves over time as I learn new healing techniques. Using this prayer as a basis, create your own, based on your needs, issues and goals.

PROTECTION AND CLEARING PRAYER

Thank you, dear God, Jesus, and Angels' team of light. I invite thee into my life to provide Divine light by placing a circle of protection around my soul. I invoke Divine intervention to remove negative energies from the core of my being at the DNA level in every dimension. Bound in strings of Divine Lights, none shall escape, rendered powerless by the All-Knowing, All-Seeing Creator. Please transform them into love and light, filling the core of my being with Divine sacred light. I request DNA decoding, portal closing, clearing, encoding, restructuring and regeneration. I ask for forgiveness from all souls in every dimension, as I understand that I create the incidents in my life as lessons. I request God's ultimate clearing and God's perfection by removing all separation and disconnection with God and Self. Jesus gives a template of oneness, love joy and peace. I release it all into the Divine light of the Creator and the Holy Host. Thank you, God, Jesus, and Angels. Amen

PRAYER OF GRATITUDE

I invite the Holy Host to walk with me in the daily journeys of my life. I ask for guidance and accept all teachings with serenity and gratitude. In so doing, I honor the Angels' presence in my daily life. By accepting my negative experiences as karmic lessons, I understand the truth from my soul's perspective. Thank you for Divine guidance.

1. I am extremely grateful to God for providing my needs and guidance for self-liberation.
2. Thank you for teaching me wisdom and clarity of truth, which clears pain from my heart by seeing God's plan in every experience.
3. Thank you for teaching me how to regain the power of the Self, Self-worth, acceptance of Self, ask for forgiveness, and create love for the Self to ultimately free myself.
4. Thank you for teaching me acceptance so I can live in total and absolute acceptance of everything, everyone, and every situation in my life by asking for forgiveness. Healing, letting go, and releasing are the keys to forgiveness.
5. Thank you for restoring my body at the cellular level, enabling all systems to function in their optimum vibration and harmony.
6. Thank you for teaching me how to be kind, loving, accepting, and have faith, belief, and trust in my Self, so I know that my feelings, knowing, and hearing are the source of Divine whispering truth within me.
7. Thank you for helping me to see my God-Self, for my will and your will are one. We were never separated and never will be. I am forever guided by your will. Amen.

HOW TO PREPARE FOR THE HEALING PROCESS

Spiritual growth in life is the process of becoming aware of the soul's agenda, karmic debts, issues, patterns, past lives, and lessons to be learned. All issues are eventually connected to fear. To begin with, everything in life is created by unconscious thoughts. If you are angry, it is your anger. If you are blaming, it is your anger. If someone is causing you grief, he is opening your repressed trauma or issue. It is necessary to remember, understand, and clear the energy of old issues, your outer condition is a reflection of your inner feelings. If you are reacting to an emotional situation, by taking inventory of your feelings you can identify where the feelings are coming from.

All past lives are happening now and all answers are within us at this moment. Everything is created by our own hands for our growth. Illusion makes us believe others are wrong. If we can accept that we are responsible for everything that happens to us in life, then we are ready to find answers within and the Angels' healing begins.

The mind needs answers in order to change perspective and most answers lie in childhood and past lives. That is why, without exception, it is important to look within for answers by connecting to our inner child with the help of an Angel. The Angel guides us and gradually shows us the cause—why we have created the experiences in the first place, and that the present, negative experience is providing another opportunity to change our perspective by healing and making a different choice.

Souls choose parents according their soul's karmic agendas and personalities. Choosing serves as a memory trigger, so that our souls can begin the journey in search of answers. Many people are stuck in lives throughout which they are repeating patterns and issues such as parental imprinting, family's karma, ego, anger, fear, guilt, sadness and depression. These issues are repeated life after life, until the soul learns its lessons. In the present incarnation, our immediate response will be to become angry at our parents if our parents have not treated us with love and kindness. That is not where the anger began. Archangel Michael said the following words about anger (written in *Emotional Healing with Angels*):

"Blaming others is a projection of your own irresponsibility. To be angry with others is a projection of your own anger. In blaming, the attention gets shifted from the Self to others. It is an easy way out, with no learning. Your purpose here is to learn about yourself, not about others. Shifted focus is looking outside of yourself and ignoring within. This shows lack of honesty, respect, and betrayal of

Self. You are not practicing the teachings, causing you to lose balance. Once you lose balance, you lose everything. Absolutely no lesson is learned in that area. If you make a choice to learn and accept, then the lesson will be learned in that area, field or category."

HOW TO RECOGNIZE ISSUES

RACHELLE:

My colleague, Rachelle, witnessed something upsetting while riding a bus to work. She saw two young mothers with their children in strollers boarding the bus. The children were crying and the mothers kept telling them to be quiet. They shoved bottles into their mouths. One of the little boys kept taking his bottle out and continued to cry. All he wanted was his mother to hug and love him. I told Rachelle that this was her issue. She didn't love herself and her little girl was crying out for her love. She was speaking words from her subconscious emotions.

Her first reaction was that she loved herself and her children. She explained that when she sees something like that she loves them even more. I told her that was because she felt the lack of love herself. She remembered that I had explained before to feel deeper before answering questions. To see how she felt, she closed her eyes and took a deep breath. She said she remembered as a little girl always wanting her mother to hug and love her, but she never did. She realized she still hungered for that. Now that she knew what the issue was, all we had to do was go through the Angels' process of healing and change the energy with Self love so she would never feel that way again.

The next day, we had a healing session. I began with a prayer thanking the Angels for giving Rachelle the understanding to know why her mother chose not to love her, and in return gave her the gift of learning to love herself. I requested that the Angels bring Rachelle back to her childhood to meet her little girl. Then I asked Rachelle to take a couple of deep breaths and tell me if she saw her little girl. She nodded yes. I told her to talk to her and tell her she would take care of her needs, and that she would never let her feel unloved because she would give all of her love to her. I told her to pick her up and give her a big hug until she felt loved and warm. Rachelle spoke to her little girl and made peace with her mother. I finished by saying a prayer thanking the Angels. Rachelle thanked the Angels and told me that her little girl's energy melted into her heart and she felt very warm in her chest.

A few weeks later Rachelle reported that she saw the same ladies with their children on the bus again, this time, without incident. She knew that her issue no longer existed.

This is a perfect example of how judging the behavior of others is a reflection of our own inner emotional conditions, also known as mirroring.

KIM:

Kim, who had attended my workshop, told me she got a lot out of it and asked for a private session. She came for a couple of healing sessions. In the first session, the Angels healed the imprinting of her adoptive parents concerning money and other issues, enabling her to make peace with them. When she came back for her second session, I asked if she had read my book. She said she was reading other books that were uplifting her spirit. I explained that while other books may temporarily help her feel uplifted, they were not teaching her how to clear her issues or heal negative energy, leaving her feeling the same way all over again. She agreed and told me she would begin working on herself. She went on to tell me about an issue that had been bothering her for a while. She couldn't figure out where it was coming from. Her issue was that she takes one step forward and three steps back. She knew it was resistance blocking her from moving forward. I told her we could spend a lot of time talking about it and never figure it out.

It was time to begin a session and ask the Angels to help to give her the answer. She agreed and I began with a prayer requesting the Angels' help. She was brought back into her childhood. When we reached age ten she remembered around age seven. She was walking home from school with her brother and his friends. She overheard her brother's friend telling him that he looked more like he was adopted than she did. This was when she learned that she was adopted and was in shock.

At home she tried to ask her parents but they did not want to talk about it. I asked her how it affected her. She said she began to shut down and felt hopeless. I asked her if she saw and felt the connection between her current issues of taking one step forward and moving three steps back, shutting down and feeling hopeless. She recognized that was the case. I requested that the Angels heal and clear this issue from the core of her being in all dimensions and thanked them.

She was very happy to have found her own answer. She felt very good knowing that she could then go ahead with her plans. I was very thankful knowing the Angels helped to awaken the memory she needed to identify, and then help her heal the issue. This is another example of how behaviors are repeated throughout our lives, and create new situations with the same emotional dynamic.

HELEN:

A mother told me that her teenage daughter Helen had an anger issue. She explained that her daughter had been very sick as a child up to the age of five. I requested that the Angels bring Helen's five year old inner child so she could ask her little girl why she was so sick. In response, her little girl said she was making herself sick to get attention from her parents. I was able to help her see that her little girl never got attention from her parent's and she was still trying to get it by being angry, but it still was not working. She agreed.

I told her that her little girl needed her attention and self love. Her parents created an opportunity for her to experience self love. She had to tell her little girl that she took total responsibility for giving her all the attention and love she needed, and anything else she needed by giving her a big hug and bringing her to her heart so she could rest in peace and feel her love. Then the Angels released the old energy from the core of her being in all dimensions. I finished the process of healing with gratitude. It made sense to her and she felt better.

It is hard to recognize our own issues but if we keep our focus on learning our lessons, knowing that outer experiences are the projection and triggers to our unconscious thoughts, the Angels will provide the answers.

CHAPTER 4

MUTUAL GROWTH WITH SHERRY

I met Sherry at work in Canada in 2006. She is a Reiki master and Yoga teacher. At first, we just talked and I answered Sherry's questions. Then we began doing healing sessions and Sherry's gift of inner sight and communication with Angels began to emerge. When I moved to Florida in January 2008, I continued writing to her with questions and she would reply with answers from the Angels. Here are some of those sessions, questions and answers. I am very grateful to the Angels for placing Sherry in my path to contribute to our continuous learning.

Canada, August 7, 2007—We began with a prayer and gratitude for the guidance.

Rekha: I would like to know about my health issues related to my thyroid and high blood pressure. I think I have a positive attitude and I'm trying to reverse the effects of my previous negative patterns to bring balance. What am I not doing right?

Angel: *You are doing everything right, but not letting it go. It is like a child to whom we are giving a plate of delicious food, yet she is clasping her hands on the plate unable to take it. Unclasp your hands, and don't think of what if, just let it come to you.*

Rekha: I would like to know why my client was having chest pain and unable to breathe or speak during a session.

Angel: *You cannot do much about her. She will have to do it herself. The chest pain is not being able to speak what she went through as a child. It's a little girl who needed to be healed.*

Rekha: How is fear in its highest form is love?

Angel:	*Because it is all the same energy: When all layers of fear are cleared, all there is LOVE.*
Rekha:	What is the difference between God, Angels, Jesus, and spirit guides?
Angel:	*All of them are an extension of "Me" (GOD).*
Rekha:	Is Bipolar disorder caused by angry past lives?
Angel:	*It is many past lives intertwining with each other like a molecule in an atom. The soul is in turmoil. They can live in control with medication.*
Rekha:	Please provide some guidance to follow in my life.
Angel:	*Sit with your legs crossed in a dimly lit room every night to spend time with God.*
Rekha:	How can I deal with a challenging negative person or situation?
Angel:	*You must have trust, courage, and speak the right words through your heart center. Change your perspective and know that you have total control over your thoughts.*
Rekha:	What is the highest experience of self that our soul wants to experience?
Angel:	*The highest experience for the soul is Self-Love. In your true essence as a soul, you are love and the essence of love is freedom.*
Rekha:	For our growth, do we have to commit murders, betrayal, cheating, and other errors in many lifetimes just because that is how the soul evolves?
Angel:	*No.*
Rekha:	Then why have we done all of these things?
Angel:	*Because you did not know that you had a choice and could have chosen differently.*
Sherry:	Why do we always choose such strong events?
Angel:	*You choose to learn your lessons in dramatic ways. You want to experience life's extremes, to test your sprit in the worst way to get the most out of your soul and to quicken the advancement of your evolution.*

Canada, October 24, 2007—Thank you dear God, Jesus, and Angels for providing answers to our questions.

Rekha:	Why do I get stressed when I am writing?
Angel:	*Take the stress and pressure of writing away and it will flow just the way you want.*

Rekha: Does life go in circles?

Angel: *Who told you that? Life goes in a spiral, ever evolving and expanding forever.*

Rekha: What is your will for me?

Angel: *Your will is MY will for you.*

Rekha: Then why did Jesus said, "Thy will be done." There was a silence and the Angels moved away. All that was left was this enormous darkness. In the middle of this dark, thick swirling energy, there was a circle of very bright, vibrant, pink-purple light. Sherry said, "Is it possible that Judas is here?" I replied, "Yes!"

Sherry said, "Judas is saying, you should have had more compassion for souls like his."

I told him that I did, and I helped you out of love and cared for you in your time of greatest need asking the Angels for your healing to ease your pain and suffering. I also told you that it was God's grand plan. There shouldn't be any guilt or shame because Jesus has already forgiven you. Maybe I need to learn more love and compassion, but I am sending you all of my love so that we can release each other.

At that point, in order to identify how Judas came to be in my life, I told Sherry about a client I met in 2005, with whom I became friends. One day she called and told me she was in extreme pain with enormous pressure on her neck, shoulders, back and had stomach cramps. I stayed on the phone praying for her healing to release her guilt, fear and pain for a long time, until she felt better. I had a gut feeling that she was a spark of Judas' soul, but I wondered why I had to meet Judas' fragment and go through this experience. After this, the darkness cleared and the Angels returned. We thanked them.

Canada, November 29, 2007—An Angel began to speak through Sherry saying that there are a few strings left in Rekha's baggage or karmas. Rekha must rest in between treatments to replenish her soul's energy. Deep breathing and relaxing of the mind help enormously to keep balance. In meditation, she must bring her little girl out, and through her eyes, see and hear God's guidance and wisdom. Love her little girl, love herself, and love God.

Then Sherry said, "You are going to meet a man. He is very tall and slender. He is very young looking with a boyish face yet very mature. His voice is very solid, not exciting, kind of serious and heavy. He knows himself so well that if someone questions or challenges him he just says, 'It what it is.' I see him standing in the house, sipping on tea, watching you through a window as you work in the garden of long stem roses . . . a garden of love of your labor. But, there will be some time before you meet." Sherry admitted she did not know where all these words came from! She just had to say them.

Canada, January 15, 2008—We sat down comfortably, thanking the Angels for guidance. An Angel began to speak through Sherry: Rekha, you have attained 93% of joy all the time and 7% of minor human irritations are left. You have mastered the ability not to sway away from the lows and highs of seven percent negative energy. You have a beautiful florescent, translucent, silvery-white lotus sitting in your chest. It is utterly magnificent. You are mentally, emotionally, and spiritually solid. That is an extremely fortunate thing to attain in life. This strength and joy is so powerful that nothing can sway you away from your path. Yet, there are some karmic physical things hanging around you from way, way back in a past life . . . a lifetime of an ignorant man and a warrior. In that time, the barbaric part of the killing and destruction of human life was enjoyed and celebrated. Now you are blaming yourself (guilt), and being hard on yourself. A part of you is not bad. Your soul is pure. Therefore, you are a good person and send love, light, healing, and blessings to the situation of the past.

I asked for forgiveness, and requested healing and clearing of all of those souls I had killed in all dimensions. The Angels changed the past. Then I thanked the Angels. Amen.

Rekha: How do we know our past lives?

Angel: *Every day take twenty minutes for meditation to think and ask about past lives. Do not force it. Think very calmly about your past life and the karmic cause of your present issue, pain, condition, or situation, etc. Keep doing it. The answer and connection of the past life will be revealed to you.*

Rekha: What will I be writing about?

Angel: *You will be writing another book. This book is big with lots of information on souls' past lives and healing. You will be writing about past lives' karmic debts that are in present lives to be cleared, healed and changed. It will take you a few years to write. It will be very laborious work and very detailed. It will be your gift to the world.*

Rekha: Thank you, but I think it will be a gift from God to the world. I began writing this book in March 2009.

Florida, July 2008—PHONE SESSION WITH SHERRY:

Archangel Michael: *You are the total sum of continuous lives lived in this moment of NOW. You are energy, and being energy, you are here, there, and everywhere at the same time. All is happening right now and you can choose to change it. Some of life's experiences are definitely destiny. The key thing to know is that you will always be the same energy, your soul vibrating the same energy. Karmic things and past lives are happening right now, in this moment. You can choose to change it. It is a misconception of time to call lives "past." Time organizes to have a human existence.*

Rekha, you definitely have a few obstacles in your life. Develop trust by allowing yourself to give kindness and healing. Trust how you are going to experience those feelings. Feel the energy. Energy has the awareness. Some may have strong emotional experiences—a difficult lifetime, returning back with the same difficulties, like in your case, slavery. Many other slave lives were repeated. There will be some people who do not have so many of the same lives. It depends on historical, karmic time, social groups, karma of the country, etc. Some of your karma was reacting to the situations that you were in. Living in a certain culture, consciousness has its own intelligence, so it is important for Rekha to experience for her soul's highest good. Then she will choose to keep it or not.

Rekha: Are people who are very sick and suffering, or born with some disease or disability, meeting karmic debts within?

Angel: *If you are suffering from a medical condition, or a child is born with medical condition, it is a more complex issue. When you look at the* *bigger picture, you see that the condition is not about the child or the individual being sick with disease. It is not always about them, but about a family member. If a person is experiencing this energy, each day is a new choice. Every new choice can change the picture. It is simple, but complex. The bigger picture has the potential to change the other person forever.*

Rekha: Why fear, sadness, and loneliness are massive running themes in humans?

Angel: *Choices are made in the very first incarnation, when we don't have an understanding of the potential difficulties with all sorts of energies and their interactions. You cannot comprehend how many universes there are. New ones are constantly being created. Their energies are having ripple effects on you. Consciousness from other universes is interacting with all of you.*

Rekha: How can I live a non-karmic life?

Angel: *Simply remember the purity in you. Use the spiritual energy of your pure soul through actions and deeds until you are completely in light. You held onto truth. You did not denounce it and you kept it open through all of these lifetimes. That is why you are able to accept your lessons quickly in your present life.*

Sherry described a past life: You were a healer and burned at the stake. People were condemning you and poking your body with sticks as you burned to death, but you held onto truth. Children in the crowd saw a bright white light surrounding you, but adults dismissed it.

Rekha: Is destiny karmic?

Angel: *Earth has its own karma. Earth is very small in comparison to other planets. An individual's karma is interwoven with planets, universes and culture. It takes an individual's karmic system to its own destiny.*

Rekha: What is the reason for my friend Nina's current issues?

Angel: *In her past lifetime she was a big woman and an old fashioned mother of four or five children. She was very controlling, very strict, aggressive, and critical. She was very egocentric and behaved as though she knew it all. There was no interaction with her children. They were not given freedom to make their own choices. Prior to this life she had been very* *fearful and submissive, and would not to speak a word about being an abused wife. She was married to an aggressive, controlling, abusive, and critical husband. She decided to become the opposite in her next lifetime and shows both characteristics in her present life.*

All characteristics of each past life intertwine within every soul and create imprinted karmic interactions with other souls. She needs to let go of her past aggression, and release control. That is how it has to be. She can't impose her will. It will take one to five years for her to learn and heal her issues. Rekha, don't give up on her.

Rekha: How many more lifetimes will I come back physically before I will cycle off?

Angel: *You have 2-3 more lifetimes until you cycle off. In these lifetimes, you will die quite young; around 22-32 years of age. You will be teaching in regular school levels of high consciousness. You won't need love because you will know that you are love.*

Rekha: Please explain ONENESS.

Angel: *You are consciousness. You are energy and there is no separation. It is all the same energy in everyone and everything. Beings of light from different universes and dimensions have been placed on earth to guide you through your journey. Human beings of pure light who decide to stay on earth are guiding you.*

Sherry: There was a past life a long time ago. You were seventeen years old and the youngest of three sisters. You had a good heart and good friends. Your oldest sister was very jealous of you, but the middle one always tried to protect you. Your oldest sister told lies about you and a young boy who was just your friend. Upon hearing these stories, your father kicked you out of the house. In those days, women did not work. As a young woman you lacked self esteem and were in shock over losing your family. You felt like nothing, unworthy and unloved. Your sadness rooted from this lifetime of being falsely accused. You did not know where to go and ended up in a place ran by an old man (your husband now). Many young women would sit in a square. Men came to this place to chat with girls, and some went for sexual purposes. You were kept by this old man and remained a virgin. You died at a young age by contacting some kind of virus. An Angel said, *"Healing had to be done on all women as a group who were sitting in the square with you because all souls intertwine with each other, creating cause and effect. Humans do not think that they have a choice or know that they can choose differently at any moment."*

Florida, November 20, 2008—SHERRY SENDS ANSWERS BY EMAIL:

Rekha: According to unresolved emotions that we die with, do we choose the parents to trigger same emotional dynamics in our next incarnation?

Angel: *Yes. Some children are born to parents again to work out karmic issues. Then there are some who are born into a brand new family simply to experience their Selves for the first time. Some children are born to parents with karmic issues of past lives and learning. Some are born more for the purpose of bringing wisdom to their parents. Children who are born without karmic history from past lives will benefit their families the most.*

Rekha: When a mother gives up her child for adoption, it leaves deep emptiness in the hearts of both souls, and a longing to find each other. Is this karmic?

Angel: *If a mother gives up her child, it is possibly because the mother is a wise woman who knows it is in the best interest of the child to experience him or herself. The mother would have agreed before birth to give her child up out of love. Yes. Sometimes it is karmic for the mother, too. Maybe she did not fully appreciate or learn certain things, so she must experience the loss of a child. There is always a reason why people experience what they do. Experiences are not always pertinent to the child's benefit, more to the parents'. And it is not always a karmic situation, but simply for energy to experience itself free of karma with a family. Sometimes there is no karmic connection.*

Rekha: Are people who are very sick and dying working out a lot of karmic debts?

Angel: *A lot of times sickness and suffering is necessary because some people are working on issues, habits, self, and karma. By going within, they become more conscious of themselves and thereby, become able* to heal mind, body, and spirit in all of time and space. Some people are not.

Rekha: Are those who are sick and dying evolving much faster than they could otherwise?

Angel: *A lot of people suffer and get sick without achieving closure through self-realization because they do not consciously choose to be active in their understanding, healing, and interaction. They don't learn that everything is one energy. So no, they are not closer to evolving at all, and yes, they leave the body angry, frustrated, and confused, etc.*

Those who are sick and suffering and choose to see deeper meaning and seek understanding to transcend, potentially evolve faster, which is why any form of suffering is actually a gift. In some cases, suffering gives you a real chance to look within and find your answers, enabling you to move forward. Eventually, you will not need to experience more suffering. To be aware that suffering is the key to unlocking healing at its most powerful level is a blessing.

Rekha: Why is it so hard to remember our past lives, to know what we did to others, when all of these lives are within us? Is there a specific technique by which to remember them?

Angel: *You only need to remember the most important parts that may be important or pertinent to you in this lifetime. You all seem to think that you have to go off and see someone who specializes in past lives, but every one of you has the capacity to sit and simply ask . . . I would like to know if any of my past lives should be revealed to me. If so, please show them to me. Thank you. There is no special way—Ask and you shall receive. Remember that part of searching yourself and figuring out links, connections, and insights to past lives is part of your journey. We give you bits of knowledge when you ask, but we want you to do some hard work too! Information is given in bits, so you can fully explore that issue before the next bit is given. But, you have only to ask us and we will give you bits of your past lives to help you if WE think it will indeed help you.*

Rekha: I think that our karma or errors create so many possibilities for us to choose when and how we are going meet within ourselves for the most growth, no matter how hard it is for us to face them. Facing our mistakes with a positive attitude and changing them, makes our soul evolve the most. Therefore, the negative actions serve us well. Do you have any other way of explaining the importance of karma?

Angel: *For this part of your question, my dear Rekha, you answered it yourself.*

Rekha: Why did I feel homeless for a long time in my life? Is this a karmic situation?

Angel: *You say you felt homeless. Can you see this is your thinking? It is not TRUTH . . . It is just a belief you have. It is not so. You are where you are. This is NOT a past life feeling based on an event. This is simply you thinking and feeling it, and giving it credibility when it is not so. You are home. However, you do have a restlessness of trying to understand. That can bring impatience and a longing to attain FULL healing and understanding, but that feeling is not the same as the feeling you need in order to understand that you are home. You have everything you need and want within you. You do recognize yourself as ACTUALLY moving very fast in spiritual terms, but you want HUMAN manifestation of the feeling of HOME. It is because you are aware you are moving forward spiritually and you want to get there FASTER, but time is not what you think. You cannot equate time and manifestation, as you know it in human terms it is not the same time in spiritual realms and dimensions. Maybe you are already sensing deep down that you are going somewhere SPRITUALY. Relax and be more conscious in every moment and try not to long for home. TRULY feel home right here right now and truly learn to feel that you have everything right now within you. Impatience does not serve you.*

Rekha: Do glandular malfunctions and excessive bleeding tie to a karmic lifetime?

Angel: *Glandular problems or any other type of ailment are proof that something in the person's emotions, mental field, and auric field from past lives may be now affecting them physically. Yes, there are certain characteristics that lead to certain diseases. The important thing to stress is that this is for the individual to explore, figure out and heal from.*

Rekha: Does everyone choose a lifetime during which they do no learning, following a lifetime in which they had a hard karmic life?

Angel: *No. Not everyone chooses a relaxing time in between, very few actually. Energy is always being transformed and often in forms that you do not know yet. There are many dimensions and energy forms that humans are unable to grasp at the moment. A lot of spiritual people at this time on earth are into healing and spirituality, gaining more openness and access to this information. But, we would overload and confuse you if we gave it all to you. You would be frightened because that is most of your ways (fear). It has to come in bits of information so you can fully integrate it.*

Rekha: May I request your guidance for Sherry and me? Thank you.

Angel: *The message for you and Sherry is to continue your search for TRUTH. Also, you, Rekha, can assist Sherry with your questions as they lead her to US. This is important for her understanding and faith. You, my dear, must learn to fully know deep in your heart, NOT always in your HEAD where you do much thinking. You need to know in your heart that you have all the answers, that, in our eyes, you are moving very fast on this path in the areas of understanding, examining yourself, and ultimately, healing to have less suffering. Patience, yes, but it is more than that. You need to cultivate a "knowing" in your HEART. Bring it from the thoughts in your head to settle into your heart, and the TRUTH will be revealed. All questions you have will be answered in your heart.*

I know it is hard for you to understand, but it is more important to us for your spiritual evolution, as you put it, than any human manifestations that you want. You are moving forward very well. We are so pleased with your urge to KNOW everything. Just relax and BE, and draw your energy down from the thinking mind into the place of truth, which is your heart. All answers lay there for you. With love, Rekha, if you want to hear us say you are doing well, then we can say that you are doing very well, and so much better than you think!!! In this last part of your life, you are moving very fast in your understanding. If you want more . . . you know only to ask.

When the time comes for you to pass from this world as you know it, you will have reduced your suffering, and so will take considerably less suffering into your next lifetime. You will have done a very, very good job in this lifetime, not only for yourself, but especially for your family and friends. We can never see in our lifetime the effects we create, but again, TRUST that you have had and will continue to have a huge impact on others' lives. Good work Rekha.

Sherry: Wow! That was a lot. Did you notice that was not me writing? It was interesting to have to write so quickly and be aware at the same time that it wasn't me. At times, I wanted to write a different word thinking that you may not understand theirs, while they insisted that I say it as they said it. Blessings and deep awe for this exchange between us. Much gratitude to you and the Angels for their love and help—Sherry

Florida, January 27, 2009—Thank you, Jesus, for providing wisdom and the answers that we seek. We are grateful for your guidance. Amen.

Rekha: How can I assist those individuals to get in touch with their inner children who are unable to get in touch with their feelings and knowing? Is there anything else I can do to assist them?

Jesus: *You need to remember and know that you are doing all you can to assist them in their journey. You can only GUIDE them and bring to their attention NEW WAYS OF THINKING AND HEALING, but they have to be ready to heal and do their work by themselves. This is not like taking a spiritual aspirin. They, too, have their journey and you guide them . . . You are the guide. Let go of feelings of inadequacy, trust that the individual got what he needed at that time.*

Rekha: I would like to have calm and positive interaction with my friend Nina. What can I do to achieve that? Is she compromising her truth in her relationships?

Jesus: *Your friend does not take advice from anyone! She is stubborn and does not want to hear about what she may or may not know, or that something she thinks she knows is wrong. Remember, as much as you want to impart your wisdom and insight to her, she still needs to grow and mature and is not ready to hear you. This can only cause conflict between you both. She needs to respect you more.*

If you allow her to be mistaken in some of her thoughts and actions, and can release the urge to help her so much . . . then this releasing

and letting go will be what causes her to release her stubbornness and negativity with you. This also applies to your children, let go of worry for them and the tension will naturally loosen its grip between you.

Her issue is not that she is compromising her truth. She just has to learn to be more flexible, more understanding of others, and less stubborn. She is still young and not fully experienced. She is more concerned with being right than respecting others who know better than she does. She needs to learn to be respectful of others who have different thoughts. There seems to be inflexibility in her attitudes. She needs to learn to be understanding of others. This is an area in which you all have to mature, experience, and gain understanding. You can be respectful and respected in your truth and still honor yourself and others. It is a fine line between understanding and being flexible and speaking your truth. She will balance this out as she ages and becomes wiser.

Rekha: I feel that I am trying to avoid writing and am not moving forward because I am confused about what to write and how to begin.

Jesus: *You need to discipline yourself and sit down to write. Let go of worry, so creative inspiration has room to enter you and then the answers will come about what to write. This is your time to write and communicate more about your original book. Write your new books so that when the first one takes off, you already have a second one ready to move on the heels of the first, to keep the momentum going. You must be clear in your head and free of all worry. Then you can create space in your heart and mind for the answers to what type of subjects to write about. You need to get clear now, or as soon as possible, because the energy is good for you to write quickly now.*

Rekha: How can I tell the difference between a feeling created by my own thoughts, and a feeling that comes from a past life?

Jesus: *This is a hard one because sometimes we do make things up and attach meaning to them. Then we understand it and heal it. As long as you understand the issue and the meaning that should be attached to it in order to reach the goal of healing, it does not matter whether the feeling is truly from a past life, collective past lives, or a product of your own thoughts!!! It isn't important if it is real, or if it is just* *curiosity and the desire to attach yourself to it. For example, this is my past life, my this, my that, and my everything else—you see, it is ego. Even an imagined one leads to more understanding of your Self and always has the same result: leading you to healing and wisdom.*

Rekha: Could you please explain the role of past lives, karma, and freedom of choice? Are people consciously aware that they are meeting karmic debts within? Do we choose when we are going to meet our karmic debts within?

Jesus: Yes. *Many people are conscious of having met a karmic debt, both good and bad karma. Remember that the universe knows the bigger picture as to how, when, and where you are to have these debts paid. Each person can, at any moment, have the potential to have freedom, but few achieve total spontaneous freedom. Each energy is specific, yet, at the same time, is connected to the whole. Energy is constantly moving, so the key word is POTENTIAL. Energy has the potential to heal and change karma at any time. There is no set answer because energy is not set. It is constantly changing and moving.*

Rekha: Do crystals increase vibrations when used in healing?

Jesus: *If you choose to use them, they can help, but no more than you asking your Angels for guidance with each client. Never underestimate the simple power of prayer and guidance. Anything else is just a tool. Just remember that you, in particular, have an affinity with prayer. Your call to prayer is a very strong link and you can access very accurate information from the Angels and stay connected with them. This is a very powerful source for you. Remember, you will have more healing and wisdom come from prayer and Angels. You are deeply loved.*

Rekha: Please give us guidance, thank you.

Jesus: *Both of you need to let go, get out of your own way, not be in the mind, and connect more with your guides, especially Sherry. Also, Rekha, you still need to let go of worry. It stands in the way of your writing and ability to get more clarity, answers, and more trust. Trust more Rekha; accept, let go, and trust. Let go of the small things and be big. Be all that you can be. Worrying makes you small and makes it difficult for you to be tall in your own power and truth. Stand tall Rekha, and stand in total trust. Remember to stand in your truth and not allow others to effect or diminish you, especially family. You are deeply loved, Rekha. Please keep encouraging Sherry as she wavers and doubts too much.*

Florida, March 5, 2009—Thank you, Angels, for your wisdom and loving guidance. Amen.

Rekha: How can we make peace with our karmic physical pain, knowing that we must have caused others the same pain in a past life?

Angel: *Do not judge. The soul wants to experience all emotions and therefore, it is your individual minds that judge and create your karmas. You may have chosen a difficult karma for someone else, so, in fact, it was chosen out of love, even if your behavior causes that person or situation much grief. Remember that you don't know the reasons behind each karma. It is often complex and intricate, as it weaves its thread between individuals and nations.*

Rekha: Are we multidimensional souls?

Angel: *You are infinite souls, but you all don't have words to explain FULLY what soul is, so you cannot at this point in time FULLY understand the nature and substance of soul. You are all still limited by words to explain many things of this world.*

Rekha: Karma seems to be a much bigger subject than I thought because souls have many fragments and many past lives are connected to family karma, society, country, nations, planets and galaxies. Do we all take some of these karmas?

Angel: *Yes. There are many types of karma as you say. But you all take on many aspects of the varying strength of these karmas. For example, if you run through a big pool of honey, some of you will run faster, and less will stick to you, while some will trip and it will be in their hair and faces and they will feel the stickiness more. Understand, yes, it is all honey—one energy—with many outcomes as to how much stays with someone and how much stays with someone else.*

Rekha: Is good karma called sanskar in Sanskrit?

Angel: Yes. Sanskar is the word for credit karma.

Rekha: Why do our DNA threads get disconnected and why do Angels slowly reconnect them to raise our vibrations? Are karma and DNA interconnected?

Angel: *This is still being investigated and scientifically explored. As far as you think you have come in your understanding of DNA, there is much left for you to discover. It is of such magnificence that if you did understand the significance of DNA, it would frighten you. The learning of all* *information, especially through scientific means MUST be a gradual process of discovery. Otherwise, it would overwhelm your system and you simply could not fully understand the power, possibly for generations to come. Because yes, Rekha, you are correct; it has its origins from other galaxies. Yes, karma and DNA are inexplicably linked.*

Yes, Angels are very much softly, softly nudging you, helping you, and guiding you. Some of you understand that far beyond the understanding you already have, there might be forces out there that you can get a glimpse of through channeling, but this information is generally far beyond what any of you could comprehend. It is not important to understand these matters yet. When respected and used for good purposes, only then can this information be understood. First, millions of people must raise their vibrations, work towards an uplifting of spirit, and make connections with God together. As this energy from humans grows in time, you will ALL be ready, not just a few. You will all be ready to receive more information about God.

Rrekha: You said, right now on earth, beings of light from different universes are guiding us. Are they in energy form?

Angel: *The beings of light are in many forms, but as I said before they would overwhelm people if they revealed themselves. Sometimes by accident, humans have realized that these beings are not humans, and people have specifically channeled and tuned into them. It is often too frightening and overwhelming for their human systems to see them. These occasions are sometimes heavenly, which is overwhelming to humans. They become scared because they don't fully realize what they are experiencing. You are all too immersed in FEAR. These experiences usually initiate great fear. There are governments that have more knowledge than you realize, as a result of having done many, many explorations. They are desperately fearful because they do not understand what they have seen.*

It is not time at all to reveal much. As I said before, collective population must shift in masses. The more people who can raise their consciousness and connect to God, the easier it will be for the next phase, until ultimately consciousness of the human race can merge.

There were and are many, many species. You humans are not ready to take on the fullness of this.

Rekha: Is human ego connected to our karma as well?

Angel: *Ego and karma are completely different entities. Each has a very different function. Both are necessary and both must be explored, overcome, and transcended.*

Rekha: Someone said that animals are created for human consumption. Is this true? I don't think it is.

Angel: *You eat meat because of how you evolved. It became part of your cellular memory, so you have continued the behavior. None of you need meat. Some of your bodies crave it because it is in your DNA and memory. In time, your body will not crave meat and you will find and satisfy the body with alternative sources of nourishment. However, the way humans eat animals also has an effect. Those who respect and bless the animal have less karma than someone who eats a hamburger from McDonald's and does not know how it was killed.*

Rekha: Why are fear, loneliness, and lack of love massive running themes throughout mankind?

Angel: *The running theme of these emotions is so prevalent because there is so much negative energy in the universe. Humans are such dense energy that it is a good and easy exercise for the spirit to struggle and overcome. These are very heavy emotions in humans. They are there for a reason. Remember, as humans overcome these tendencies the energy of other universes will also be changed. As we refine this negative, heavy energy into pure, positive, faith oriented energy, it extends into space. Other universes and races that struggle with negative energy are in turn enabled to purify their energy, to get into balance and alignment with God. Humans are one of the heaviest energies. Remember, you cannot experience positive without experiencing negative.*

Rekha: I would like to know the meaning of my dream. I was watching a big man standing in a river. He saw my husband and me, and challenged my husband to a fight. I told him not to listen to the man, but he went. Within few minutes, the big man held him under the water. I couldn't watch him gasping for air, so I turned my face away feeling helpless. Does this indicate a change in my husband's consciousness?

Angel: *This is actually his awareness trying to fight through and overcome his physical ailments.*

Rekha: I have an issue that sometimes I am not hearing and seeing Archangel Michael, only feeling him. How I am creating this block?

Angel: *You can hear, feel, and see him only if you believe that you can. Remove the fear that you can't. Trust, trust, and trust in your Self. Change your language from I can't hear, feel and see to I wish I could. Change the negative to a positive. WHEN it doesn't happen straight away, THAT is the time to choose to have FAITH that it will. Then you will hear, feel, and see him as you wish to. Remember, he is at your RIGHT side and whispers in your RIGHT ear. Ask him to make his presence known to you more. He is always guiding you. Connect with him and ask to feel him more. Know that he is right beside you.*

Rekha: If Sherry uses her gifts to assist others in their spiritual growth, what can she call it? Do you have any suggestions?

Angel: *Humans like labels. You can call it Energetic readings or angel readings. It doesn't matter what you call it, as long as your intention is true. Then we will all be there for you.*

CHAPTER 5

HEALING PAST LIVES #1

In January 2008, I moved to Florida. I read other books and learned many things to increase my knowledge and self-awareness. I started working in a new age spa. Angels began to send people who needed their help and healing.

DONNA:

In October 2008, I met Donna. She was going through a difficult divorce. She started asking questions and I answered them. Then she asked for a session. I began with prayer and the Angels awakened her memory as I asked what was going on in her life 10 years ago. Through every event she described, she could connect her emotional condition to her childhood or to parental imprinting.

For the first time, Donna recognized her issues and the parental imprinting that was repeated throughout her life. When we got to five years of age and established a dialogue with her little girl, I sensed Jesus' presence and told Donna that for some reason Jesus was there for her healing. I asked her if she knew why. She told me that as a little girl she always wanted Jesus to love her. I told her that he was there to fulfill her wish and heal her. Then Donna saw Jesus put her little girl on his lap and love her. He said to her, "Suffer not little one unto me." He loved her as much as she wanted, as long as she wanted, and was with her through eternity.

Jesus told her, "Rekha is a teacher of truth. You are very fortunate to have found her. You are safe with her and you are in good hands. You will find your path." After that, Jesus told her that his death was karmic. We thanked him, and finished the rest of her healing with her parents making peace with them. We thanked Jesus and the Angels.

MUTUAL GROWTH WITH GINA SESSION # 1

I met Gina in January 2009. She is an intuitive reader and massage therapist. She needed to clear her emotional body so we agreed to an exchange. On February 3, 2009, she came for a session. I began with prayer and the Angels guided her to see that her financial issue had its roots in her childhood environment. She agreed and said that there was never enough money as she was growing up. She saw then that it was parental imprinting and mental recording. They always told her that there was not enough money.

The Angels started to show her incidents as I brought her back to around the age of 30-31. I asked her what came to mind. At 31, she was going through a divorce. The treatment she received from her husband was similar to how her father treated her as a child. Moving back to age 21, she was having miscarriage after miscarriage. When I asked her to tell me how she felt, she had a whole list of adjectives: not good enough, unworthy, unloved, inadequate, afraid of failure, empty, etc. She added that her mother made her feel these emotions up to the present time.

We moved back to ages 10-15. Her family arrived to the U.S. from Cuba when she was seven. As the oldest child, she was pressured to learn English, which she did fairly quickly. Through the young ages of 10 through 15, she had to take care of her younger siblings. She had to take care of their paperwork for school, plus her own studies, and house work. She was still, to this day, taking care of everyone. She was sick and tired of it!

Then she met herself as a five year old. I told Gina to hold her hand and explain to her that we were going to work with her parents and the Angels were helping us to release their imprinting. The little girl's heart was filled with fear and she refused to face her parents. I requested that the Angels show why she chose her parents. She moved into a life of prehistoric times. She saw herself as a young, pregnant woman being beaten to death by the same mother. I asked her why? She became pregnant by a man from another tribe. She said she felt the fear of losing her baby, mixed with anguish, pain, anger, and rage as she and her baby died from being beaten by her mother. She never asked for her mother's forgiveness, either in that life or in her present life. She was continuing to repeat the same issues of fear, anger, and guilt in many lives.

She asked for forgiveness because her soul knew that somewhere, somehow she must have created this experience to meet within. Then she moved into another life when horse carriages were the means of transportation. She described her father as a wealthy, prominent man. He sexually abused her. When she protested and had a lover, he locked her up in a room without food and water. She banged on the door and asked servants for food and water, but the door was never opened. She died of starvation.

Again, we saw the pattern of her anger, anguish, fear, and being controlled. She experienced intense, emotional trauma during many lifetimes. When I asked if she was tired of carrying this karmic burden, she said she was more than ready to let it go. She had been working on herself for a long time. I wanted to know if her little girl was ready to deal with her parents then. She was ready. The little girl was holding onto Gina's hand, tightly, as if for dear life. I asked who she wanted to deal with, first. She chose her mother.

The Angels gave the little girl a garbage bag and gave her time to fill it. When she was done, she asked for forgiveness and gave her filled bag to her mother. The Angels cleared both of them. I told Gina to see her mother as a soul who chose darkness for her soul's growth. Inside her dark energy she was a pure being of light. As soon as Gina saw her mother as a being of light, her mother was filled with Divine love and light. She chose the light and was gone.

Then we approached her father with his bag. She told him that she had come in peace with the help of the Angels to clear their issues and imprinting, to free both of them. I told him that he could choose differently, just as Gina was making new choices for herself. She saw her father as dark energy. A huge Angel was standing behind him putting his hands on his shoulders. Her father broke down saying that he did not know any differently. He did not know that he could choose anything other than what he knew. The Angel cleared him. Then I requested everyone's healing through prayer and thanked the Angels.

At this point, Gina's little girl felt freedom, joy, love, and peace. She was in a state of Nirvana. The Angels gave her a white dove and it perched on her finger. Gina felt the whole universe open up, layer after layer, dimensions after dimension and galaxy after galaxy. The multitudes of angels started to pour in singing in celebration for the freedom of their souls.

Each dimension had its own vibration and sound. When the next dimension opened, more angels poured in. Musical notes changed into higher vibrational notes, then blended into each other, creating celestial music. Dimensions continued to open. Angels continued to come in, and music continued to blend into higher and higher frequencies, until the very high, dimensional vibrational notes opened up, almost next to God. The angels in this dimension are like diamonds—translucent with magnificent, infinite facets of light. The light was so bright, it could blind human eyes.

The infinite, dimensional Angels said, "Rekha, you need to look into the diamond's characteristics and qualities. Remember that diamonds come out of carbon and carbon is very black and dark. Within its heart comes this beautiful precious stone. So no matter how dark a soul, no one is left behind in the ascension process. Because you are able to see and find the light, or diamond within a dark soul, you hold the key to ascension as a facilitator for Infinite, dimensional Angels. Once you accept this, you are already there. The shift has already begun. You will be teaching this method of healing to others."

Gold Angel (Jesus) said, "Go beyond mind so you can reach heart. In truth, you will reach the diamond within. You will need to do a lot of work with tuning forks to break down the lower frequencies of the root chakra where energies are stuck in many of souls. We will be sending many souls to you of this nature. Today is a new reality of the manifestation of your truth because all the rest was your illusion. Do study characteristics and qualities of the diamond to know what we have assigned to it through its multidimensional vision."

When we finished, Gina was still in a peaceful state with her little girl holding a white dove on her finger. She saw a small pot of gold overflowing with coins. At the very moment she was thinking that the pot was awfully small, the Angels made it very big and it continued to still overflow. I told her that she now knew the meaning of her physical experiences. She needed to practice what she learned instead of reacting with negative behavior because the Angels would be testing her for those issues and patterns of anger, unworthiness, and fear. These are tests of self-awareness. It means all this time she was just reacting with her pre-set emotions. After her session she was able to be aware of the issues and chose differently.

The following week her tests began. She was sick, but she was aware of her lessons. It is a slow process. Along the way, an individual learns faith, trust, patience, self-love, humility, gratitude, and appreciation for every lesson. The Angels continue to work with us, showing us answers until we reach total and absolute acceptance of our Selves. At that point we clear our separation from God.

GINA'S SESSION # 2

Gina's second session took place a week after her first. Jesus, also known as the Gold Angel, came to assist us. When I asked her which issue she wanted to focus on during the session, she chose fear of success. That showed me that she was working on another level of fear, so I requested a garbage bag. Gina chose an extra large garbage bag and began putting all kinds of fears originating from her childhood, present and past lives, and other sources into the bag. The bag was filled to the top.

I then recited the next part of the prayer: I invoke Divine intervention, binding negative energies in cords of Divine light. None shall escape, rendered powerless by the all-knowing all-seeing Creator. As I spoke these words, Gina saw a white dove fly from her finger. When she saw it, she felt badly thinking her Angel was leaving her. Instead, the dove circled around the top of the garbage bag and began to tie it up with threads of gold and white Divine light. I continued my prayer. Please transform all negativity into love and light, filling the core of her being with Divine sacred light. Her vision continued, seeing the dove flapping its wings, propelling the bag forward, sending it into Jesus' golden heart. He then changed the negative energy from the bag into pure, Divine Love. The white dove then returned to the little girl's finger. I finished the prayer, asking for healing, cleansing, forgiveness, and blessings for all souls. We thanked Jesus and his Angels.

This was an illustration of the prayer—what goes on behind the scenes. Prayer always works, whether the individual sees Jesus and his Angels in action, or not. Healing is an ongoing process, during which, we may experience the same issue many times, until it has been cleared on all levels.

At the end of the session, the **Gold Angel spoke through Gina and said,** *"People continue talking about the second coming of Christ, but they don't realize that he has already come because he is with each and every one of you. He already came and died in his first life. His death was karmic because the minute he took a physical body, he needed to experience what it entails to be a human. Going back to karma, he needed to experience meeting within, due to some bad choices, and he also took upon himself some of humanity's karma—so called "sins." That is why he needed to experience such a gruesome, physical death. But, once the debt of karma was paid, he was resurrected into a new body. That is what ascension is all about. Once you have paid your karmic debts, you release that energy, or vibration, and resurrection comes about. Resurrection and ascension are one and the same because your vibrations become higher by releasing the old energy."*

Rekha: Does the soul have many lives in each soul age cycle, such as infancy, toddler, young child, adult, and elderly? Each of these age cycles has many levels and each level has many lifetimes. Do we create most karma during our toddler and young child soul cycles?
Gold Angel: *Yes. I will describe the answer using the best example I can think of. You develop certain skills during your preschool years. Then you graduate to the next grade or level. It doesn't matter what the age of a soul is. If you choose not to learn, you repeat the grade, and of course, as you go through higher grades, the material becomes harder and more complicated. Some pass, while others don't. There is no comparison. When you compare one soul to another, you belittle*

yourself and others. You are unique and have chosen differently. Therefore, you should not compare your soul to another's. Some of you go faster and some of you go slower. Some learn faster during childhood. Others learn slower and later. Humans limit themselves with linear time. When humans develop the ability to let go of perceiving lifetimes in linear time, they are able to see that all is happening simultaneously. You can create what you want at this very moment. Like attracts like; as your vibrational frequencies become higher, you will lose the people around you. It doesn't make them inferior, nor does it make you superior, or vice versa. There is no comparison, but at some point in time, you will meet again because everyone is given the opportunity to raise their frequencies.

We re-establish the connections within your DNA, gradually on a daily basis. It is a slow and gentle process because your bodies are stuck in third dimensional dense energy. We have to go slowly in order to not do damage to your physical bodies. Sometimes you understand it in the spiritual sense, while the physical body still has aches and pains. You have to love yourself and accept that it has been taken care of. A lot of human frustration comes from not trusting that there is a process. If you get everything fast, there is no appreciation. Many people have been punishing themselves because of being controlling, and the lack of patience with regards to respecting the process. They are angry. This is why they are stuck and not moving forward. Look at the animal and plant kingdoms because they understand and accept the process unconditionally. They are totally connected.

Rekha: Do animals have a separate heaven when they die? I ask this question because I had a vivid dream that I was in "Animal Heaven." The first thing I saw was a bull dog chewing his food and talking at the same time saying, "I wanted to share my story with you."

I told him that dogs don't talk in human voices. He said, "Yes, we do."

I asked, "Why can't you let go of your food and talk."

He answered that he can't because his owner in his earthly incarnation starved him to death and now that he has food, he can't stop eating.

Then I saw some cows in the distance and one of them started to come close to me. I stopped her because she was so huge and I felt fear being so little. She said, "I am not going to hurt you. I only wanted to tell you my story."

I said, "Ok tell me your story."

She said, "I was on a farm and I gave a lot to the farmer and his family by producing a lot of milk and babies. The farmer killed all of my babies for money. Then I became old and of no use to the farmer so he killed me and made more money."

Both of them were sad because of how they were treated by humans, but they did not show any anger. They wanted me to hear about the unkind treatment they received at the hands of humans.

Then I moved into the cat section. There was a big mountain and millions of cats were everywhere. I saw a cat dragging her hind legs. I asked, "Why are you in this condition?"

She said, "A car ran over my back and I died like this."

Then I saw a security vehicle with two officers inside. One of them saw me and said to other, "What is she doing here?"

As soon as I heard that, my dream was over and I woke up.

Gold Angel: *They are more innocent and pure than humans. They have higher consciousness than humans are unable to attain. When animals are taken to a slaughter house, they know what's happening and feelings of terror are imprinted in their cells. When you consume them as a meal you are consuming their horror, fear, and disease. That is why humans suffer so much disease. Overindulging, greed, hurting others for self-gratification creates karma. God's plan is perfect. He provided you with everything you need. When birds wake up in the morning, they sing greetings of gratitude to God without worrying about their daily food. They know that everything is provided for them. The same is so for each of God's creations. It's just like the grass. It has a process. It grows and provides food and shelter for creatures. Each living thing supports each living thing. If I have provided for animals, so have I provided for humans.*

Humans have decided to play God. That is why disease and karma have been created. Your actions dictate your lessons. It is a lack of respect and separation from light. Free will is the ability to choose with no interference. Humans make poor choices; hence, the birth of karma, which is a law of cause and effect. Wild animals kill what they need to sustain life. They leave nothing to waste. There is always a balance. Everyone has a purpose in serving each other to grow and sustain.

Humans really made it challenging for themselves by the choices they made. You chose to move away from light. Your choices will provide challenges to teach you lessons. Every time a soul chooses an incarnation it chooses a set of lessons. During that lifetime an opportunity will come up to experience and learn those lessons. If at one time you choose not to learn that lesson, you will pick it up the next time or times. Therefore, you have free will to choose where and when you want to learn that lesson. You cannot run away from your lessons knowing that you will have the experiences needed to bring you face to face with them.

These are exciting times of ascension that are truly for your benefit. It seems that the media and the world are constantly overwhelmed with negativity. The earth is also ascending, and releasing its toxicity as negative energy. The less baggage you have, meaning karma, the faster you will increase your vibrations. The planet earth is not being destroyed. Not everyone is going to ascend at the same time, but there is no comparison. No one is superior or inferior. A family means no one is left behind. We use media to give you messages and you are not listening. We are one soul family. You are all related, and came from the same source. That is why you need to be like children. Children are all going to ascend because children are pure and open up a pathway for you to experience Divine Love and healing. Once again, there is no comparison. No one is superior and no one is inferior. You are all unique and worthy.

Children are and have been coming to the planet for a very long time. They are very advanced, old souls. That is why parents are noticing their children's boredom and frustration. Listen to them. They have a lot of knowledge and wisdom. Look into their eyes. They are the masters, the teachers, and the Angels who have chosen physicality to bring light and higher vibrations to help raise the vibration of the planet. Pay attention to them. They live in the moment of now. They have a lot to teach. They are the master souls. Some of you don't totally trust yourselves and are in the process of ascension. Don't beat yourself up with doubts and frustration. Remember that no one is superior or inferior. You all support each other, including animals and the plant kingdom. They all serve a purpose. We need to simplify the meaning and bring clarity to the process of ascension.

Time limits your perception, yet everything is happening at the same time. You are in an expanded state of awareness, so your new issues are in a continuous state of now. You learn new things depending on your love, passion, and path. We request that you go different ways and take different paths as a part of raising the vibration of the planet earth.

The Creative Source is continuously creating. It is infinitely creating new dimensions. It has no beginning and no ending. It is calmly flowing and changing and changing and changing. You are in constant evolutionary growth. Change, growth, and evolution are secondary to the vibration of ascension.

There are an infinite number of possibilities for you to choose from. That is why it is important to be in the moment of now. Every choice has a consequence. There is a ripple effect. That is why it is so important to know the law of karma . . . action of cause and effect. One affects the whole and the whole affects one.

PAST LIFE'S KNOWLEDGE ALONE DOES NOT HEAL—LENA:

Lena came for her second session. She came in with a very heavy heart, sadness, and extremely angry feelings. She spoke about her childhood issues connected with these feelings. I began with prayer asking the Angels to show Lena where these feelings were coming from.

Having been regressed before, Lena saw a lifetime during which her parents sold her as a slave to work for a rich family. She endured a very hard life. At one point, she was accused of stealing a bracelet. Lena realized that this is the reason she is unable to wear bracelets in this life, and feels that her parents secluded her from the rest of her family. She felt unloved and unwanted. I told her that we needed to heal the past life and free her from this pain. It is karmic life, and she must ask for forgiveness from everyone because she must have done the same to them. Then, I requested the Angels help to heal and clear her from core of her being.

After healing, she saw herself as a little girl in beautiful curls, jumping up and down with the joy of healing. Lena then understood that knowing a past life does not necessarily mean that you are healed. It is healing that changes the energy. After that, she felt much lighter, as if a heavy weight had been lifted off of her chest.

At that point, Archangel Michael communicated a message through her for both of us. She explained that for me, the message was to quiet my mind and hear the Angels whisper in my ear, so that I would be able to teach this type of healing to others. The message for her was that she would be learning and doing this work as well. We thanked the Angel.

March 2, 2009—ILENE'S SESSION # 1

I begin the session with thanksgiving and prayer. I asked Ilene to take a few deep breaths and tell me what the Angels were showing her. The first thing she saw was her little girl so angry that she was pounding her fists on the wall. She was surprised to see that because she never thought anger was her issue.

I requested that the Angels show her little girl why she was so angry. Right away, she moved into a past life and saw a big man in anger and hatred beating a woman with stick. The woman was on the ground trying to protect her. He continued to beat her and didn't want to stop. I told her that the man was her and the woman was his wife. She had to confront him and tell him that she came to make peace with her anger and hate. To her surprise he froze and stopped beating his wife. I told her to tell him to kneel and ask for forgiveness. He did and then he picked her up and they hugged each other.

I asked Ilene what else the Angels wanted her to heal. Ilene was horrified when she saw herself as a Nazi general in a camp, killing thousands of souls. It seemed like a countless number. She was overcome with guilt. I told her she needed to ask for forgiveness from all of those souls for being so hateful, cruel, and angry. Then I requested that the Angels bring all souls from every dimension to hear his prayer of forgiveness to release each other from their karmic bonds. Thousands of tiny lights came and kept coming in. Then they all left as they made peace. She realized why she couldn't kill any living creature in her present life.

I asked her if there was anything else that the Angels wanted to show her. She watched her own horrific death. It was when women healers were burned at the stake and healing was considered to be witchcraft. She saw that her present husband and step daughter turned her into the authorities. Her feet were tied in a sack with rope and the sack was ignited. It was a very painful, slow death. Seeing this made her realize why she couldn't cover her feet at night. She didn't like wearing socks, shoes, or anything on her feet.

I asked her how she felt when her husband and stepdaughter turned her in. Her response was, "very sad and betrayed." I pointed out that this feeling of betrayal still existed in her and that this was her karmic debt meeting within. She had to forgive her husband and daughter. She said she already had because she was regressed to this life before. She thought she had been hung, not burned. I requested healing and clearing for her.

After healing, she found her little girl full of joy, playing, and jumping up and down. Then her little girl integrated peacefully into her heart. We thanked God, Jesus, and the Angels. Ilene told me that Archangel Michael wanted to tell me something. He was there, telling me that his love for me was beyond the galaxies. Then Ilene was overcome by immense love. I asked her if it was the blue Angel. It was. She saw a beautiful, translucent, blue flame, and then a blue lotus with translucent, shimmering, blue lights. He told me I would be teaching this method of healing to others. I thanked him.

The next morning, after my prayer, I was thinking about Archangel Michael and what he said. When I went to blow out my candle I heard these words in my mind—Our eternal love will live in people's hearts long after you leave this planet.

To my surprise, I saw a lady drinking poison from a bowl (cup) saying the very same words before she drank. I knew who she was—a famous 16th century Indian poet—Meera Bai. She sang her love songs for Lord Krishna. I asked him if he was telling me that this was my past life. I heard him say, "Yes. This is your homework to find out about your life."

I read about Meera and learned that there was no written account of her death. In short this was her story: Meera was born to a Royal family in Rajasthan. As a little girl she watched a marriage procession of a bridegroom and asked her mother who her husband would be. Amused, her mother pointed to a statue of Lord Krishna. From then on, she was totally devoted to Krishna. At age 18, she married Prince Bhoj Raj, the eldest son of King Rana. Meera still regarded Krishna as her Divine Lover and primary priority. She frequently visited temples, sang devotional songs, and mingled with wise people of ordinary class. She refused to worship her in-law's deity, Shiva. This angered her husband's family. They did not approve of her piety and devotion to Krishna.

They became increasingly disapproving of her actions. Her sister-in-law started to spread false gossip that she had an affair. Her husband believed the stories to be true and tore into her room with a sword in his hand. He saw Meera praying and talking to Krishna's idol. She was persecuted in various ways by Rana and his family. He once sent a cobra in a basket with the message that it contained a flower garland. After finishing her prayer she opened the basket and found a flower garland inside. In his last attempt to kill her, he sent her a bowl of poison with the message that it was nectar. Meera prayed to her beloved Krishna and drank the poison. It became nectar.

Meera's devotional love songs were sung across northern India and they reached the ears of Mogul Emperor Akbar, a powerful Muslim ruler in India. He was respectful of other religious paths, but visiting Meera would have caused a problem for both of them. Disguised as beggar, Akbar visited Meera and was so enamored by her soul-stirring music that before leaving, he placed a priceless necklace at her feet. Unfortunately, the necklace revealed his visit. Bhoj Raj was furious that a Muslim, his historical enemy had seen his wife. Bhoj Raj ordered Meera to commit suicide by drowning in the river because she had defamed his family and he did not want to see her face.

She intended to honor her husband's wish, but Krishna appeared to her and told her to leave for Vrindavan. So she left with a few followers. She went on a pilgrimage with saints. They arrived at Dwarka. Krishna's temple became her shrine. Meera, living alone in the company of monks would bring a bad name, which the royal family did not like. So, Rana requested that she return to Chittor.

Having suffered many tortures, she refused to return. Then Rana sent five holy men to bring her. She still refused. The holy men tried many different ways to convince her. They finally used their last weapon telling her that they would not return without her. If she did not go with them, they would go without food and water until they died. Meera would not be responsible for the death of these holy men. She agreed to go with them. The next morning at dawn, Meera was not to be found anywhere. Only her dress was found lying in front of Krishna's Shrine.

March 4, 2009—I called Sherry and told her about my experience. We decided to have a session. I began with prayer asking questions. Sherry said she saw nothing and was receiving no answers. We waited for few seconds and saw nothing but an empty cave. I thought it was very strange. Then Sherry said she saw a man standing behind her with his arms crossed. I told her to ask him what he wanted. He did not say anything. Then Sherry sensed that this man lived in her apartment and died but never left. I began talking to him telling him that he no longer needed to stay there and could choose to move on for his soul's growth. Then I asked the Angels to assist him in making his choice by bringing in loved ones from other dimensions to lovingly guide him and show him where he needed to go in order to move on. His loved ones came and he left with them. He had told Sherry that he just didn't know where to go.

After the man left, the Angles returned. I asked them with whom Sherry communicates during our sessions. They told me that when she is with me, she is talking to Angels. When she is alone, she gets answers from souls of other galaxies. I asked them how Meera died. Sherry saw Meera walking barefoot on dry land. She saw that Meera was ambushed by three people and had no place to run. Her mother-in-law was in front of her. Her sister-in-law was behind her, and her husband was beside her. They had plotted her murder.

Having tried to kill her and failing so many times before, this plot was her husband's idea. Many people were involved and they were all warned that if they spoke about it they would meet the same fate. Her mother-in-law threw a big rock hitting Meera on her forehead. She fell to ground. Then many rocks were thrown by all three of them, hitting and brutally injuring her.

After being brutally stoned, she was still alive, so her husband picked her up by her throat and strangled her. Sherry saw both of his thumbs pressing hard right over her thyroid gland. "Now I understand why I had so much trouble with my thyroid in this life," I said.

Meera's eyes were open and looking in horror. She saw the hate and anger in her husband's eyes and couldn't understand why he and his family hated her so much. Because she was naive and innocent, she never thought they would do that to her.

I requested that the Angels clear Meera's horror, fear, naiveté, innocence, and disbelief of her death. I began telling her that her death was her karmic debt from another lifetime. She created her experience of death in this manner. Her in-laws and her husband were not at fault. They were mirroring her past life's personality. She needed to ask for their forgiveness so they could release each other from this repeating karmic pattern.

As I was speaking to her, Sherry saw Meera who was dead lying on the dusty ground, stand up and shake the dust off of her clothes. She said that she had never looked at it that way before. Then she joined hands with all of them in a gesture of forgiveness, gratitude, and love. They made peace with each other. Then I requested blessings, healing, clearing and changing of the lives off all of them in all dimensions. Amen.

While the Angels reprogrammed my cellular memory over the next couple of days, I needed extra sleep. At the same time, I was getting more insights on this life. Archangel Michael told me, *"There is only energy of love and you create karma for each other's growth out of Love no matter how negative an experience may look."* Therefore, karmas are tools for growth. Karmas are not bad or good. They are lessons but the choices are. In the end everything balances out by itself. This is God's perfection in every experience of life."

March 19, 2009—ILENE'S SESSION # 2

Ilene told me that she felt that her husband didn't love her. She was doing so much for others but felt unappreciated. I told her that maybe she did not love herself and needed to be kind, loving, respectful, and appreciative of herself. She said that she does love herself and in her daily meditations, fills herself with white, Divine light and feels loved and peaceful.

I told her that if the light had filled her, then she would not continue to feel such a lack of love and emptiness. She recognized this and realized that it was due to parental imprinting. She had another issue: nobody was showing up for her group discussions. She realized that as a child, no one showed up on her birthdays. I asked her how she felt when no one showed up. Her answer was sad, ugly, and unwanted.

I asked if her mother had these issues. She did feel ugly, but never called Ilene ugly. Her mother didn't have to because Ilene carried the parental imprinting in her DNA. She also realized that her husband's treatment of her was like her mother's: controlling, unloving, cold, and putting her down. She inherited her habits of being loud and talkative from her father, while her memory loss came from her mother.

After this discussion, I began to pray and asked the Angels to bring her little girl and parents for Ilene. She saw herself as a three-year old waiting for her. They hugged. I asked Ilene who she wanted to deal with first. She chose her mother. The Angels gave her a garbage bag to fill with her mother's imprinting of control, feeling ugly and unwanted, fear, and guilt. Then she began filling her father's bag with his loud voice, and endless talking. She remembered that her mother didn't like it when she stood up for herself. Her mother used to wait for her father to come home and beat her with his belt to discipline her. He would apologize to her telling her that he did not want to beat her.

Ilene said that her ex-husband used to beat her and was very controlling. I told her it was karmic and she accepted it. Then her late father-in-law came and she remembered what he told her when he was dying as she did Reiki on him. He told her to stay on the path of helping others because when he was living in Africa he had slaves and used to beat them. He would tell them that the floors had to shine enough to see their reflections. This was his confession. I told her he had come in for his healing and the Angels took care of him too. We finished the session by her giving the bags to her parents. The Angels cleared them to choose differently. Then I requested healing with gratitude. Amen.

March 24, 2009—GINA'S SESSION # 3

I began with prayer and asked Gina what she was being shown by the Angels. Her answer was guilt. She saw her little girl sitting peacefully under a tree with a white dove perched on her finger. Then she saw a past life as an Indian Hindu king and noticed a sense of disdain and boredom in him. As this king, she (he) affected the lives of many with no thought but the flick of a wrist. She had no interest in the often terrible results of her actions. As the king, she was very arrogant and totally self absorbed. People's lives didn't have much meaning to her. She had a total disregard for human life and suffering.

I told her to tell him that she had come to make peace with this life's karmic consequences. He needed to accept his responsibilities and ask for forgiveness. I requested that the Angels bring all souls from every dimension that had been affected by his ignorance to hear his prayer of forgiveness. Then I requested healing and clearing in all dimensions with gratitude. Gina noticed a red dot on her third eye as it came from the distance. When it came closer into her vision, she noticed it was a heart made of rubies of beautiful vibrant red with white and pink roses around it. As she stretched her hands to receive it, it became a dot and rested in her third eye.

When I asked her little girl if she understood the meaning of asking forgiveness, she turned her face stubbornly, and told me that it wasn't her issue—it was an adult's issue. I asked three times and got the same response. I realized that she was only fooling herself, not me. For some reason she had become very rigid and angry. I told her it wasn't an adult issue, but her issue all along. She was in denial and acceptance was the only way to heal. Upon hearing this, the child recognized that it was, in fact, her issue. Then Gina saw her little girl surrounded by green and yellow light sent by the Angels to heal. It was healing her rigid, stubborn state. Gina saw her resting on a bed of feathers. I told Gina to bring her to her heart and let her rest there. After the session, Gina channeled these words from **yellow and green Angels' light:**

"Life is not all about intellect, wisdom, knowledge, and experiencing God, or Angels' communications. The price you pay through duality's law of karma through anger, judgment, sorrow, guilt, pain, sickness, sadness, and lack of love, allows you to reach the goal of going back to the beginning. You make the journey to return to your SELF."

"Rekha, you are now in the process of creating your next lifetime as determined by the law of karma: how much karma you have paid and how much karma credit and credibility you have earned. You are learning that behavior can either credit your karma or create karma and understand how credit karmas can balance out the negative karma. The outcome depends on how you choose to deal with your experiences. Michael has a lotus flower for you."

I asked what it symbolizes for me. Archangel Michael said, *"The lotus symbolizes compassion for yourself and others."* I thanked him, knowing that I needed to have more compassion. I did not take the lotus from him, knowing that I would take it when I learned this lesson. Gina asked what color Archangel Michael was. I told her he was the Blue Angel and that HE had been teaching me since I was a child. She saw a big blue aura around Archangel Michael and a grin on his face as if to say that it was about time that she recognized this truth.

Archangel Michael: *Faith simply knows the connection that something greater than yourself is always within you, guiding you, watching over you, lovingly taking you to your path, and allowing you to make your choices. When you get confused, it is a challenge to your beliefs because you have labeled your belief system as faith, but it is two different things. Belief systems are based on whatever society, religions or teachings dictate: believing in someone or something other than yourself. Belief systems kill your curiosity and questionability. With the belief system, your faith bails out because faith is the inner knowing, inner truth. You give away your trust, belief, and faith* *in yourself. Life moves and evolves in a SPIRAL. You can move upward or move downward on a spiral, depending upon your choices, whether negative or positive.*

The concept of HELL is simply connected to very low frequencies. There is COLD HELL and HOT HELL. Cold hell's frequencies belong to souls with a very rigid nature who refuse to change, evolve, and grow, denying everything, and are stuck in their belief systems. Cold hell is based very much on issues of fear. Hot hell is where very angry and violent people go. They have allowed their rage to take over, instead of their higher selves. All these souls can evolve, but they have to start from the very beginning of the spiral. There is a transition happening now. It is a constant wheel of movement. In the beginning, there was God, you, and choices. Karma is created by choices. Your first few choices created karma, which led to more choices, which multiplied into more karma. Each previous choice leads to new choices, as well as back to the original choices. There are good karmas and bad karmas, random acts of kindness are good karma because you start creating karma credit. Sometimes you can draw on credit karma. For example, you get assisted in your despair, saved in a fatal accident, cured from a fatal disease.

Rekha: Why can't beings of light have physical bodies?

Archangel Michael: *What makes you think that they cannot have physical bodies? The physical world is an illusion. It is like a big Broadway production to assist you in learning your lessons. It's like fiction. The reality is another dimension where everything exists at the same time as in your three dimensional world. So even though the illusion is that you are not with Archangel Michael, in reality you are together. Maybe you are stepping into his reality, in order to have him, not the other way around. He is real and living in his reality. You are living in an illusion. Learn the lesson and let it go. Each lesson that you are learning, draws you closer to reality. Every Broadway play has a beginning and an end. You can still have a physical body and not live in the illusion. When illusion ends, you become the MASTER. Souls evolve to the point of becoming masters. Process this information and believe that you are a master.*

Then the yellow and green light transmuted into purple light and was gone. We thanked Lime Light Angels.

Two days later, March 27, 2009, Gina got back to me with a splitting headache where the red dot was and asked me what to do. I told her that we would simply ask the Angels to take it back. When we did, she saw it as it had come. It moved out of her third eye and disappeared. At the same time, her headache became less intense.

March 25, 2009—I was frying vegetables and wasn't thinking about anything. I was turning pieces over and watching them fry. All of a sudden, I saw a man thrown into hot oil. My immediate reaction was that it couldn't have been me who'd done that to him. Even though I had no reason to doubt it, I still asked. Further information came to me. I was in Egypt, but I was not the one who actually threw slaves into hot oil. I was a head priest who made decisions for slaves to die. My consciousness during this lifetime was very low. I was very self centered and abused my power. I prayed and requested that Jesus and the Angels heal this karma and change that life by bringing the priest and telling him that in his power and ignorance, he did not value human life.

Then I requested that the Angels show him how many lives of being enslaved he had to experience with horrific deaths in order to pay his karmic debts. After seeing this, he was ready to ask for forgiveness. I requested that the Angels bring all souls from every dimension to hear his prayer and change his choices so that he never made those horrific choices. The souls were released from their karmic bond, freeing all sparks from hot and cold hell and mending all souls' fragments into their higher Divine selves. Then I requested every soul's healing and clearing in all dimensions, with gratitude. Amen.

March 26, 2009—ILENE'S SESSION # 3

Ilene mentioned her fear of people leaving her. Even though there is no love in her marriage she is afraid to move on. I began the healing session with a prayer requesting that the Angels bring her little girl. Ilene saw a past life with me. We were walking together wearing long dresses in

England, a long time ago. It was a beautiful day and we were having a lot of fun. We were very close friends on a spiritual path, talking about how we are going to help people to become awakened. We knew that one of us was soon going to get hit by a car and die, leaving the other behind. As soon as she said this, I knew it was me. My whole body shivered and I had goose bumps. Then Ilene said she was crying for her loss with enormous sorrow, fear, and pain. She was overwhelmed by being left alone and had this same issue in this life.

Having seen this, she was able to release it because she knew where it came from. The Angels were telling her that Rekha had to leave because she was more evolved and had to learn more to her further evolution. Ilene was left behind to teach others, so she is teaching awareness now. This was the missing piece of the puzzle. I requested healing and the clearing of her emotions in all dimensions and thanked the Angels.

Then the Angels showed Ilene my past life in Egypt. I was a Hebrew slave and the mother of three children living in fear for the life of her newborn child because of the pharaoh's orders to kill first-born boys. Ilene said, "You put your baby in a basket and left him in the river. Then you were stricken with guilt, sorrow, and sadness."

Jesus said, *"Rekha you now have learned the value of love by choosing to bring in Moses' soul who later changed consciousness in great numbers. He took some of the karma of the mother who raised him onto himself. He was the chosen one then, but you are the chosen one now. He gave you a gift of a change in heart. It all had to work out this way."*

I realized that after that life I may have ended up in COLD HELL. Jesus replied, "Yes. Do you know there is a male and female hell? Hot hell is male and cold is female." I requested healing and clearing for this spark and it mended into my original soul. Amen.

Rekha: I would like to know why I have to write Jesus' and new comers' healing and teachings and why it was not written by the masters before me.

Jesus: *All of the masters before you were raising consciousness by teaching awareness so people could awaken and begin to clean up their karma.*

They taught awareness of the present moment. Now the consciousness is ready to grasp more. Therefore, new comer's awareness and teachings are available for their further evolution to shorten their incarnations.

Then Ilene saw Archangel Michael. God's enormous light extended way beyond him and it kept on moving as if never ending, telling her, *"HE (GOD) functions with WE and HE is within, through, and around us at all times. WE are collective consciousness. Peace and blessings come out of all this that you are doing and that's how generations will come to survive. Angels are able to inhabit physical bodies with an agreement with that person who already accepted for them to be a vehicle."*

April 1, 2009—GINA'S SESSION # 4

Gina had been very sick with headaches, nausea, and stomach pain. When I called she was in bed, feeling pretty sick. She told me that everyone in her home was also not feeling well. She felt she was absorbing everyone else's energy and issues. She had been asking for clarity and discernment for this condition and the message she received was that she needs to let go of her attachment. Then she had stomach pain and felt like throwing up.

I told her to close her eyes and place her hand on her stomach while I did a healing prayer, asking the Angels to provide her with understanding and answers. She kept seeing an Indian king sitting in an arrogant position. I heard "guilt" and told her that it was causing the nausea and pain in her stomach, as a result of what she had done to many souls. I knew that the king had never accepted that he had done anything wrong. I told Gina to look into his eyes and tell him that he had never accepted how much pain and suffering he caused to others and earned karmic debts. He needed to accept this and only then, could he ask for forgiveness from others.

As I was speaking, Gina saw a multitude of souls come to forgive him and the king's demeanor changed. Instead of sitting in a tilted, arrogant position, he sat up straight as he saw that none of the souls were judging him, but had come in love to forgive him. He began to cry. Then a joyous smile came to his face. He began to throw his gold coins into the crowd. As their karma was released, change took place. He changed that life by giving back what he had taken from the people. I finished with prayer by asking for clearing the entire dimension, with gratitude. Amen.

Gina's inflated stomach went down and the intensity of her migraine left, but she felt numbness because her healing was still in process. The Gold, Yellow, and Purple Angels came to heal her. By the end of our session she had recovered to the point that she could function through her daily life.

GUILT

Jesus: *Guilt and non-forgiveness; these two energies are the biggest causes of human suffering and pain. Guilt makes you obliged to do things for others and you can't say no. Guilt has a hard time receiving anything but do, do, and do for others, out of that urge to fill the deep emptiness, but it remains empty. You become a go, go individual who hardly has time for yourself, and so stressed out that you are very hard on yourself. Therefore, you are hard on others. Then anger, arrogance, blame, control, and unkindness are the additional emotions created out of guilt. You are mirroring your very image in every day life's experiences, but you refuse to see it. The soul knows what you have done, but you don't want to see the ugliness of yourself, and you keep on affecting others.*

   The actions of one, affects the whole, and the actions of the whole, affects one. It is the universal law of karma. This is how you multiply your karma in each incarnation from that original issue. Recognizing that your issue can trigger your soul to search for answers and in this journey, the soul could become awakened. Pain and suffering is a trigger to your soul that propels you to look for answers and makes you feel that you need to find freedom. That's when everything falls into place and the Angels come in.

Rekha: How is this king's energy still living in hot hell while he has been reincarnated as Gina?

Jesus: *A spark of your soul remains in hot or cold hell and continues to re-experience the same attitude, act, or karma over and over until* *an enlightened master comes to free you. There can be hundreds of fragments (lifetimes) of yours stuck in cold and hot hell until you heal that memory or imprinting. That's why you continue to be reincarnated, to clear one fragment at a time. But, in each lifetime you keep creating more karma. You are living life very unconsciously. Rekha, your book is a trigger to souls to search for answers and truth within and ultimately find freedom.*

In serving others out of love, you automatically make a direct deposit into your spiritual bank account. If it is not out of love then you are doing it out of attachments. When you serve out of love from your heart, without any exterior motive attached to it, money will come from sources that you have never imagined. When you learn to serve totally out of love without any expectations then you have finally found the balanced account. You have redeemed your karmic balance out of love.

CHAPTER 6

TESTS AND LESSONS

April 4, 2009—HOW TO BE KIND AND COMPASSIONATE

This lesson came on an evening walk, as I began to ask the Angels how I could develop more compassion. I heard Archangel Michael in my head, "Where does compassion begin in the first place?"

I answered, "Of course, with me." I understood that Michael was telling me that I didn't have compassion for myself for the hardship and challenges I had gone through. Because of my guilt I had been very hard on myself, and was therefore hard on others.

When I got home I prayed and asked the Angels to bring my little girl so I could tell her that I am committed to her, that I will always honor her and never be hard on her. She will have all my love, compassion, care, kindness, and anything that she needs. I gave her a hug and told Archangel Michael that I was ready to accept a lotus from him. He gave it to my little girl. I saw my little girl holding it in her hand and smiling. I thanked Michael for teaching compassion and kindness for myself. Amen.

FEELING UNWORTHY

The next morning during my prayer, I was told that my guilt had created unworthiness in me. Guilt set in as awareness grew and I saw how I caused suffering, hurt, pain and damage to other souls in past lives. I requested that the Angels clear all pain, suffering, and guilt from the core of every soul's being, changing the past. Amen.

May 6, 2009—GINA'S SESSION # 5

Gina complained about so-called "friends" asking for readings (for free) as soon as possible, leaving her no time for herself. She felt as if it was her responsibility to take care of everyone. As she was speaking, I could hear the Angel saying that it was her issue. In some other life, she didn't accept the responsibility of an obligation towards all of these souls. Now it was coming back to her through these people.

Through prayer, I asked the Angels to show her where and how she created this issue. Gina took a deep breath and began to search. A lifetime came up in England. She was the eldest and only boy in a family with 3 or 4 sisters. Their father had passed away, so, as the only boy, the responsibility of his family rested upon his shoulders.

I asked how he felt about this situation. She learned that he hated it. He was miserable because he was gay and planning to leave for USA with his partner. But he was stuck with the responsibility of his family and his partner left without him. He was emotionally devastated. I told her that this lifetime was showing her the repetition of the same issue. The Angels needed to show her when this issue first originated.

She asked to be shown. It was in the 1300's on a pirate ship. She was under the command of the ship's captain. It was a very late at night and very dark when the captain gave her the responsibility to watch over the ship. He left to get some sleep. Instead of doing her duty of watching and protecting the people on the ship, she was drinking. Another pirate ship attacked them and she could not warn the captain or anyone else. They were all killed because of her negligence. She was responsible for all of those deaths. Upon seeing this, she understood why she does not drink in this life.

I explained to her that all of the souls who were on the ship were now in her life, demanding her time and attention so that she could complete her karmic debts with them. She needed to make peace with them by asking for their forgiveness. Then I requested healing and clearing for all souls in all dimensions, changing the past. Amen.

This clearly shows that if something bothers you, it is your issue. Souls cross our path and create situations for us to learn about ourselves.

JESUS REVEALS MARY'S LIFE

On June 4, 2009, I was at Gina's place, looking at her books. One book entitled *Lives of the Master* jumped out at me. After further examining the book, I found out that it was about Edgar Cayce's readings on Jesus' life. I became anxious to read this book because I had read a couple of Edger Cayce's books on different subjects and loved them. A week later, while reading the second Chapter, *Story of the Master*, Archangel Michael triggered a memory from 1995 when I had asked him why I felt such deep sadness about Jesus' crucifixion and why Jesus had to die the way he did.

In turn, Archangel Michael asked me what else I felt. I felt heartbroken, a great loss, injustice, sad, in pain, and cried a lot. Then he told me, "You feel this way because you were in his life." I couldn't figure out who I was, but it stayed with me and all of a sudden, I began to realize that I was Moses' mother. I had inherited the pattern of suffering the loss of a child and was filled with guilt, sadness, and pain.

I hadn't finished connecting the similarities when in my mind I heard, "You were Jesus' mother, Mary. Now you can make the connection about why you have felt this way about him all this time!" My mind was flooded with experiencing Jesus. I had always wondered why he was with me and why I loved him so deeply, even though I was not raised a Christian. I had thought that since he was a grand master healer, he was there to guide me and to heal others.

Once I went to a friend's house to assist in healing her two year old son. She told me that there was a young man with long hair standing behind me dressed in white robe. I told her it was Jesus and he was with me to heal her son. After the session, her son never had those issues again.

Over the next couple of days, I began to assimilate this information and pieces of the puzzle began to fall into place making total sense. I realized that I carried forward the same emotional trauma from Moses' life to Jesus' life. The same trauma repeated in this life when I lost my daughter's bird. I felt sad, devastated and depressed, as if I had lost my child. This story was described in my first book.

Then I thought of Judas' experience and realized that I must have blamed him for Jesus' suffering, instead of having compassion for his soul. Judas was addressing me as Mary when he told me that I should have more compassion for a soul like his. Then I heard Jesus say, "You had forgiven neither Judas nor yourself for having gone through the pain of losing your son. See the perfection in God's grand plan in every experience."

I understood. In Mary's human ignorance, she held Judas responsible for Jesus' suffering. She had to ask for forgiveness to be freed from her karmic bond with Judas. I told Mary that Jesus had never left us and that it was His Divine plan to raise human consciousness by taking upon humanity's karma to bring love into their hearts. She had to look at the bigger picture of how and why souls are doing negative things in order to raise each other's consciousness. I requested that the Angels clear her attitude, mindset and perceptions so she could ask for forgiveness from Judas, Roman soldiers, the people and the king to free herself. Then I heard, "Now the rest of my disciples are waiting for you to be set free." Mary asked for their forgiveness. Then I requested clearing and changing the life thanking Jesus and His Angels.

One morning I woke up hearing "Jesus is here." I wondered what He wanted me to do. I heard "You have released everyone but ME from the mother and son's attachment." I asked Jesus for forgiveness to release me from my attachment and thanked Him.

HEALING PARENTAL IMPRINTING AND KARMA

I chose my parents because of my soul's karmic agenda. It seems that spiritual growth works in phases and cycles, and on different levels. I had been working on my parental imprinting for almost sixteen years. Yet, some imprinting that I had already worked on was still showing up, along with others that I had not connected to my parents' issues before. I had been working with my parents for a long time. They already knew what I was doing and as I continue to change, they do as well, and we are all healed together.

CHAPTER 7

HEALING PAST LIVES # 2

July 17, 2009: GINA'S SESSION # 6

Gina wound up in the emergency room with severe abdominal pain and found out that she had diverticulitis. Her colon was badly inflamed, but she began to respond well to antibiotics. The doctor also found a cyst on her right adrenal gland. She stayed in the hospital for three days and was told to return in two months for a biopsy. When she got home, she called asking for help. An Angel told me to give her a couple of days to rest.

When I saw her two days later, she was anxiously waiting for me. She broke down and cried. While we were hugging, I told her it was a good cry and she needed it because she hadn't cried in a long time. She told me that she hadn't cried in thirty years. I assured her that everything would be fine as long as she saw this experience as an opportunity, blessing and lesson by which to get to know her Self. She explained that she felt broken inside, as if her soul had died. She had no desire to live. It was as if the world was coming to an end. I told her that she had felt this way before. This was not the first time and I knew she did not want to repeat this life after life. She agreed.

Then she lay down and was able to relax. She told me that over the last 2 days, she had received Reiki and another type of healing that helped to relieve the pain in her right foot. She was able to walk instead of dragging her foot. It also brought her to a breaking point. I told her that the Angels wanted me to wait until she could reach a point of acceptance. Knowing everything has a process and Divine timing, she agreed.

Then I explained that any kind of inflammation in the body symbolizes a swollen ego. She realized that her issue was that as long as she was constantly on the go and always doing something for others, everything was in control. At this time, she felt that all control has been shattered. She felt very tired and drained. She admitted that she had an angry episode that morning with her son and she knew that she needed to learn acceptance and to be humble.

I told her that her soul had not died. It was her ego that had been shattered. The veil of illusion was lifting and her soul was emerging. Her soul was very sad, lonely and buried because it was totally controlled by her ego. Now, she was in touch with her true feelings, which is why she was able to cry and feel for her soul. Her ego had killed her soul. It made sense to her.

I began the session with prayer and requested the Angels' assistance to provide answers on how she could release her negative, poisonous energy of guilt and anger. She took a few deep breaths, while thinking about why she had created this illness. She said she saw Satan sitting on a throne and that she was his agent, collecting souls to follow him. She saw two doors, side by side, one white and one black. She was very afraid to open the black door because she had chosen the light. She felt frustrated, angry, and fearful, and her guilt was so powerful that she wanted to break free from this chain of negativity. The hold was so powerful that she was unable to. She said out loud, "I am not a bad soul."

I agreed and told her that all souls are beings of Divine Light, including Lucifer. She was not able to see that. I understood her struggle. We choose darkness for our soul's growth, so that we can eventually experience Divine Love and Light. She needed to ask for forgiveness from all of the souls she had hurt. I requested that the Angels bring them to her from every dimension to free each other. She had to shake hands with Lucifer as her final good-bye. Gina said it wasn't his hand, but his claw that she shook with. The handshake began with blood red energy and then changed to orange, to yellow, to soft yellow, then purple, and shades of pink. Then Lucifer turned his back and all his followers turned their backs and walked away. She saw only the white door left.

I asked her how she was feeling and she said broken up, lifeless like a rag doll, bitter, discarded, and tired. Then Gina and her little girl filled up an extra large garbage bag with all of these negative energies. I said, "Well, give it to Lucifer!" He came back, took the bag, turned his back and walked away. Gina felt a nasty, oozing sludge being pulled out of her stomach. She felt like throwing up but settled down and noticed that the heat radiating from her colon area was gone. I finished my prayer asking for healing and clearing and thanked Jesus and his Angels.

I asked, "Are you ready to leave your body so I can get further information for you to follow?" She was ready. She fell asleep, went to her favorite place, and sat near the water. I asked the Angels if they were ready to give her more information . . .

"Yes. We are here. The first thing is that Gina has to love her Self. Second, she has to add movement in the form of exercise—walking—and connect with the nature. It is so readily available to her. Third, it is very important that she let go and not be involved with toxic people, for there is a lot of toxicity around her. The way she has been eating is also very toxic. She should eat organic foods; no red meats, no shellfish or fish—too many pollutants. Salmon may be a good staple. Chicken is okay, but not to be abused. Juicing would be important for her. Fresh vegetables and fruits with all their nutrients intact will benefit overall health. She can have calming and soothing treatments like massages or baths with lavender, rosemary, peppermint, or eucalyptus to cool down her systems. Her nervous system needs rest. Her entire nervous system is weak and hyperactive. It's creating too much heat in the body that needs to be cooled down. Fresh, soothing, calming, and cooling herb tea will help."

"No canned foods. They are not good for her. If she calms her nervous system, her stress level will be somewhat released. I don't see anything wrong with her adrenal glands. What we see on her right adrenal gland is a cyst that her body will absorb with the proper diet and rest. Although her colon is compromised, with a proper diet and rest it can be healed. The pain in her right foot is connected to her bladder, kidney, and liver because they are totally full of toxins. It will be wise to add some kind of air filter to her surroundings because she is very susceptible. This is how her physical body is being compromised. She has come through a lot of challenges with toxicity, even though they are not visible to physical eye."

"Meditation on only the spiritual body causes imbalance. Balanced meditation incorporates emotional and physical bodies. Use the meditation process to release and excrete, and build new cells to strengthen the body and organs. Balance is very important and must incorporate all three bodies. It is important to calm the nervous system down. It is ok to allow emotions to flow. Resisting emotions creates blockages. Releasing emotions through meditation is helping, assisting, and building the nervous system. It is important to integrate the process of resting and calming the nervous system in meditation."

I asked who was speaking through Gina and an Angel answered that Edgar Cayce was speaking through her. I was happy to hear what he was saying, but had to ask why she was compromising her nervous system.

Edgar: *She had been fighting with her conflicting thoughts forcing her to manifest more negativity. She couldn't dispel it, which is why we have given her a title to write a book and focus her energies on a non-essential project. She also needs to read and do non-essential things. Now we are integrating her energies. Everything has a process.*

She had a hard time connecting with her true Self and lost her joy for life. Affirmations are important to bring back the joy of life. Before this healing she was afraid to connect to her Angel. Now she is clear to do so, but it is a process and she needs to know that it takes time. Integration of energies cannot be rushed. I learned this the hard way and compromised my nervous system because of my deep desire to serve and assist others, and did not take rest to integrate new awareness.

Rekha: Is Gina aware of our conversation?
Edgar: *Somewhat, I am speaking through her higher Self.*
Rekha: Who did you channel in your life readings?
Edgar: *Jesus and Collective Consciousness.*
Rekha: Is there anything wrong with my physical body? (I had stopped taking medication for thyroid and high blood pressure a few months prior.)
Edgar: *Your Physical body seems to be ok. Your thyroid is very slightly out of balance, but not much.*
Rekha: Why I am having a problem digesting rice and grains?
Edgar: *We are changing your physicality.*

Rekha: Am I taxing my nervous system?

Edgar: *No. The Angels take good care of you. I have two or three books in me. Would you write them for me?*

Rekha: *Yes. But you know I don't like writing books and I am having a difficult time writing this one.*

Edgar: *Don't worry. I am like you in writing books. I will help you to complete the Angels' book. We are headed into happier times. It is a calming, peaceful and healing time; a time of changing consciousness. Changed consciousness will create a new, happier and peaceful world. The world is not coming to an end. There is no such thing as dooms day.*

Rekha: Are you doing the same work in other dimensions and for us in this dimension?

Edgar: *Yes. I am helping many healers and others in the physical dimension with information, guidance and readings by allowing them to connect with my energy. Life never ends. Leaving flesh gives you more freedom of movement because flesh limits you. Lifetimes continue to evolve by learning and growing. Evolution is infinite growth of knowledge and wisdom.*

Rekha: Will you be reincarnated in near future?

Edgar: *Not for a while.*

Rekha: I thank you for Gina's reading and answering my questions. Do you think it is time to bring Gina back?

Edgar: *Yes. It is a good idea to bring her back.*

July 18, 2009—I read what Edgar Cayce said about love: "Love is a law unto itself. Love is a channel of miracles because it can transcend the law of cause and effect. It can break the rules."

I was thinking about love when I noticed Lucifer with his followers entering my room. I remembered that while I was assisting Gina an Angel asked me to assist Lucifer and his followers in their choices, but I forgot to do it. Now they are here. This means they are willing to choose light. Then I prayed for their clearing in all dimensions and to fill the core of their beings with Divine Love releasing them into Jesus' Holy hands. Amen.

July 20, 2009—I was told about my past life connection with Edgar Cayce. He was one of Jesus' disciples, Mathew. I had a hard time believing this so I wanted Edgar to confirm that it was true.

July 23, 2009—GINA'S SESSION # 7

I went to see Gina. She was feeling a lot better and the light in her eyes was back. Gina was happy to have a session. So she lay down and I gently guided her conscious mind to connect with her higher Self. Then I asked guidance for both of us and thanked the Angels.

Gold Angel: *You are on the right path. The color yellow is very significant to both of you. Yellow has a lot to do with sunshine, light, happiness, intellect, vision, knowledge, and the logical mind. It integrates into your heart and soul. Yellow is one of the colors connected with happy times, joy, and the flow of information.*

Rekha: How is Gina doing?

Edgar came through smiling and said, *"Now you are becoming more familiar with me and yes, our past life's connection is true. Trust in yourself. Gina has made tremendous advancement. She is finally consistently making positive changes. It is not only nutrition, but the mindset, as well, that is very important. It is shifting her perception, adjusting priorities, taking real steps towards her personal power. She finally understands and accepts that we are guiding her, teaching her as a light team. She was never alone when she felt alone, but it was by her own choice. She wanted a lesson. We were always there for her."*

"Now she is more receptive to receiving her messages. She kept complaining and screaming that she was tired of climbing a rocky mountain and feeling exhausted. Now she is on a plateau. The road to her journey is rest, relaxation and healing. It could be a soft, natural, peaceful valley. You all have the wrong conception about reaching plateaus. Throughout life you reach plateaus where you heal and rest and have an opportunity to recreate a different perspective to add more life, light and joy to your journey."

"Continue working with emerald green light, meditating, and doing healing work. It is time to receive healing and accept the nurturing care of the gentle souls around you. We are very happy that you have changed your eating and living habits and are taking better care of yourself. The process has a beginning, middle, and end. Honor time—it cannot be rushed. Rushing will not accomplish anything. It is essential that you know how to break your hours and days into

times to read, play, work and rest. You will accomplish more in this manner of being. Rekha, you have to learn to trust yourself."

Rekha: How can I tell the difference between my test and what I had been asked to do?

Edgar: *All tests are of your ego. You test your Self by choosing from your ego or from your higher Self. It will either build or destroy your Self. Just know that when you give too much power and attention to your ego, it will take you on a negative journey. Ego is part of the personality and it does not go away, but you learn to keep it in control. You will always have those tests. They are part of the soul's ascension. The key is allowing yourself to see the difference between your ego and your higher Self. Challenges will always come up. You must resolve every problem with peace, serenity, joy and faith.*

When you visualize every situation and come entirely with the energy of love, the negativity automatically shifts and falls away. If there is any negativity, bring in peace, love and light. Your perception will change and negativity will not have the power to pull the ego in. Ego is similar to your inner child. Once you have done the work and healed your inner child, it is lot easier to keep ego in check and in balance. You will never get rid of ego because it is a part of your personality, but you can have it work for you in a positive way by not feeding into its negative energy. The antidote for ego is love and light. There is peace, tranquility, faith, hope, mercy, compassion, humility, healing, relaxing, laughter, and joy. Now I want to address Gina's physical body if I may!

Rekha: Yes please, thank you.

Edgar: *Her nervous system is doing much better, but it is still compromised. Water exercises, walking, and nature outings are very important. Her colon is still compromised, but it is coming along.*

Rekha: Why are we not aware of your presence or able to receive your assistance when we need it the most?

Edgar: *It is very simple. We never leave your sight. We love you and respect your gift of free will. We will never interfere with the choice of your free will. When you ask, you shall receive. Gina has been asking, but wasn't putting her heart in her words of letting go and letting God in.*

Once she did that there was an opportunity and permission to step in to assist her. We stepped in to assist her from the inside. While her physical body was resting, we came in and started working with her because there is no ego, worry or negativity.

Only in a state of peace and balance are we able to come in and start energetically cleaning the body and organs, cell by cell. Each thread of DNA creates new cells. It is the same thing as running a vacuum cleaner on a very dirty rug. You will have to run it several times. First it will pick up some superficial dirt. Then it will pick up finer dirt. Sometimes it needs to clean deeper to get to the dirt that is embedded in the threads. This gives the carpet a fresh, clean appearance. Healing is equivalent to vacuum cleaning. Energetic healing cleans all threads of emotionally, mentally, physically, and energetically.

Rekha, you wanted to know how healing is done. People like you assist others on physical, emotional, and mental levels. This makes it much easier for us to go in and work at the energetic level. When everything within is clean, the body is given the opportunity to emerge balanced, healthy, and energized.

What goes on within, affects you at all possible levels. Disease is not outside in, but inside out. We revitalize the organs by raising their vibratory frequencies so they can function in harmony with each other. For example, when the colon is compromised, it has a very low frequency because it has been storing negative energy and toxins. We are working to bring it to its normal vibratory frequency by going in deeply in adjusting its memory at the cellular level. We are creating brand new cells on a higher vibration where disease does not exist. If you want a different outcome, you need to change your thought patterns and perspective. For example, if you plant potatoes and expect bananas, it won't happen. The intentions of what you want have to be clear. You must plant that new thought, and create a new perspective by releasing your old perspective. Doing the same thing or having the same thought over and over will produce the same results. It is a vicious cycle. A shift will create a ripple effect of transformation.

Rekha: Could you please shed some light on Gina's move and her financial issue?

Edgar: *It is a very positive move for her. WE actually brought this for her because it was on her wish list. She wasn't ready to believe it. We proved her wrong. She is really doing well. When all of her negativity and darkness clear up, her new financial picture will be her reward. Her finances will continue to improve as her physical, emotional, mental, and energetic bodies continue to improve. The light is going in deeper and driving darkness out. **Money really is a positive energy. It becomes negative when you abuse it.** Her finances will continue to manifest.*

Rekha: Could you please provide a reading for my sister's grandson? He is suffering from seizures.

Edgar: *I see neglect of "Self," rejection of life, fear of the unknown, fear of the future, a sense of terror, and always trying to escape reality. He was an abuser who caused lots of pain, suffering, and terror to others. High position, misuse of power, and manipulation are connected to Napoleon Bonaparte's fragment. He incarnated as Napoleon in that lifetime. He was very powerful even though he felt insecure because of his small stature. He created a persona of terror and showed strength, power, and cruelty on the outside, while he was fearful and insecure on the inside.*

I asked who I was speaking to. The answer was "Universal wisdom, Creative Force, I Am Who I Am."

I said, "Oh I know—you are GOD—Jesus. Thank you. I would like to know if this is how evolution of the soul works; awakening of the soul, Self-mastery, become an enlightened master, an ascended master, an angelic being, and so on."

Jesus: *Yes. It is in this manner, but new dimensions, new realms and new positions are not created yet. Evolution of love, light, and soul is infinite. As you evolve your love grows. At the same time, your creativity grows higher and higher. As you cleanse your energy, you get closer to the purity of Divine light. You have the ability to create new realms and dimensions. You are the ones who will create new realms.*

Once you have power of creativity, with love and compassion, you can create anything and everything good and positive. Unfortunately, a lot of that creativity is used negatively in creating an atomic bomb—a tremendous creative negative force for destruction, but still a creative energy. Nuclear medicine is a positive energy and has infinite potential of creativity. Creativity is at your fingertips. It is available to every one of you. You attract it to yourself by what you choose. Make your choices in the face of sunshine. Step boldly into the light and claim creative, positive energy for you and for others.

Rekha: Could you please provide guidance for my work? Thank you.

Collective consciousness: *You are ready. Be prepared because WE will be bringing forth a lot of souls who have been searching and asking for a long time. You are a part of the team of assistance. Work on yourself and know that any doubt you manifest is the ego. You know how to lovingly keep your ego in check. When all of those negative feelings come up, take a deep breath and look within with love, light, and understanding. It will lose its power and energy, and not take you over. Be grateful to your ego. Allow it to work with your soul. It is not a bad thing. Appreciate it and make a different choice to create a different outcome.*

CHAPTER 8

GROWTH BY HEALING OTHERS

On August 4, 2009, I began working in a metaphysical center. I met Lorna. She did channeled readings. She came over to sit with me. She saw two figures standing behind me. One was short, and one was tall. She asked if I knew them. I did. The tall one was Jesus and short one was Edgar Cayce. Edgar Cayce began to channel information about my diet: *No sugar, white flour, eggs, caffeine, breads, canned food, or margarine, and eat less salt. You can eat fresh, raw vegetables, honey, butter, soybeans, rice, whole grains, fruit, dried fruits, pure Swiss cheese, pure peanut butter, nuts, and seeds.*

We are adjusting your body's vibration so we can communicate through you. Start meditating 10 to 15 minutes at a time, and increase to half an hour, to an hour, then longer. The transition will be slow and easy, as if preparing for a marathon. This is your next step towards ascension. The purpose of your books is to raise the consciousness of the masses, and to help you prepare for the prophecies of the years 2012, 2013 to 2020. The predictions are to change awareness and show you what you need to do. It will be for the masses to change conscious awareness. You need to tape record all of our sessions as a proof. Save them so you are able to write exactly as WE are speaking. (Edgar Cayce is part of the Collective Consciousness.)

August 6, 2009—LORNA'S HEALING SESSIONS:

I began with prayer, and the Angels brought her little girl. She was abused as a child so I requested that the Angels show her why. She saw herself as an abusive man in a past life. I requested that the Angels bring all souls from every dimension that were abused by her and told Lorna to ask for forgiveness for making bad choices. Then I requested Angels' healing and clearing with gratitude.

I told her that I could see that she was struggling for growth. She told me that she wanted to grow to a point where nothing could bother her. When I told her she could do it, she looked at me and said, "I see the purest white light around you. It is so pure that I have never seen it around anyone before."

August 12, 2009—Lorna told me that the Blue Angel told her that I was put in her path for her soul's growth. He told her to ask me for a healing session. I was happy to assist her. I began with prayer asking Lorna to take a few deep breaths and describe what the Angels were showing her. She saw three soldiers: Roman, German, and British. We asked the Angels to show us what she was doing in her Roman life first. She watched in horror and began to cry. She saw him killing men, women, children, animals with his sword—anyone and anything that came into his path. He slaughtered them all and would not stop. He seemed to enjoy it. An expression of rage, hate and anger was on his face.

I told her to tell him to stop his mindless rampage because she was there to clear her past with the help of the Angels, and to heal that karmic life. He stopped killing and told her he was following orders. I explained to him that by following orders without thinking, he had earned a lot of karmic debts that he needed to meet within in other lifetimes. The only way to make peace was to ask for forgiveness from all of the souls he slaughtered mercilessly. He dropped his sword, knelt down and took his helmet off. I asked the Angels to bring all souls from every dimension to hear his prayer for forgiveness. Then I prayed for healing, changing the past, and clearing for all souls. They changed into orbs of white light and went up to the sky. The soldier's face softened with peace and this fragment integrated into Lorna's original soul. We thanked the Angels.

We worked with the German soldier next. I asked the Angels to show her what he had done. He was a high ranking soldier during the Holocaust. He herded people from the train compartments like cattle into gas chambers. He opened door after door and sent them to their deaths. He was heartless and merciless and showed no remorse over what he was doing.

We confronted him, made him realize what he had done, and showed him that he had to pay his karmic debts life after life. He knelt down to ask for forgiveness from all souls. Lorna saw the Angels weaving through the souls, cutting off their chains to free them as if they were tied to earth. They became white orbs that lifted into sky. It went on for a long time because there were so many souls.

Then she saw a huge Gold Angel with a golden orb in his hand and a Red Angel standing in front of her. I told her that the Gold Angel was Jesus. He was there to bless her with Christ's consciousness. The Red Angel is Uriel. He came to open her heart so she would be able to find Self love. She had to let go of her anger. I asked her to tell me who she was so angry at. Lorna said, "I am angry at my friend name Sharon. She was a good friend, but now she is doing things to me that make me very angry."

I asked the Angels to show Lorna what she had done to Sharon in a past life. Lorna saw herself as German soldier, taking Sharon away from her parents. First he raped her. Then he dragged her all the way to the gas chamber. Her skin was being ripped off by stones on the ground. She was in agony when he threw her into the gas chamber and closed the door. She was nineteen years old.

Now Lorna knew why Sharon was so angry with her. I told her that being angry with Sharon would not serve her soul and told the soldier to ask Sharon for forgiveness by picking her up and sitting her on a thrown to honor her soul. The soldier listened and took his helmet off. He began to rip all of the medals from his uniform while asking her for forgiveness. He made peace with her. I requested healing and clearing for all, including earth, with gratitude. Amen.

Then we worked with the British soldier. Lorna saw that he was afraid to die, so he didn't fight. He ran away into the forest and survived by eating animals until the battle was over. I asked, "Are you still fearful and constantly running away from situations you don't want to face?" She said, "Yes." I asked the Angels to release the energy of this pattern from the core of her being. We thanked the Angels.

August 13, 2009—Lorna channeled: We are here, but first WE are going to answer the questions you had. I asked who I was speaking to. She said, "Who you always speak to. WE are the Collective Consciousness." I did not have many questions prepared, so I asked if I was following my diet correctly.

C.C: *You are doing everything the right way. We will tell you all in due time as we always tell you.*

Rekha: How many people should I have in my workshop?

C.C: *Have limited people in each workshop and then add an extra night, with a limited amount of people. About ten would be fine. Just make sure you bring your books to each workshop. Offer to sign them. Don't worry about the amount of people coming in. It will happen. Those who need OUR help will be able to come in. WE want you to start going to other metaphysical book stores. WE want you to have a book signing event in each one of these metaphysical book stores so you can spread the word. Is this something you are comfortable with?*

Rekha: Yes. I have done it before and I can do it, but what would I write for them?

C.C: *Don't worry. You need not prepare. What each person needs to know will come through. The reason we wanted you to have this channeling session was so that we could tell you about another thing WE would like you to do. WE want you to hold workshops in these other metaphysical stores in the area. This can be done once a month, but you need to spread out. The more people you see the more exposure you will get. Don't worry so much about technical things. WE really want you to just expand. Don't worry about learning how to use computers or recording. Everything that needs to happen will happen. WE want you to expand out like white light that spreads out and touches people with its rays. You need to do that. You are going to be very busy. We want you to be fluid. We don't want you to be stagnant.*

August 14, 2009—I began Lorna's session with prayer and asked the Angels to bring her inner child. Lorna's voice changed into her little girl's angry and crying voice saying, "I don't want to do any healing." I told Lorna to tell her that she loves her. Hearing this, she replied that she does not believe her and the little girl began to shut down. She just wanted to suck her thumb. I told her she could because I knew she felt neglected. Then I told Lorna to pick her up and put her on her lap. The little girl spoke, "You left me."

I said, "Lorna abandoned you because she did not know how to keep communication open within, but the Angels are helping you to heal and Lorna is taking total responsibility. She will love you and fulfill all of your needs."

Lorna said in a soft, calm voice, "I will give all my love to you and I take total responsibility for your needs."

I told Lorna to comfort her and tell her that she was on a path of growth by making different choices. Lorna saw the Angels circling around her. The little girl was on her lap whispering that she wanted love and to trust people. She wanted compassion. I told her she was in the process of having all of it. She cuddled up to Lorna so she could feel her love. Lorna told her that she would protect her and allow her to move forward.

Then I told Lorna to put all of these repeated patterns of negative emotions in a garbage bag and ask for forgiveness from the Angels. Then I asked the Angels to remove and clear her stubbornness, filling the core of Lorna's being at the DNA level with Divine light. Lorna saw herself and her little girl in bright light. The Angels were kissing the little girl and holding her in their arms. Lorna felt her disappear into her heart. Lorna began to cry. She saw her little girl so pure and beautiful as the Angels continued to work on her. I explained that it would take the Angels a couple of days to completely integrate her new energies. We thanked the Angels.

August 20, 2009—I found Lorna's mind was too busy and there was no peace. I asked her why she was feeling this way. She said she was very angry and couldn't stop thinking about it. That told me that another level of anger had opened up for her. I asked Lorna to take a few deep breaths and tell me what the Angels were showing her. Her little girl did not come. I told her that wasn't important. The Angels decide what you need to see in order to heal.

She saw three lifetimes as a female with her present husband. She had the same abandonment issue in all three lives. In the first one, she saw her husband working, suddenly dying of a heart attack. She was in shock. She was young and very much in love with him. In the second, she saw her newly wedded husband commit suicide by hanging himself. This was another lifetime during which she experienced shock and trauma. In the third life, she saw them as a young, engaged couple. He left to fight in a war and never came back. She saw herself looking at her ring in tears, wondering if he was dead.

In her present life, Lorna is afraid that her husband will leave. She lives in fear of being abandoned again. I explained that her abandonment issue had begun many lifetimes before and was present in her childhood as well. The energy of this issue remained in her cellular memory and DNA. Her husband gave her three opportunities in the past to recognize this issue each time he left.

Lorna saw all three women were listening to me and understood that their focus on anger took away the opportunity to learn their lesson and change the pattern. I told them that the Angles were giving them this opportunity to change their perspective by focusing on the lesson. All three of them understood and let go of the anger of being abandoned. Lorna felt them disintegrate into her higher Self. After that, she felt peaceful. Her mind was calm and there was no anger left from those three lives. She saw a blue light exploding like a fire crackers in her eyes. Then she became silent and the next words I heard were "WE are here. Ask your questions." It surprised me, but I began to ask.

Rekha: Was I with my husband in any other life?
Collective Consciousness: *Yes. You were husband and wife in another lifetime in Egypt. You had many gifts then and were healing people with crystals, but you misused your gifts through five lifetimes. Now you must learn not to misuse the power.*
Rekha: Is this why I don't use crystals in this life?

C. C:	*It would be ok to use crystals in this life. It won't be as bad as you think.*
Rekha:	It is sad that it took such a long time for me to achieve this awareness.
C. C:	*Yes. You had many lessons to learn so you could be ready for this life.*
Rekha:	Have I finished my karma with my son?
C. C:	*No. Your karma is not done with your husband, your son, or your daughter. There are still some lessons that you all need to learn from each other. Lessons go both ways.*
Rekha:	Is it true that I had a lifetime as high priest in Egypt sentencing slaves to death by boiling in oil? How many slave lives did I take?
C. C:	*Yes. It was boiling water and boiling oil in Egypt, in 17 BC. You were quite a punisher. You had ten lifetimes of being slave. WE are very satisfied with what you are doing now. You have followed directions very precisely. Do you have any other questions?*
Rekha:	No. Thank you.

August 26, 2009—CHANNELING WITH LORNA

Rekha:	I am not able to meditate because I fall asleep and I am not doing it regularly.
Collective Consciousness:	*WE told you in the beginning that it would be wise to begin with 5 minutes, and increase to 10-15 and so on. Meditation is a habit you have to get into. While you are sleeping, WE are working on you. You are still under a meditative state. You are doing quite well.*
Rekha:	What are the reasons for money and weight issues?
C. C:	*All WE have to say about the money issue is that the Universe is filled with abundance, but the individual might be blocking their abundance for whatever reasons. The weight issue, you are quite aware of, it is emotional, it is also circumstances, protection of self, and vulnerability.*
	Now everything is going as planned. WE will let you know. WE do have one more thing to say. Try not to get so entrapped in thoughts of

worry. Let things come and go, and drift through your mind. Don't take them so seriously. Everything will be fixed as it should. You should not be distracted by the mundane things. WE know it is hard, especially in this reality. (I was stressed because the air conditioning in my car wasn't working.)

August 21, 2009—CATHY:

During an Angels' workshop, Cathy saw a very angry Voodoo Man with a painted face standing in front of her. I told her he was her in a past life. As this man, she killed many souls and created fear in others. That explained why she had been seeing many lifetimes in which her head had been chopped off. Cathy told the man that she is his future and that the Angels are helping us to heal and clear this lifetime by asking for forgiveness. He understood and knelt down to pray. I asked the Angels to bring all souls from every dimension to forgive him. They did and he became calm and peaceful. Then I finished the prayer releasing all souls into Divine light. They all became white doves and flew to heaven, and his peaceful energy integrated into Cathy's original soul. We thanked the Angels.

September 2, 2009—CATHY'S SESSION # 1:

Cathy came for private session. She brought an empty grocery bag with her. I wondered why. She said she had a weak stomach and it was bothering her that morning so she brought it just in case she needed it. I began the session with prayer and asked if her mother had a weak stomach. She thought for a minute and realized her mother has a weak stomach. It was simple. The Angels brought her back in her childhood so she could give her stomach problem back to her mother. It was cleared from her DNA and she was free of this parental imprinting. Then I told her to take a few deep breaths and tell me what the Angels were showing her. She saw herself dying on a cross, which explained why her feet hurt so badly and her arms felt oozy, as if she had no strength in them. I asked the Angels to heal and clear this life. She felt lighter and her feet and arms felt better. We thanked the Angels.

September 13, 2009—I gave a free class on Angels' healing. Cathy saw her little girl choking and gagging on chemical fumes, while her mother was using bleach and hair spray. She was telling her mother that she was killing her because she was allergic to the chemicals. I guided them through the Angels' healing process thanking the Angels. A week later Cathy told me that her allergies were gone and she was able to smell normally. She also mentioned that since our first session, her stomach had not bothered her again.

GRACE:

September 19, 2009—Cathy brought her friend Grace to my workshops. They were both continuing to grow and heal as the Angels showed them more issues and past lives. In one of Cathy's past lives she was Japanese Samurai. Her grandfather, who was also a Samurai, appeared because he wanted to be healed and cleared as well. They put their swords down with the blades facing away, knelt in surrender, and asked for forgiveness. I asked the Angels to bring all souls from every dimension to heal and free each other. Then I requested clearing for all souls and released them into Divine light with gratitude. Amen.

October 2, 2009—During this Angels' workshop Cathy's friend Grace saw herself as a man named John, being beheaded. I was told that she was John the Baptist in her past life. I requested her healing and thanked the Angels.

Grace wrote: Rekha, I have been in and out of my chiropractor's office for two years with chronic neck pain. Since my sessions with you I have been pain free. I have to say thank you. I would still be in pain if I hadn't found you. Because I have, I feel like I have been able to open up my heart and soul and follow my true Self. Thank you for helping me with that. Grace

DORIS:

Doris had been attending Angels' healing workshops frequently since I began in August 2009. She was gaining self-awareness. In this workshop, she saw her little girl at the age of four or five in her bedroom. She saw a man pass by her door and she became deeply frightened. Because of this fear, still forty-five years later, she was unable to sleep.

After the workshop, Doris told me that she could still feel the weight of her fear sitting on her chest. I asked the Angels to help her see her little girl again. This time, she was able to see more and told me who the man was. He was a young man who had committed suicide by hanging himself in the house before her parents moved in.

The Angels told me that his name began with a D and that he had never left. I told the young man that suicide did not end his life. He had lost hope. The Angels were there for him so he could choose differently and move into the light. He left and the Angels cleared his energies. We thanked the Angels.

The next day Doris called and told me that she had slept for the first night in forty five years. And her mother confirmed that the young man's last name was Denison.

During another workshop, Doris worked on her parental imprinting. She had a habit of collecting lots of papers, old receipts, bills etc. She wanted to know why she had this habit. I asked her to think about her family. Someone else must have this same habit. She realized it was her mother's habit, so she gave her back. When we give an issue back to a parent, the Angels always give parents a choice to change as well. The Angels cleared it from their DNA and I thanked them.

Doris' mother lived in another state with her sister. A month after this workshop, her sister called and told her that she didn't know what was going on with their mother. She suddenly started cleaning up all of her old papers, clothes and clutter. Angels' healing is truly amazing. It is effective in any area of life. It heals the whole family at the same time in all dimensions. Amen.

In the next workshop, Doris told me that she hated to get up to go to work and hated working. I asked her who was like that—who else in her family felt the same way? She thought about it and knew it wasn't her mother because she did not work. It was her father. She remembered a friend of his saying that he cursed everything at work. The Angles helped her give this issue back to her father, and they cleared it from their DNA. She called me the next day and told me that she had no problem getting up and that she enjoyed her work.

October 9, 2009—In the next workshop, Doris' issues of worrying and being overly concerned about things came up. Her mother and father both worried a lot. During the Angels' healing process, she tried to give the issue back to her mother, but she wouldn't take the bag and put it on the side. I had a big class that night and couldn't give too much personal attention to her.

After the workshop Doris said she felt like crying to let it all out, but she couldn't. She hoped she would be able to at home. I told her to call me if she couldn't, so I could assist her over the phone.

She called me the next day and told me that she couldn't cry. I prayed to the Angels and asked them to bring her little girl. She saw her sitting on her lap with a garbage bag in her hands. I told her to ask her little girl if her mother told her that she couldn't cry. Doris said her mother told her not to worry.

I told her to tell her little girl she was giving her permission to worry. She can cry to release this worry. After that, the little girl got up and gave her bag to her mother and the Angels cleared them. Doris was able to have a good cry after that. We finished healing and thanked the Angles. Amen.

CHAPTER 9

MUTUAL GROWTH WITH HOLLY

September 5, 2009—I first met Holly at the center when she asked if I could give her messages from the Angels. What came to my mind was that she needed to journal, to cut sugar and white flour from her diet to be a better channel, and that she is on her right path, etc. She told me that she saw a big blue light as I was speaking and that she is getting similar messages. She feels that she needs guidance, yet doesn't need channeling classes because she already has channeling skills. I told her I can guide her, although I do not channel like her, and advised her to attend Angel's workshop. I also suggested that she read my book because she will need the protection prayer and basic foundation in spirituality offered in the book. She bought the book and left, feeling happy.

September 11, 2009—Holly came to Angel's workshop with her mother. I began with prayer, working on parental imprinting, but Angel showed Holly a past life and she was crying profusely. She described it as follows: "I, my son, and many other people are hiding in a big house during war and a bomb fell on the hose. There is fire everywhere and we all are burning, screaming and crying, but there is no place to run."

I told her only the physical body feels pain and suffering. Your soul is not harmed and feels no pain, so take a deep breath and get in touch with your soul. She did, but her son was still afraid, screaming, and wasn't listening to her. After talking to him, he finally released himself. Then I told the same to the other people who were screaming. They all began to raise as a ball of light, feeling coolness—no heat or pain. Everything was quiet, peaceful and all souls were released into Divine light. Then I requested Angels for everyone's healing and clearing with gratitude. Amen.

September 25, 2009—Holly attended the next workshop with her partner, Amber. By this time, she had done channeling and wanted to share what she had written: I would like to know about Rekha Vidyarthi—why I feel she is so special to me:

"Holly, when you saw her, you felt a feeling in your "Gut." This is a tug of "Love." She is special to you because she is special and full of Knowledge. She offers very simple patterns of how things are to be. Do you feel like you should question her? We want you to watch her. Watch the way she loves us. Watch the light in her eyes. Her life has been a road of necessary things—things that were cornered off to present her in the place she stands now and the place she longs to be. Her heart is pure. Her lifetime and her lessons are what attract you. You were there in some of her journeys almost holding up signs to cheer her on, now she does the same for you; here we have the chain. She speaks with, a tongue of ancient times. She holds truths up to a windowpane for the light to shine through. She has worn the cloak of hardened awareness or lack of awareness, so that she can be here now. Look at the lines on her hands. They tell many stories of where and why she has been. There is a diamond in her heart and she is marked; marked in the light. She is holding a lantern for you."

After class, Holly, Amber, and I, sat down and Holly began to write, saying, "Jesus is coming through and telling me I was His apostle, Thomas, who doubted himself, and therefore, Jesus." I asked about my son, who he was. Holly saw my son as Jacob.

Jesus answered, *"AAH-HA, tell her Jacob, too, gave me troubles. That is why I placed him with her. I never left her. Even in bed at night, there are times your head is on your pillow and it is heavy, but your pillow it is not holding your head, it is I!"*

I thanked Jesus. He said, *"No need to thank me. Marigolds for you, Marigold means life, joy, and celebration. You should wear more yellow."*

Jesus: *Amber, I am Jesus. You almost giggle at me, my existence. I am human—no more, no less. I bleed like you. Your mother bleeds like me. Your mother has a wound in her side, as I have. Love her. You gave her the wound. You have jobs to do. Rope, lasso—lasso up the crew. There are people coming to you. You three are not alone. Amber is not Judas.*

Judas lived a life of doubt, which led him down the dark path. He fell out of love within himself and then, not loving Me. Amber, you fear that same path. Walk this same pasture like a child and I pick flowers for you. Lilies. You must reconnect. Go with her (Rekha). She is my mother, as every mother knows how to lead you to healing your wounds. Cycles repeat with you and this is what is happening with Holly.

You three bring hope, healing and happiness to many dark souls. **There will be many books. You appear in my Love and in my Name.** *Do not be afraid of what happened to me—doubt and persecution is a small price to pay. I am living a life of GOLD.*

Rekha, you hold gold coins in your hands and on your eyes. Sit with me, child, cross legs, meadow, and pasture, and un-tape gold coins from your eyes. It will come off; peace does not have a space in need and greed. The grass we are sitting on is soft and wet and so are our hearts. Pieces of your mind pop up throughout the day and I kiss your forehead. I hold your head.

Rekha: What do the gold coins represent?

Jesus: *Drop it; watch it spin. It keeps spinning, heads or tails, no more, no less. Don't dwell on it. It is to remind you of ego for the road that lies ahead.* **Life is for learning and tests give meaning.**

Holly: Has Rekha worked through all of ego's issues?

Jesus: *I am afraid not. Most souls have ego as a primary source of contamination.* (Now I understand my ego's greed (gold coins) of a past life and cleared these issues in January 2011 as Jesus taught Jill and I through His advanced healing prayer. It will be included in book 2.)

Holly: What must she focus on?

Jesus: *She has worked on many lives; however, one life will always work backward to the previous. She will need to continue working backwards, allowing her a chance of seeing. Seeing is her biggest obstacle right now. Feeling opens primary doors, but seeing completes it. In seeing, her vanity was in her way. Ego is a snake in the grass. Ego is a cooking pot of everything.*

I was stoned, as all were stoned, as all are stoned, as all stone each other. You must take the stones and build a house.

Holly: Jesus is thanking you for cleaning his body after his disciples brought him down from the cross. And you must cleanse everything, the cloth, cross, nails, water, earth, and every soul.

Jesus: *The Bible is as you are doing now; is as was done then; channeling, seeing, living, writing stories to prove points, and teach lessons. Too many people now miss the beauty of the story. The nativity should be the beginning and the end; doubting Thomas, doubting in Self, no more.*

Holly: Is Rekha supposed to treat us as a family?

Jesus: *As pebbles fall from a mountain, falling gaining, gaining speed, picking up speed so should the amount you carry on your back. You sat with me on the bench under the tree outside of where we lived. There is a breeze. This breeze holds many answers. The breeze washes over your third eye. In the space on your forehead, I kiss. You hear mild chimes. I made something for you—beautiful music to surround you when I was away and now you shall listen to the messages in my songs.*

FAMILY:

Your family is a tribe. They are strategically placed like feathers on a bird. Feathers are not only beautiful, but they give the bird flight. All families offer energy to their members. There are individual tribes on the earth that must learn to work together to survive and do as any tribe would. Families are very intricate pieces of this whole process because much of all existence flows through the family. And this is where yours comes in. Your tribe; this family, must learn to raise each other up so the bird can fly.

September 26, 2009—AMBER'S SESSION:

I began with Prayer. The Angels showed Amber her issue of not being able to talk about sexual orientation to her parents. I requested the Angel to show her where it began. She saw, as Egyptian soldier standing in crowd watching Jesus' Crucifixion. Amber described it as a huge crowd. She knew in her heart that Jesus was innocent, but couldn't speak her truth because she was afraid of being persecuted.

I said, "Can you see how you continue to create the same issue with your parents now? I want you to speak to this soldier and tell him his fear is holding him back from speaking his truth, but Angels are giving us an opportunity to speak our truth and change this issue by asking forgiveness. Jesus will forgive us and set us free." Upon hearing these words, the soldier knelt down, took off his helmet, and prayed.

At this point, Amber was crying. I began to pray to finish the healing process. She saw Jesus put his hands on the soldier's head. Amber felt good. Then she saw this soldier telling the rest of the crowd by waving his hand and asked them to do same. They all wanted to admit they were wrong and wanted to be healed and freed from this burden. They all threw their armor off and Jesus waved his hand over the crowd to free them.

Then, in the same life, Amber saw her brother's jealousy with him (as the soldier). Her brother in this life is her mother and she has same issue with Amber. I told Amber to ask forgiveness from his brother as she must have done the same in another life. Then Amber worked through her little girl on parental imprinting and was able to tell her dad about being gay. She made peace with her parents. Her little girl felt lighter, happier and loved. I thanked Jesus and His Angels.

HOLLY WROTE HER SESSION:

Rekha began with prayer. I was very relaxed and looked down at my feet, but they were not mine. They belonged to a man and I could see pants that were cut and jagged at calves. When I looked up, I saw a village from long ago. There were small "houses" and items hanging by ropes. There were mountains off in the distance, behind the houses. There were no streets per se, rather paths of dirt and pebbles. There were dogs running loose and goats tied by some of the houses.

I had olive skin and saw myself sitting on a bench. I looked at myself as the man with short dark brown hair and brown eyes. I could also see I was angry and sad. I saw Jesus and he was waiting for me with his other disciples. I was Thomas. I was the only one dressed differently. They all had robes. I had pants. This explained my separation of Self-doubt. I "felt" different.

As per Rekha's instructions, I stood up from the bench and told Thomas he didn't need to be so angry. There was nothing different about him that separated him from others because Jesus equally loved him. I could see Jesus standing there waiting patiently and lovingly. He was smiling. Thomas started to lighten up and feel more at ease. Thomas then handed me a red sash and walked over to Jesus. They began to walk as a group.

The whole village/town approached me as I stood by the bench, and started handing me red sashes. I held a HUGE bundle of red sashes. The dogs started running in circles excitedly and there was a feeling of "lifting" and happiness. Thomas was able to return as part of the group rather than an outsider looking in. Now he was wearing a robe and walked away with Jesus.

I asked Rekha, "What should I do with all these sashes?" She prayed that all sashes of fear, doubt, and negativity of all souls were bubbled and tied by Divine chords of light and cast away, never to return—filling every soul's core of being with Divine, sacred light, thanking Angels. Jesus smiled at me and they continued to walk as a group out of the village.

I felt at peace and a HUGE heaviness was lifted. It was a very beautiful and relaxing experience. I have much more healing to do with Thomas, as he still affects me to this day, as all of my lifetimes affect me. I am what I always was, what I always did, unless I heal. Healing is a very important part of my journey.

September 29, 2009—Holly and I got together to receive messages from Jesus:

Jesus: *Big smiles you have come.*
Holly: We are here in your name.
Jesus: *Yes, and I am giving both of you peonies pink flowers. Sit. Let's start.*
Holly: Thank you.
Jesus: *No need to thank me. This is our project.*
Holly: I am a changed person because of you.
Jesus: *You are a changed person because of yourself. I supply the road map, God supplies the scenery.*

Rekha: You put words so beautifully together with a profound meaning.

Jesus: *Words wrap beauty and words are like butterflies. The more different ones you piece together and let go, the more beautiful it will be.*

There are many, many hearts now on earth that are hardened beyond words, darkened, and in need of light as many of them walked in my time. Many walked in light to spread MY word, so shall you do in writing. Both of you receive ME as I AM HERE. This is my second coming and this is important. This is a foundation for the whole MOVEMENT.

Holly: What is coming next?

Jesus: *I have glorious things in store for you. My disciples are already around you, but they do not know nor will they be able to find you until you get the information out. You are writing the Light. The light will open the darkness in these hearts, one-by-one, and soon they will come. **Many books are to be written.** Love and learning are houses tall and years long. One book cannot hold it.*

Holly: Must we read the Bible?

Jesus: *You will skim through and certain stories will stand out. Please pay attention to the stories of my life day-to-day. When Devil was mentioned, it is devil within, not actual. **This is the devil that plays all conditions that the human spirit must cleanse.***

I want you to focus on happiness on celebration. I say again, the Bible should begin and end with nativity. I want this book to focus on BIRTH and LIFE. Too many have written about my death. My birth is more important than my death. My birth brought LIFE. My death brought lessons. Hold out your right hand, open all fingers, and bring down your two middle digits. On the front of the book I want my hand with my hole—a ruby placed on the hole. My BLOOD is now a JEM to see and this book comes to the world from ME.

PURE AND TRUE
LOVE FROM JESUS

Rekha: I told Holly, my husband was Joseph.

Jesus: *Joseph is as a beam in a home. He was there. He held the structure. No more, no less. I learned what I needed to have sturdiness from him.*

> *He is solid as a rock. You lean on a wooden beam; you will never be without a need to lean on that. You will not be done with him for that purpose in this life. He is there to hold you on that footing.*

Holly: My friend Sarah is Mary Magdalene.

Jesus: *She was a flower, a lotus that was picked too early. Look in Sarah's eyes; they will lead you. She is almost as poison and honey. The poison is her ignorance and doubt. The honey is her white and forever honesty and light. She must be cleansed so she can walk on water with ME. (Holly asked, "Why on water?") Her feet are so soft like velvet. Water is pure, she sees and speaks truth, and it is through her path and your guidance that she becomes part of this movement.*

> *One mouth feeds many, as a mother bird feeds her young. Rekha, you are this one mouth, that feeds the young, and it creates the chain. You are like my boat in the ocean. Get in the boat with her. She explains the waves.*

September 30, 2009—EMAIL CONVERSATION WITH HOLLY:

So much is being revealed! Like a flood gate has opened! Jesus says: "It is as I promised it would be. Continue . . ." I met **Peter**! Peter is Pam! On top of finding this out, a few weeks ago, she was awakened in the middle of night in a dream with the name Peter. Today we were discussing some things from last night and I looked in her eyes. It clicked! I said, "YOU ARE PETER!"

Then Jesus said, *"She is pure of heart. It is her purity; read about Peter's purity and loyalty. His stories match her stories. She is my right hand. She knows this. I have been trailing her for a long time. She has Positive connection and Lower fuel. She needs to build her fuel—connect with stories of Peter and she will find her light."*

Jesus says, "Happy Wednesday, my Mary. Happy day, Ama." (Sounds like Ah-Mah.)

Rekha: Did he really use this word? Amah is a Hindi word for mother. I think Jesus wants me to accept that I was Mary.

October 1, 2009—HOLLY WROTE A MESSAGE FROM JESUS:

*Rekha, any soul that comes to you in my name will be learning fast and growing. This is why you are so important because you are the spark that begins the flame. Through you, clearing begins. This clearing is imperative to this movement. This is the Chain. All will be involved to some degree of this movement. That is why it is called 'A Movement.' It will be a **big beautiful movement of many in my name!** The name of **LOVE**, I am LOVE. LOVE is ME. We are all ONE in LOVE. REJOICE! It has begun.*

__The jointed core will be the 12, including you.__ You are to lead and to council them. You are also to receive their gifts of wisdom and fruits from my tree. This will bring clearing of your own. We will continue from there. It is important now because all will begin filtering in. Everyone here was there. All souls are recycling now for a reason. __This is the second coming.__ It is time now on earth for Love to start spreading in my name correctly. Not because of fear. __Souls are to receive ME as easily as the day receives the moon and the moon receives the sun. There is no work for Love. When one must work FOR love, he has LOST Love.__

Rekha: Jesus is uplifting the world.

Holly: Yes! He is so beautiful, bright, and STRONG! I love Him working through me. I love being the window from which the light of His sunshine will filter through and it is only partial because He filters through all of us.

Rekha: Holly, you could work through the center to teach Journaling classes.

Holly: Jesus said, *"PRAISE! PRAISE! PRAISE! All is falling into place."*

October 8, 2009—Holly was out of town investigating haunted houses. When she came back, she wasn't Journaling much. I had a feeling that lost souls got attached to her, but she wasn't seeing. Finally, I wrote that she needs to clear these souls first and cleanse her energies in order to get in touch with Jesus again.

Holly: Done! It was a sweaty man with a beard, who was eating and choking. I could feel and see him breathing hard. I am afraid, but I need some time to meditate and connect on that level. I haven't meditated in a while, where I've isolated myself.

Rekha: This man wants to be released. An approach should involve Angels. Tell him, Angels are here to free him from his experience by choosing to follow Angel's light. Then thank him. We need to think and become creative with these souls and honor their choices. Use any idea with prayer it will work. Meditation is not necessary if you see him so clearly just talk he can hear you.

Holly: Rekha! He is gone! He was beautiful! I started talking to him. He felt he did not deserve to go into light. I started to tell him, he can go into light and I reached out to touch his face. He was ashamed, sad and confused. I also started to see the Angels lining up to my "right" and they were there to welcome him and bring him over. He started moving towards them and kept looking back at me and I kept praying and I requested Angels to bubble his confusion and said the prayer. Then I also asked them for cleansing, forgiveness, blessings and healing, thanking them in Jesus' holy name. And he was in the light. I felt "freeness" and now I feel so good and ALIVE inside! Thank you, Rekha!

October 9, 2009—EMAIL CONVERSATION WITH HOLLY:

Holly: I know my issues are opening up. Maybe we can channel a bit tonight after workshop?

Jesus: *When you do not journal or meditate, you are not identifying the connection. You must write and continue with your purpose because when you are not on this path, others cannot follow and learn of the movement. It is imperative that you do this. The movement must start with you.*

Rekha: Jesus will provide guidance for your inner movement. You are learning fast because He is helping you to grow spiritually.

Holly: Yes, we have to become strong within ourselves and in each other. I will get there early tonight. We have work to do!

Jesus: *Both of you are as necessary in this movement as the other. Both need each other. You will learn from and shine light on each other.*

SARAH'S EMAIL CONVERSATION:

Hello Rekha!

I haven't talked to you in so long, and the past couple days I haven't been feeling very spiritual, but today I am feeling it. So I thought it would be a perfect time to write. I had a question: Is it possible that other spiritual people can bring out my spirituality and my spirit guides more? Being around Holly and you, I feel, hear and see more things than normal.

Rekha: You are very spiritual, but you doubt. We create space where your doubt disappears and you get in touch with your soul and feel spiritual. But the Angels are always with you, have faith and ask guidance. They will provide you directly. Holly and I are with you to assist you in establishing direct connection with your Angels so you can receive your messages and healing.

Sarah: I do have a lot of doubt in myself, and I know it's not from this lifetime because I have had no experience that would hinder my Self-confidence. I need to sort it out, so tonight will be perfect to work on this problem. I feel like I am being pulled to just be quiet, listen, and meditate, but I have a hard time doing it at home. I have such a strong feeling I am going to get a message tonight, like I am waiting to hear from a long lost friend. I saw a tall ray of light today in the corner of my eye for a split second, and I knew in my heart it was Jesus, trying to show himself. I don't know why! Today is the start of a beautiful day, Rekha. See you later tonight.

Holly arrived early and we thanked Jesus for His guidance:

Jesus: *So be it tonight shall mark a festival within us-three. Wash away doubts because it is strong. Doubt that is the strongest is your own doubt that lies within you. When you can cleanse, remove, and get past it, you can then see and welcome ME. There will be much questioning with the two (fear and doubt).*

Sarah and Holly had many in-between lifetimes that are the starting points of fear and doubts. They focus on such petty things, when their soul's purpose is alive within ME. By removing the blockages you will begin to taste HONEY. Rekha already tasted HONEY. She has acquired jars upon jars and this is why the MOVEMENT is through her in great numbers. She will continue healing herself.

Do not worry about those who are local, who attempt to stop and question this FIRE. They are as swine and will be as small as a mustard seed. They may or may not grow in this lifetime. But you cannot allow their false, large persona to intimidate you.

Velvet grasses and your toes and feet will walk on soft grass. Stay with ME we will continue. The light is now shining. People are now thinking it must continue. It is only beginning. This is why it is important for Holly to continue cleansing and journaling. Write themes. The pen meets the paper. The more you write, the more you are adding oil to the FIRE within. You are the one sparking your flame. This is important. People can smell, taste and breathe through your writing. This is MY SECOND COMING. I am here. I have arrived. The sky is opening and trumpets are blaring. Souls now are able to be touched. Let them not hide and wither any more.

It began with twelve people, but many more are coming, that lifetime is recycling, yet the 12 are coming to you. One-by-one, you will know it internally, as if another log has been placed on to FIRE. They will be led to you now. They are already here on this plane and have filtered in and out of your knowing. When they filter back to you, you will feel it. Holly did her job with contacting and bringing in. The rest will filter, almost like a magnetic attraction of souls to you. Do not try to name and classify just yet. They are still filtering. There are things that must be done with those you already have. One log that is here now is darker, thicker, and older than the others. She is also the youngest in form. She bears much witness to my soul. It is imperative that layers and layers of darkness and dead wood be removed, so we all can rise. (Holly saw Jesus holding Sarah's soul in his hands like a flower.)

Mary, please have patience and go slow. Sarah and Peter have no idea how precious and important this is. And your speed in the delivery of my Angels is imperative because I am sending some special helpers.

Tonight you will feel a lot of love and warmth in the room because it is a celebration.

October 12, 2009—GINA'S SESSION # 8

I was told about Gina's past life with Jesus, but I wanted her to hear it. She wanted to do channeling. So I prayed and connected with Jesus:

Gina: Jesus is standing on a mountain with open arms, looking down, viewing lush vegetation, grass, trees, and abundance of nature, saying: *"Embrace the beauty, peace, and tranquility of the nature. Nature provides everything you need. Have gratitude, compassion, kindness, and love for nature. I AM Jesus. Yes, she understands that she was Andrew in her past life. The pain in her sacrum that she recently healed was from this lifetime. She was brutalized—a spear going through her sacrum area, severely beaten, and tied to a cross to die, as she refused to give up in her truth.*

The Bible is misinterpreted and manipulated by man. There is a thread of truth left of my life, a thread of truth. Mary Magdalene was my wife. I came to do an experience in human incarnation in that lifetime. And I experienced it all. I had a daughter, Sofia. After crucifixion Mary Magdalene went into hiding because they wanted to kill my blood line. Mother Mary was not virgin.

Jacob is your son now. He was a rebel. He had a hard time in believing and trusting his work in discernment and truth. He challenges everything, thus, shows very little faith. He will come around. He wrestles with his internal Self and with his beliefs. He questions everything. But faith is believing without seeing. It is a knowing in your heart. He needs to learn compassion, needs to open his heart. When he understands there is only love and is grateful for love, then the compassion begins from his heart. His arrogance will change into love. He will do that in this lifetime very soon. Everything is falling into place. The temple he has built around himself is crumbling. His thought forms and beliefs are falling apart because it is not the truth, therefore, not on a solid ground. So they are crumbling."

Gina began to take deep breath and said, "There is a wolf coming. It means there are difficult times coming. Then an Owl follows. Difficult times followed by expanded consciousness, togetherness, wisdom, love, and peace."

Collective Consciousness: *The difficult times are coming, but at every time in the history of the planet, there is conscious awareness growth of Divine of ALL THAT IS. It is like you need to expect the rug to be pulled from underneath. You call it chaos, you identify chaos with pain, suffering, mutilation of each other, and in the times to come there is more of this; more wars and more destruction. In 2012, it's the implosion of this reality and the awakening into new consciousness, into new light, into a new world; the promised years of peace and abundance. All those souls who have chosen to stay in chaos and darkness and have refused the gift of light, knowledge, and wisdom will continue their suffering, their confusion, their darkness until they choose, once again, to evolve, grow and seek Light.*

There is a lot of evil, but there is also much Love and Light to always conquer darkness. No fear. Fear is nothing more than an illusion. Darkness produces fear to bring confusion and inaction, which freezes you, stops you. (I was wondering who is speaking through Gina.) We are the pillars of light and when I say WE, I am talking about Collective Consciousness. It is a body of God. There are many souls that have reached mastery and immersed back with their twin flames, losing their identity, but each fragment had played an important role. The blending of energies creates a magnificent energy of love, gratitude, and compassion. WE rejoice in your choices, advancement, growth, and evolution because more of you are making the choice of Light.

There is "MORE LIGHT" in the planet right now. The planet is already anchored in fifth dimensional consciousness to heal and balance. The fifth dimensional planet is already in existence. We are there waiting for your arrival. A lot of you are already visiting and connecting to fifth dimensional consciousness. It is so awesome to see. It's like a blooming of flowers. It is ok to let go of third dimensional consciousness. You can still assist and help, even though illusion seems to be real.

Difficult times are coming, harder times of much fear. Each and every one of you on the path are totally protected and provided for. All of your needs are taken care of. Just continue doing your task because it's not a job, it's a TASK of LOVE. All Light Workers are connected to this consciousness. There is "MORE LIGHT" on the planet even though appearances seem to show otherwise. I am pleased and look at the planet in this consciousness. I place it in between my hands, sending down compassion and MY LOVE. It is a DIVINE PLAN and it's manifesting and unfolding just as it should be. It is my FATHER'S PROJECT of LOVE. It is perfection because the motivation and driving force is LOVE. Once we embrace the energy, it is capable to support and create this love.

All of darkness will dissipate. Everything that is negative and dark will cease to exist. There is so much light, so much creativity, and so much love in so many of you, that already, new dimensions and new universes are created because you are evolving and growing at incredible speed. Each day, you come closer to acknowledging and accepting that you are a spark of Divine, that you are the spark of the creative force, capable of manifesting all your dreams into realities.

You no longer need to live in this illusion that you have created for yourself with so much pain, darkness, suffering, fear, and anger. It is time to WAKE UP. Those who have chosen darkness are asleep. Their souls are asleep and WE will wake each and every one of them up. That's why things are speeding up. That's why there is so much destruction. That's why there are going to be so many challenges. It is not for you, but to give opportunities to those souls to wake up because WE love them too. WE don't give up because they are also a spark of Divine. Each and every one of you came from the same Creative Source, from the same Love Energy. Some of you decided to choose experiments and see other things, but WE will continue to set the alarm to awaken souls from that deep sleep of unconsciousness. Wake up! WE say wake up! Wake up!

All of your needs are taken care of. Wake up. Do not worry; you have our love and our support. WE understand the energy of money in third dimension, but you have little time to spend in third dimension. Continue to work as you are. Enjoy each day. Be peaceful and focused. Know that all your needs are provided and taken care of. **Believe because when you trust and believe without seeing, then you are awake and then you manifest.** Prepare yourself for journeys. WE will start taking you on special journeys where you can start creating your new place of being—the center of healing, center of teachings and learning. Allow yourself to dream big and allow your dreams to become realities. WE are always by your side, always guiding and protecting you. Your loved ones are protected and guided as well. Just focus on the task at hand and all your needs will be provided.

WE will meet face to face very soon. We will be celebrating at a beautiful table that WE have set for each and every one of you; bounty of wisdom, love, and abundance. WE are all at the table awaiting your arrival. What a feast and what a glorious day of celebration when we finally embrace each other in recognition, love, gratitude, and unity. Table is set; the feast is ready; continue doing what you are doing. Everything is revealed to you naturally and effortlessly. Do not concern yourself with the clarification and clarity you need. It is there when you need it and when you are ready to do next step—like climbing a ladder or staircase, one step at a time. The worse is already behind; just look forward.

WE are also providing energy and information. You are still processing and downloading information, energy, and wisdom from the gateway that WE just opened on 10/10/09. WE have been sending those messages for a long time it is just to wake you up in your awareness. There is yet another gateway opening with a lot of download and healing energies being multiplied and sent to assist each and every one of you.

This year you have three downloads. There is one in November on 11/11/09 and one in December 12/12/09. Those are gateways that WE open, bringing more light and consciousness and wisdom. It is for ALL. Every single one of you is getting downloads. Some of you are catching on, moving very rapidly, others are receiving downloads and will eventually awaken. Everyone is getting information; some of you are responding faster than others. These downloads are not discriminating, they are for each and every one. This information and energy is bringing *clarity, vision, love, gratitude, compassion, and continues to multiply Divine Light.*

WE have devised this plan of opening gateways of information and light because it is a concept that resonates with each and every one of you. WE have been sending messages for a very long time and you have resonated and responded very well. You are all very aware. When you look at the clock and you see 10:10, 11:11, 12:12, 2:22, 3:33, 4:44, 5:55 all those are just little codes triggers for soul to awaken. They are special codes guiding you, bringing information, knowledge and wisdom. Only there is Love. That's why I say: Do not worry; all your needs are taken care of. Just continue on your task with love, confidence, and the dedication that you have shown. Everything else, leave it to us.—Thank you—

Gina told me that this time she was more aware and even felt going through many layers of dimensions while coming back into her physical body. Our journey together will continue.

October13, 2009—HOLLY'S EMAIL:

There is a lot that will be unfolding and taking place. This center is like a magnet for believers. It is imperative that we are there now. It is interesting that I am there.

Jesus: *Not interesting, it is as planned.*

Holly: Thank you Jesus! Thank you for your messages and your beauty and your love!

Jesus: *Process the information. There will be a lot to tell, a lot to feel. Go inside of your mind. There are instructions there. I will give detailed information as to how this all must be. There will be messages and classes—classes of light and love on "How to journal from within." They are to guide people in getting in touch with their inner-selves through Self exploration and Self-love. **The key to unlocking true happiness and being able to love is through the Self.** The classes will be full of messages and instructions and you are to use your daily themes* *that you write. These will be your daily guidance of class literature. They will need to bring a notebook and writing utensil. They are to write what comes to their minds. This will begin their own journaling process and will light the fire within them.*

This process will also lead them to Rekha in which their soul's journey will be cleansed and their paths will be able to light up and begin THE MOVEMENT! Continue. Do not fear or doubt. You have an army of the Angel's support behind and beside you, carrying you all the way. People will come. They are already internally being projected toward your path. It is important to place yourself where they can find you. Do not stand behind false windows that will not light your path, but dim your message. You MUST stand firm on the single stone we place you on. The stone (again as we have stated before) is larger than it appears. You must realize that you are surrounded by many Angels who will guide you on your way.

Rekha has much to be thankful for. She is beyond pure of heart. She offers purity and clarity to those she encounters. But she must listen. There are a few small important notes she is missing. These are the missing keys that are needed to unlock doors ahead. All is happening as it should. All is unfolding as instructed. Please continue to glow and go forth in Jesus' name. Amen.

SARAH'S EMAIL: Good morning Rekha! I hope all is well. This morning was an interesting morning because something happened in my mirror that I have never felt before and couldn't translate. I was wondering if you could explain. I asked what it meant and got nothing back. I was brushing my teeth this morning, looking at myself in the mirror. I started looking deep into my eyes. All of a sudden it became so intense, all I could see was my blue eyes (somewhat glowing) and nothing else on my face. It wasn't a scary experience, but it was so intense and overwhelming that I had to look away. It wasn't a spirit, but whatever it was gave me a tunnel vision and I was almost like in a trance. I have no idea what they were trying to tell me. It was a strange experience and I wanted to ask what you thought.

Rekha: It is beautiful! You just met your "True Divine Self" your "Soul" that is much larger, purer, and with infinite knowledge and wisdom. That is "Who You Really Are." Physical aspect of you is a temporary outer casing, holding a fragment of your true form. This world is illusion. In your soul is truth and pure love. That is your goal in this life, to constantly live in those pure blue eyes. They are showing you your path and you will find it.

Sarah: Wow! No wonder it felt so powerful. I felt like it was trying to tell me something, although I don't know what. I can't get over how amazing it is . . . When you ask the Angels, they begin to show you things very quickly. Thank you Rekha.

October 13, 2009—CHANNELING WITH JESUS THROUGH HOLLY:

Rekha: Was Mary a virgin?

Jesus: *Mary was pure of heart. The heads (leaders) changed many things to suit their personal gains, including falsifying information about my life and my family. But Mary gave birth to others than me. There is a girl (one), and two boys, one died young. I was the only boy and my sister, Elizabeth of Noels. We were a quiet family. This was our tribe and our family, yet the heads tried to change it their way.*

I was human and lived a human life. I felt human pain and suffering. I bleed like a human, and I broke a toe. I loved feeding animals and I loved Liz. We would feed our parent's goats and donkeys. We did many things normal families would do. Amah knows Elizabeth. She is your daughter now. The two of you have many, many previous lives together. She is strong for you. She is also your set of wings although it may seem not. She married young and went away. You—Amah—missed her and cried greatly, and protected me more. Elizabeth, John's mom, was my second mother. She protected and watched when we were boys. You did the same for us. Joseph took it very hard when the eldest brother died, he drowned. He was three. I came two years later and Liz was two years after that.

Your daughter is on her own path. There were several lifetimes she went alone and did not learn what she was to learn. She has very deep Self-perfection issues. In turn, it suppresses her love of "Self," when she does not meet her own expectation. Her intelligence handicaps her soul's evolution. As her mom, you need to step back and know how to deal with her—use instinct, innovations, trust, impulses, and intuition. Trust in me and in your inner child. She still needs time. Stand still and unwavering; do not put your beliefs onto her. She will find her way.

Focus on prosperity with change, change comes with time. When you feel uncertain and it seems that "Nothing" is happening, that is when "WE" are working and everything is happening. Holly, you must have patience. She does not focus and plays with other things, items that take away her focus and time. Time is very important because she won't be here very long. She has a long road ahead of her with her many obligations to fill. She needs maturity of the brain to match her soul. She needs healing as Holly has much bloodshed in her past. She has caused much pain, she believes she knows it all now and she has only skimmed the surface. She cross references to all of her disabilities. She picks apart at things that mean nothing to her. She wants to dive deep without putting feet in the water. She does not want to do her work. Truth scares her because she is afraid she will be forgotten . . .

Suddenly, Holly saw herself as Thomas in his childhood. His mother abandoned him and she saw his mother as dark energy and was afraid of her. She also realized that his mother is her father now. I requested Jesus' clearing for his mother's dark possession and requested to clear Thomas' abandonment issue. Then Thomas asked forgiveness. Jesus hugged Thomas and Holly felt peaceful.

Jesus:　　*Rekha you reached a very important place within Holly. Amah, please keep doing the healing work. Holly, this is very important for you so you can reach the levels you need to reach. Holly, your book cannot and will not even begin without reaching this level. The more you neglect, the longer this takes because the fire is within you. The movement has begun and you are doing well. Fear within your surroundings and those around you, both seen and unseen, should not even be an issue. In ME is never fear. Fear is opposite of me. I* *have your hands as a father would hold his daughter. Stop looking for this in your dad; you have this in ME. I am healing her day by day through journaling and I will be doing more when she begins working with people. However, it is imperative for you, Rekha, to please walk her through time. She has many blinders on and cannot yet visualize everything on her own.*

Rekha: What was the relationship between Pat and Doris (two friends of mine) in a past life?

Jesus: *Doris and Pat were sisters and they are coming together in your classes for path crossing and for soul evolution. Doris has come a long way in a short period. Pat is still cloudy and attracting things that are not necessary. She keeps herself open and stays in a state of meditation. The meditation is important to receive information and quiet the body, but it is her openness that is a threat to her evolution.*

Grace is brilliant. She is so big inside because she has many, many big accomplishments. She is John the Baptist. Her compassion and love is cleansing and she needs to learn how to direct this from a pure state. She has a lot of internal issues of doubt and fear. Once cleansed and diminished, she will create Self-love and will be a figure of light.

Rekha, when you are healing, please be firmer with people. There are those who listen and grow, and all is done within reasonable time. There are others who will stay at your finger tips for hours and you will become exhausted.

Sarah must heal from my death. She had my child; she was a single mother and survived. I came to her many times; I still do. She knows this, yet she still questions.

My blood line is still living on earth. I am everywhere, literally. I have a very big family. My family fights with themselves; Israel versus Palestine. My blood line is in both. They do not even realize that they are fighting amongst family. Sadness falls on Jordan. Please pray for them. I pray every day. They still do not listen, as children do not listen to their parents. My blood line is in both Israel and Palestine. It is important that all know who I am and where my blood is still living and, in turn, being shed.

It is most important for Israel and Palestine to understand this. They MUST NOT continue to take what is not theirs, never was theirs, and never will be theirs. No land belongs to anyone but to the moon and stars. The earth is for all souls to borrow and coexist on. To use it as an "item" and then turn brother against brother, in literal terms, brings great sadness to all. Much of mankind will be watching what is taking place in Jordan. Sadness falls over Jordan. My children, my blood line, my gene pool has continued within the lakes and mountains, the hills and country sides of both Israel and Palestine. Both should RISE ABOVE the history of hate and betrayal and realize that the future lies in their hands. Put down the maps and plans of destruction. I see all. I see all that is hidden; plans of destruction for all races. This is and SHALL NOT BE! I tell you now! Remove and destroy what you are planning. The only punishment will be what you receive within your souls, should this carry out. Take down your weapons. Behind these plans are broken hearts of HURT AND PAIN, which is the root of all lessons. You MUST learn. You ALL are not learning! CHILDREN OF ISRAEL AND PALESTINE! PLEASE COME FORTH AND BOW YOUR HEADS AND LOOK AT ONE ANOTHER! YOU ARE FAMILY! You always were and always will be. You are a tribe greater than you know. You cannot undo what God has already done.

Holly: Will Rekha and I travel to Holy Land?

Jesus: *It is my wish. Beginning steps now must be taken so the future can take place. Right now, the Holy Land will come to you. Like I said before, all souls from my human past are recycling now. Rekha, your healing is important and by healing others, you are healing yourself, but listen to Holly because through me she continues to bring awareness to areas that are neglected.*

POSSESSIONS:

I ask Jesus to help me understand possessions. I had been clearing them with His help, but I need more clarity.

Jesus: Hmm . . . *She needs help! A body is a holding of soul; soul gets pushed out of the way, while another takes it's place. Yet, original* *soul is never gone. Through cleansing, you will be able to speak with parasite soul and send it into the light. The host soul can then return. Possession is no more than this; a parasite soul to be released into the light so host soul can regain the body. Any person, who is possessed, needs constant cleansing from then on to build spirituality, which will lock in the host soul and push away any negativity.*

You will know who is truly possessed by looking into the eyes. If they are possessed, another soul will speak back through the eyes. If they are not, you will notice the host soul is in place and safe. You are to use the Angels and send these parasite souls on their way, no more, no less. No different from cleansing. Do not be afraid. Some may be bolder than others, but we are all together and are one. WE ARE ALL OF GOD. ALL SOULS KNOW THIS WITHIN. They choose to forget this because of soul's stains. You know the process. This now brings you back to your life's work and research. You are protected and safe. Continue to heal and believe in us and be strong. You are Light and Love.

October 14, 2009—HOLLY'S EMAIL:

Holly: I just wanted to know why I am having SEVERE butterflies. It's a feeling when you go down a rollercoaster and you get butterflies in your stomach, but it won't stop. I think I know what it is: I am being shown Fourth dimension. I am also told not to doubt my "hunches" because everything that has been promised is happening. My consciousness is shifting. It's like I am shedding skin. I am also feeling a great sadness because ego's attachments are loosening up deep inside. I am seeing leaves falling. It is not bad. It is change.

Rekha: This is wonderful. As I was reading your email I asked Jesus to show you what is going on as He is right beside you. I never felt any of these shifts. You got your answer and you are moving very fast. Amen to that.

Holly: Yes, thank you. I also got a vision of Him standing by a donkey. He was brushing the donkey and asked me to stand by Him. I did. He smiled and took my hands and said, "This isn't going to be easy, but I am right here with you through this. This is all ok. Remember everything you have learned . . ." I had a sudden feeling of sadness and crying like something is going to happen. He kept holding my hands. I began to cry for real, maybe just a release. Not sure. I just feel uneasy and nervous.

I have been talking to Jesus. I feel like He is saying: to trust myself and my intuition. I am making this bigger than it is and everyone is going to be ok. This is more of a lesson for me and to trust my intuition instead of something actually happening. I need to trust Him and me alone.

October 15, 2009—HOLLY'S EMAIL:

Jesus: *We all have ability for different purposes; Holly is able to "see" because this is how she will work best to heal others through her work. You are able to "hear" and use your hands because it is mostly a pulling of your heart and because this is how you are able to work best to heal others. Please do not see this as negative. NOTHING is negative. It is how you look at it. Shift the light. You are far more advanced than others and therefore you do not need to "see" as much. You are there. They are still growing; learning how to use their gifts as one would use yarn to crochet. You have already made several garments!*

October 16, 2009—HOLLY'S EMAIL:

Holly: Ok, did Angels give you any other information about what is going to happen?

Rekha: Holly, please get in touch with your feelings and you will know all your answers. You can choose to be happy or sad. If you only look at your feelings and not focus on emotional drama then you will recognize your issue and know why you brought this experience. Outer experience is only a trigger to your inner condition. It is your sadness inside that is bothering you, not that something is going to happen.

In Mary's lifetime when Jesus temporarily left his body, I cried and cried, not knowing He had opened my issues that I had carried for lifetimes. This morning, it was part of Mary's pain I released. So you see Jesus' suffering on the cross served many souls' purpose by mirroring their own pain and suffering to this day. Meditate and find out or ask Jesus when and where you created this pain. He will gladly answer your question because we are primarily here to learn about our "Self," not to become psychics. But once you know your lesson, these feelings will make sense to you.

Holly: I went in my quiet place and the Angels showed me a life during the medieval period, where I was a drunken man abusing his wife. But it was deeper than that. It went back to his childhood because his father did the same thing to his mother. He couldn't forgive himself for making such a mess out of his life and hurting others, so over the years he gave up and stopped caring. He drank and became hopeless. He opened his shirt and there were a lot of little dark faces in his chest. I explained that he has to forgive himself because it is preventing him from LIVING and loving his wife, whom he does love (Amber). She was sitting and watching. He had lost control over himself and he controlled everyone else.

He was crying and I saw his parents. He gave all issues back to them. He was in such despair. After talking to him for a while, I said healing prayer and the heavy feeling lifted. I saw many Angels and told the woman I loved her. She smiled and said she knew. Then I saw a little boy walk out. It was their little boy and his father said. "I needed to go because I had work to do. There was a lot to fix and I had to tend to my yard that I had neglected." The woman was smiling like she got her family back. He was glowing and there was a feeling of a father and "the man of the house, the caretaker" has returned.

I then saw my mom and my aunt. I don't feel anything is going to happen. This is VERY REASSURING! Jesus is smiling like "I told you I would provide." I will be ok. Thank you Rekha!

Jesus: *Life does not justify happiness. Life reports, repairs and prepares you for your happiness . . . You set the pace.*

Holly: Jesus wants to say something to you: *"Long time ago, there was an issue with spouse. Let that go. It holds you back. Trees sway in the winds. The wind is what moves them. You must allow your issues of the past to move you."*

Rekha: Holly, could you please get more details from Jesus. Thank you.

Holly: I am seeing teeth, (I don't know why) bad dreams and money problem in the past.

Jesus: *Holly, please focus on what you are seeing. You have the ability to connect to me, within me and in me. You also have the ability to connect to others on my plane. There are many. They are walking and they all have many items in their hands, messages to give. You see them and feel them.*

You need guidance on how to use this ability because it will be important in your classes when helping others. There are souls that connect through you with symbols. Understanding these symbols is necessary.

Rekha must understand what was written before. Teeth refer to gnawing or gnashing. Bad dreams are how she was communicated with at one point and money was an issue she dealt with early on. Spouse is not an issue. Sponsor is. She will understand this. She, too, must go within. There are many lessons in this lifetime that she is still learning. We do not stop. She has clenched onto a part of her soul currently for something that has happened early on in this lifetime. She must go back and realize that "fervent emotions" binds you until you can let go within. Even younger children can lock things within. She was very intelligent when she was young. This separated her from other children at times. She remembers this feeling. She was not different just evolved. She knows this too. However, there were things that were done when she was a child that she must forgive herself for and understand, in her doing—small, but Meaningful Releasing.

Rekha: Holly, I wanted to tell you about Crystal and Rainbow Children's Class starting from next Saturday. It is not my idea; it is Jesus' idea. What do you get about it?

Holly: Before I even finished reading this, it came very clear and "loud" "*YES, It is important. There are mountains to be moved. You are instructional in this process.*"

Jesus: "*Currency for souls . . . Double-time, treason within.*"

Rekha: I have no clue about this, but it does not sound good. Please ask Jesus for more details.

October 19, 2009—JESUS' INSTRUCTIONS FOR OUR CLASSES:

Jesus: *Prepare for what is coming. Write. Pray. Think. Your minds are your best tools. They connect you to the levels within. Holly, there are many, many levels and you have much to focus on this week! Tomorrow night will be very important because I will need both of you to focus on the outline of your classes and how you will carry out what will be done when someone comes to you. Then this will open information about the journaling class. Rekha will also receive messages for herself. You both are interchangeable. Both of you are very important together. You both share much information from different Angles. You are ONE MIND—TWO SOULS. You two are very old souls on a very high level together; very intellectual and interchangeable. Lotus flower brings fruit to both. Open up with music. Music opens parts of the mind, which opens parts of the soul and creates connection. Openness is an ability to think and receive on a different level.*

October 20, 2009—Rekha: Please ask Jesus about "Currency for soul, double time, treason within." I think he is describing my past life, but I cannot figure it out.

Holly wrote:

Jesus: *Currency for soul: a previous life where you took money for saving souls. You did not have the ability to do this. You brought in dark magic and used the innocence of many for financial gain. Double* *time: Dual Purpose—darkness served its purpose for now you are in light. Treason within: betraying your own soul. Holly and you were both in this previous lifetime where you attempted to save souls for financial gain and it caused treason within. Release all to me. All souls are for God's handling. You know this now, but you did not know this then. Heal this in that previous life. They need to know that greed got in the way of what started as something in the light (the task you are completing now) and turned it into dark. This lifetime you both are in the completion of your previous tasks.*

Rekha: I didn't know that it was for both of us. We must be priests in that life. We will clear this life when we get together.

Holly: Very interesting! Yes, I guess I need clearing for this life, too. We were evidently partners in this. We allowed this. We used dark magic to entice people and also during the ceremonial process. This is all that I am seeing. I see us as both men. I see us both being greedy—money, money, money. We lost sight of what was really important. I think this is also a lesson for me now.

Jesus: *Channels are opening. Each cycle of the moon brings more awareness. Souls are starting to sense a deeper understanding of what is happening within them. They are sensing that they are connected to something. But proper awareness is a key right now. As you sleep, your souls download information. It will help you carry out your purposes on your path. You all develop at your own speed and in time, all souls will be ONE.*

Holly: It is very interesting! I feel like Jesus has much to say today in general.

Jesus: *Systematically, you are overanalyzing. All souls are doing this. They have been taught how to do this. It is imperative that you undo this and retrain your thinking. Thinking is the soul's way of programming the body. This is why it is difficult. You must surround yourself with like-minded souls so this process is easier.*

Rekha: Over analytical mind is often inherited from parents' DNA as parental imprinting. When we clear this issue we clear our parents, as well.

Holly: I need much help in this area. I can trace everything back to my parents. I have done the exercises multiple times without much success and still feel overwhelmed.

HOLLY'S SESSION:

I began Holly's session with prayer requesting Angels to bring her little girl. The little girl stood there with stone-like eyes and told Holly, "I have to let you go."

I told Holly, "You became little girl's mother. You were too busy fulfilling your inner need from outer means. So your little girl is viewing you as her mother because you have all your mother's imprinting. Now tell her you love her that you will fulfill all her needs and never abandon her."

The little girl's eyes started to soften and she began to listen. Angel gave her two bags and she filled them with parental imprinting, giving them back one at a time. Her father had a hard time taking it back, but I explained that he has an opportunity to release it and make a different choice. Then I requested to clear these issues from the cores of their beings and finished process of healing with gratitude.

Holly said, "I wasn't connecting with my little girl all this time when I was doing healing process. I was giving bags to my parents in my mind." I told her it can be done and cleared on a certain level, but not the level you desire if you intend to release it completely.

Then we worked on our past lives as priests, promising souls their salvation. Holly saw me standing in back and she was doing the work. They came as bodies without souls, knowing they are leaving. She slashed their wrists with rituals and chanting. I confronted the priests by telling them to open their eyes and see what kind of karmas they are creating with their greed and ignorance. I said, "Stop this chanting" and requested Jesus and Angels to remove their possessions.

After that, they were ready to ask forgiveness. Angels brought all souls from all dimensions and we made peace. I requested to change this life and our work into light by directing souls into God's hands and doing God's work Selflessly; cleansing everything, including earth, underneath earth, and releasing it into Divine light. We thanked God, Jesus and the Angels. Amen.

Rekha: Do we deal with many personalities in every lifetime?

Jesus: *Yes. Not too many personalities, but several. From several personalities, others grow or stem from the initial ones. But all souls are born with the basic personality kit (parental imprinting). Through people, relationships, events, and circumstances, these kits open and "free will" blossoms in the personalities as they began to take on karmic debts. This is where the karmic cycle takes place, but not every lifetime many personalities exist only few.*

Rekha: I must have worked on at least fifteen-plus personalities.

Jesus: *That is different. Do not confuse past lives and the soul's healing progression with the basics—parental imprinting in your DNA. You are born as detailed and intricate as you can be, so it should be simple. Not understanding the basics will create continuous problems if not dealt with. The basic "personality kit" is the tires on the car. Without basic threads of personalities (character, issues, habits), no one would realize their issues because so much is learned behavior, inherited from their parents' DNA. If they fought, you fought. If they were secretive about things, you will be doing the same and it must be cleared from the entire generation.*

Rekha: What else do we need to work on today?

Jesus: *Yours are much easier because you have worked from a forest and now have a desert with a few scattered trees left. Holly has a forest.*

Suddenly, Holly tightly closed her eyes and said, "Oh, my eyes hurt so badly and I have headaches for last two days, as if someone is poking in my eyes. I had been taking painkillers since yesterday with no relief.

Jesus: *Clasp this information tightly and go where it hurts. Go where this shadow is coming from—a black shadow from a dark past.*

I told Holly, "Close your eyes. Move back into a past life and Jesus will show you why you had created pain in your eyes. She saw a tall, handsome man with blue eyes and married, but women were like farm animals for him. He was in a high position, punishing women who had children out of wedlock by blinding them. But there were innocent women who did not have children out of wedlock and very young girls as well. His name was Rosario during 797 AD, in Greece. I told Holly, talk to this man and tell him you are his future and came to make peace with this life."

He replied, "My mother was old, blind, and single. She did not teach me anything. I did whatever I wanted. I stole, lied, did bad things, and was ruthless."

I told him, "You are only making excuses. Stop that and begin to accept responsibility of bad choices you made."

He said, "I did not know that I had a choice." Then he knelt down to pray asking forgiveness.

All the women and girls arrived, crying. Tears were flowing out of their empty sockets in joy to be released. Then they all went to pick up their children. They were vibrant wearing colorful dresses, happy, healed, and left.

Then there was one young girl standing quietly. I told Holly, "She is your daughter now and was punished by your hands." He went to her apologizing, giving her hug and kisses. As I finished praying, everything turned into white light and healed. He was very smart, read books, and told me that he chose this life for his solitude so he could look within, but it was easier to look without.

Rekha: I would like to know about rashes on my face caused by a mosquito bite on my hand two weeks ago.

Jesus: *Bacterial channel is sweating. Bacterial infection is causing a heat rash. Infection is now within. Mosquito bite brought bacteria. Bacteria are absorbed into cells and now reacting, while body is fighting resulting breakouts—need antibiotics.*

Rekha: Is this karmic?

Jesus: *Not all is karmic. Some moments are just moments. Some bugs do nothing but bite and they are beautiful nonetheless. The rash is inseparable and could not have taken place without bug, as life in general. The rash is to serve a purpose of knowing a presence. She must feel because her soul is moving and evolving so fast at times, it is important to keep her human. She is much evolved and sometimes her soul is not encouraged. She is on earth and it must be this way for that purpose.*

JESUS' INSTRUCTIONS FOR CHILDREN'S CLASS:

First Rekha, please know that anyone who takes concern in children realizes the depth of where my love begins. All of eternity lies within the magic and knowing of children. They possess ALL that adults and mankind are to know, especially now when they are entering oldest souls in youngest bodies. Collective Consciousness is entering because of all that is to take place. This is the strategy. We are placing our strongest with our wisest because those on earth need us most.

You are to teach them how to unlock the pier. There are to be no blockages. All beaches will connect to each other. They are naturally born with separation, they will, in turn, be teaching you. The souls stepping down and coming in are part of the bigger existence. They are the breath of a total body function. They do not have identity yet, but they will now because they wish to experience this and that is what makes these children so powerful.

First, start with prayer. Have them sit in a circle like I would do with them. Start with a name game. This will open their thinking on their level. It will be enough to open creative channels within them. Creativity is everything within children. Creativity in children is a meditation in adults. You will then ask: What are their biggest hopes and dreams? This will also set precedence in themselves.

This circular format also teaches respect and no cross talking (I said that I didn't know this). Most of them do not know this. You will then begin to share your dreams as Angels will give them to you. Write these dreams down. Please also take this time to explain and glorify all Angels. They need to understand how closely Angels work with children. They are on guard 24-7. Children sense them, but do not even know of their existence. These children even see them. You are to guide them in describing all they are seeing, feeling, and hearing because this is how they will be developing their abilities. Like WE said before that, you are the match. This time, they are the fire, and the movement continues in them.

You will ask if any of them have any messages to deliver. Have your recorder ready, they have many dual purposes. At the end you close with a prayer and fun. Have a special treat box to let them pick crystals. Use oils. Oils are senses to open children's awareness. Do not stress or worry, Holly, also with your classes too. Everything will fall where it supposed to. You will say what is needed and where it is needed. You are here doing perfectly, so do not worry. Rekha, focus on classes and on your book.

October 21, 2009—Holly wrote: I just wanted to thank you for the healing session last night. Something beautiful happened in general. I was showering this morning and my little girl and I talked. Then we went to my boss and made peace with her because I realized that there was something I did in a past life that is causing this karmic debt with her now. I went to her office with my little girl and apologized for anything I have done in previous life that has caused her to do what she is doing now. She showed me her teeth. I then told her that she, too, has the same option to go back and make peace, just as I am, and handed her the issues. Angels were there. I did a healing prayer. She said, "You partly chose this for lessons," which I firmly believe. But it was very peaceful and beautiful. Then my little girl jumped into my arms and disappeared into my heart.

I had a problem in the beginning with my little girl because her eyes froze again, but I spoke to her and pink flowers were blooming in her eyes. She smiled, "came to life" and took my hand to do healing. This life MUST be about healing the past and recognizing "why" it is important so we can make peace. Thank you so much.

Rekha: Thank Jesus and His Angels. I love to hear when people begin to work on themselves with their Angels.

I would like to ask: Why my light was going off and on and I am concerned about the mosquito bite spreading bacteria into my blood and now swelling, causing fear of death in me. I remember having Jaundice as a child and I had fear of death then. Now my head is hurting, my eyes are burning. Jesus mentioned "Mosquito bite" wasn't karmic. It made me think that the mosquito infected me to re-experience my past life's death, so I can heal this trauma that had been stored in my cellular memory and recreating same experience. Angel showed me: I was an old slave woman, no longer useful to Romans so I was to die from snakebite. I died in fear, loneliness, and horrible pain.

Jesus: *I take you now and hold you as close as a child. You are to remove this fear for I am removing it. Go to that lifetime of a slave woman and see what she was doing when she was bitten by the snake. This will make much sense when this is done. This is where healing is needed. Other than that, you are fine. I protect and bless you every step of the way. I lay down a path of Gold for you to walk on, for you are guiding MANY behind you. Please do not focus so much on this. Heal and move forward. The bite itself is not Karmic. The life before is. Remembering the jaundice as a child is purposeful because it is opening up MANY memories that are necessary NOW of your childhood. These memories are needed for your children's classes. Smile! This is all purposeful and beautiful. Your lights going off and on are for attention to wake you. I will do it again. Love and light always; Love and Light.*

Holly: Rekha I am typing a message from Jesus: *"Good morning MY beautiful child. You are as fresh and bright as the morning sun for all to see! You bring much needed hope and reassurance to those who cross your path. Please know that as you are reading this, I am placing my hands on your shoulders. Can you feel me? There is warmth radiating. You will feel it, a tingle. I am healing you. This healing is about to bring MANY blessings. Your internal clock is about to go off. Get ready because this journey is going to be very beautiful. You are very special and beautiful to me, as all souls are. You are just realizing this now. You are WAKING UP! Holly is a whisper to you, but you will be a bigger voice. You all have a purpose, as you chose previously. This is the Movement! Continue opening like a Lotus. It is happening. Do not question ahead. Do not look behind. Focus on where your feet are standing now and imagine them rooting deep into the earth. Your soul is deep within there. You have lived many beautiful STRONG lives and they are all now coming into fruition."*

Rekha: Thank you Jesus and Holly. I love you very much.

Holly: You too! Thank you Rekha! I could not have gotten here without you!

Rekha: I requested healing and it was in Egypt. We were many slaves, old, sick, and children. Although I was old, I was taking care of children. Roman soldiers brought many snakes in baskets and placed our hands in it and my bite was exactly where I was bitten by the bug. This life was karmic so I requested to change the past as I must have done to others. Amen.

Holly: Beautiful! Thank you for healing that because it affects me! I can almost see the baskets and snakes!

Rekha: Yes, I requested everyone's healing. Angels never heal one soul, but all souls in all dimensions. Maybe you were one of them and got healed. I get you were an old man.

My face was on fire, so I asked Jesus if this was another life's memory opening up.

Jesus: *Yes. In Egypt you were doing healing work and helped many, but pharaoh's people caught you and burned you to death.*

I realized that I caused suffering to others as an Egyptian High Priest. Therefore, I requested healing by asking forgiveness from all souls and clearing karmic debts, thanking Angels.

October 22, 2009—Holly wrote: Jesus is saying: *There is much bricklaying today; much mortar in the cracks. Removing this mortar will remove these bricks and you will be able to see clearly into many layers.*

Classroom begins within. All too often, we look outside of classroom and pick flowers because it is easier to distract ourselves from ourselves. Cathy does this quite a lot. Holly needs to bring people back into the classroom. Rekha is already there. There is chalk. There is a black board. Life is the blackboard, soul is the chalk. Holly has much information to offer. She is flowing with energy and light. MUCH flows through her.

Rekha is a pivotal tool in this teaching process. Others will filter in and out, but it is in you that they find the necessary information needed to apply. You studied many books and much information in the past and you obtain much information within. You must go within to pull out this information. Your soul houses this knowledge. The Angels also assist you in finding this information. Time is of the essence. Not everyone will remain within your classroom. They will come to you. You will deliver messages of Truth, Love and Light. They will leave and continue the process.

Holly, do not stall or waste time. You are good at this. You run in circles around yourself. Focus. The rest will follow.

Creativity to children is what meditation is to adults. Meditation opens the mind so one can see. Without meditation, one cannot see the plane on which the soul goes to converse.

October 25, 2009—Holly: I am at work on Sunday. No one is here and I am taking a moment to channel. I do not clearly understand all that is happening lately.

"Waves are necessary for balance. When one is surfing, they rely on waves, combined with their skills of balance. Without waves there is nothing to learn to balance with."

Holly: Ok, right now, I am going through waves to learn how to balance. Why does the process have to be so hard?

"Without the intensity of the wave or the number of waves, a surfer would never be doing just that—surfing. Life is like surfing. Once you can make it to the top of your board and maintain that position, the scenery is breathtaking. It is worth all of the work to get there. Unless you learn how to stay on top of your board, you could never experience the view. Life is about hard work, awareness, balancing, and learning—all combined so you can enjoy the scenery."

Holly: It's a good way to explain it to me.

"We are wording it in ways that younger people can understand. Too much information has been relayed to older people for their understanding. But much has been missed in younger generations. They hold so much data that they brought with them to this earth. This data is unusable unless they are nurtured, loved, and valued. The generations of today have lost some value because the generations that have gone before them have lost all value."

Holly: I am trying to teach my daughter things that I never learned: calmness and love. That was never taught to me because it was never taught to my parents.

"Don't you see? Without your parents being who and how they are, you would never be how you are, which, in turn, helps to mold how your children will be. Human kind reflects on itself and affects the current generations from both ends to the middle. It always has, from the beginning of time. History teaches you patterns, which give you road maps on how to change what has not worked before. God has created this pattern for a reason. The present time gives you the opportunity to learn from all that has taken place prior. This is what prolongs lifetimes.

Many souls don't learn from the past, from previous mistakes. **Mistakes are one of God's best creations**. They are gifts for the future. On small accounts and much larger accounts, humans have always made mistakes for their own progression, but MOSTLY for the progression of others. People do not realize how essential their interaction is for promoting each other's growth.

Life is not about comparison; in general, it's about learning what to compare with certain things. You cannot compare Albert Einstein with Thomas Edison; both are intelligent on a very different physical level. One was intelligent of the mind and one was intelligent of the heart. Albert was gifted with many additional areas within the mind, which he was able to transmit and receive brain waves at very high/fast frequencies. Thomas was lead by his soul, directly to and through his heart. His heart leads most of his reasoning behind most of what led his thoughts and inventions. Both were triggered by waves—waves of the mind and waves within the heart; both are neurotransmitters waves, which fuel intelligence. Regardless, both men could not be compared.

In life, people are to learn how to compare likes and be pulled toward the likes, rather than the dislikes. When you compare dislikes, it is like comparing two negative ends of a magnet. They repel and will never, and can never be compared. Comparing is like "clicking." Look at life like "clicking." What two things can click and what two things cannot. Who can you click with and who can you not? What feelings click within you and what do not? We have clearly gotten off subject here, but it has been a long time since we have been able to speak. The point is that God has created everything to take place as it should. All human kind will click or not click, and it's all up to them. You all have the ability to click within yourselves and, in turn, you will learn how to click along your path. It's a progressional process. It's God's most perfect plan for Humanity."

Holly: May I know who you are?

"We are twins within Collective Consciousness. We have been marked as twins. There are two of us. All have been marked here—super souls who are eternal and the most loving. We all have evolved to the highest light and because we are connected with all of humanity, we are here."

Holly: How are all of you marked in Collective Consciousness?

C.C: *We are marked by our eternal umbilical cord as all of you will be marked. This is how you came into the existence with your connected soul. We do not say "soul mate" because there is not a permanent mate of soul, but your connected soul is the exact equal soul that was created at the exact same second, moment, and space as your soul. Two souls must spur; created at the same moment in order for a soul to come into existence. That is the key to life in general. Not shocking or beautiful, but necessary. We literally could not exist without each other. Each and every one soul is exactly tied to another, equaling two halves to equal one whole soul. It is like a yin and yang. Your soul could not have sparked without the other. All souls are a spark.*

Each set of two halves comes in with one eternal umbilical cord—a Divine cord, which keeps two halves forever connected. When both halves learn all lessons needed to achieve the level desired of learning upon soul creation, then they will connect again and be risen to Collective Consciousness and marked. You are already pre-marked. The final marking is just your crest, your final "grade," school complete, for example. We were marked twins because that is what we are—true pure twins, also of Gemini sign with knowledge in Pisces (our complete opposite). You will always have knowledge in the complete opposite; Balance.

Holly: I understand this to a point but each question creates more questions and so on . . .

C. C: *And so it should, it always will; more questions, more answers and more questions. Be careful though because there is a limit of what HUMAN mind can understand. This also has to do with your lifetimes and your personal level of awareness.*

Holly: But back to the "connected soul" thing! Where is this identical connected soul during our lives?

C.C: *Each soul will ultimately work through life back to each other. You are TYPICALLY learning lessons to lead yourselves back to one another. Once you meet again—sometimes this takes many, many lifetimes—you will have a few final lifetimes together for final internal lessons and then you will move on within the Collective Consciousness.*

Once here, we work together to guide and offer the best case scenario for each soul who needs guidance and help. We cannot change paths for you, but we collaborate the best possible way. You can still learn your lesson, while others still learn theirs and still stay remotely close to the same path. The littlest things can bump and deter several paths at once. It is our job to try to keep it all organized. You have the choices to remove or create roadblocks within your path, but your path never changes. You can change the scenery, but the path is the same. Sometimes, you THINK you can stop, jump or alter your path, but you cannot. All humanity travels on their own eternal umbilical cord to and from God. ALL PATHS LEAD TO GOD.

Holly: I have heard that saying before.

C. C: *It's true. Again! Not strange or shocking, but necessary. People often stand in awe or shock when a miracle happens or something catches their eye. This is a fraction of what happens on the Other Side. Soul only knows miracles; it creates them.* **You create miracles every day.** *Miracles come from within; they are a God-given right—a gift. There is nothing shocking about that. Necessary! Miracles create hope. Hope creates faith. Faith creates breathing WITHIN God.*

So yes, Miracles equal God, but it is humanity that must work through the miracle and realize it in order to enjoy it and for it to equal God. There are MANY Miracles each day, each second. Every relationship, moment, smile, trial, lesson, and life are all Miracles. People put too much emphasis into things. God makes them simple. **You put emphasis into things you shouldn't and miss the areas that require your attention.** *This creates lessons. It is all one big lesson. This channeling is a lesson."*

Holly: Thank you, for working through me to deliver light to dark places and bring love and hope to those who have a hard time with loving themselves. Amen.

C.C: *Your life was the way it was because you needed to learn how important clarity and Self-love and nurturing are. It's the only way you are able to be compassionate with others. Go in love and light—In Jesus' Holy name. Amen.*

October 26, 2009—Rekha wrote: I would like to ask Jesus about being sick with Chicken Pox as a child. In high fever, I use to leave my body and remember being in bright light, looking down at my room. I could describe what was going on and tried to explain to my mother. She thought I was hallucinating. I had another experience of being lost and dying in a forest, but an Angel brought me back to my parents (written in my first book). Are all these childhood experiences past lives' Karma? It is pretty hard to figure out and I need help to understand if I need to heal these experiences. Thank you.

Jesus: *No. They happened to show you just how attached to the chain of consciousness you really are. Keep remembering your childhood. There is more. More that was revealed then, to be remembered now. Not everything is Karmic debts. There are credits and debits and there are still lessons that create both. Then, in-between, there are moments where additional information and events take place for karmic/learning of others through you. This is what is happening with your childhood, so many pure and beautiful gifts were bestowed on you. Many things were revealed to you that have been revealed to some of the children coming to your classes. This will be a combining of information and data. You cannot combine with that which you do not know. Now you will know. One thought will bring others, which will bring memories.*

October 27, 2009—Holly: Why am I not smarter than I think I should be?

Jesus: *Book smart is very different from soul smart, you are very soul smart.*

Holly: I have a big test at work that I am supposed to be studying for. It is to be done by November 16, 2009. Why can't I complete it?

Jesus: *There are lessons within this book. You do not want to complete it because this is yet another mountain you created. Should you have*

	completed each chapter per week or month during the original time allowed, you would have been done already.
Holly:	Now I am behind. What do I do?
Jesus:	*You must focus and juggle your time wisely. We will help where we can, but your finishing is important in your progression. It's not the lesson within the book; it's the lesson of the book. It is about accomplishment.*
Rekha:	I would like to know details about my Chinese King's lifetime.
Jesus:	*Chinese emperor—many, many murders, many even within his family. Same parents you had then, but not same issues. He was the one who held the axe. Thousands were killed, but many were sacrificed for your learning. You were lonely, miserable, could never be comfortable, and had many problems with your knee and feet. The more that an individual misses the ability to learn, misses their lessons; the more miserable they are, and the more resentment and blame set in, fueling the ego.*

It's an irritable circle. Much emotional inflammation of disgust, anger, hopelessness, depression, sadness, violence, and it all equals to the same thing, separation from the Light. You had many moments of solitude in that life, but painful knees and feet made you uncomfortable because you felt you deserved disarray from a previous lifetime. You were a bagger and a thief. You stole from many and your life was so empty. When you were caught, your legs were severed from knees. You were a man, forty years of age.

Holly, you had many lifetimes centered around and for money. Money was used as the item of choice for your lessons. You chose this. Vanity is a big issue for you; you cover up your ego with money. You have killed for money, now you are changing your pace in this lifetime, but it will sneak up on you.

Holly:	When someone close dies in the family, why do some feel more pain than the others?
Jesus:	*It's the level of connection of soul's attachment. This is the level of how close or how removed you are with the cord in a physical soul connection—meaning the souls were spurred ignite onto and tied with*

the umbilical cord. When there is no longer a distance between the souls and they have come together, another set of souls were created, and so on; thus soul cluster, but in literal terms of measurement like distance between souls being spurred. The closer you are on your cord at creation to another, closer your connection in life will be—your soul connection.

Rekha, detachment is one of your issues. Do you truly believe you can make peace with the absence of your spouse and those close to you? Peace is interpreted in many different ways. Do not be confused between peace and solitude. A life alone is not peaceful. They are in your life for lessons and you must learn how to give them your joy. Your spousal soul needs your joy for some of his lessons. Your joy is mirror image; give it, receive it. By bringing joy to him, he will teach you how to bring joy to yourself and to others. You must realize that there are levels of joy and you are missing some of them. You work hard, but there must be balance. Your daughter is a mirror image of yourself in this lifetime. Classify the connection in your meditation.

October 29, 2009—Holly wrote: I am in a fog. I am in a moment of learning how to juggle, but it's HARD. I am overwhelmed. There is SO much information out there to channel and I am running out of time. In any event, this too shall pass. Jesus has never ceased leaving me signs of his presence. It still doesn't change the fact that I want to curl into a ball and cry. It's so hard sometimes when soul wants to run and the body can't keep up. I feel like I have lost control of my surroundings and the world is whirling around me. Tomorrow, I have Maria (7 year old daughter) again for two weeks and the pace picks up again. (Jesus says, "Such is life.")

Do Angels say anything to you right now about me? Like I receive information about you, do you hear anything for me?

Rekha: You are not any different than me, the only difference maybe when I am in fog, which I have been since yesterday. I begin to search within and sort out my feelings, tracing them back to my childhood, but lately to my past lives. And I learned to trust what I feel and hear from the Angels. You need to do the same.

Angel is saying, *"Set your priorities. You come first and as you clean up your issues, you will begin to see what is next. You will have to work hard, but WE will provide. Say to yourself, you have time for everything and you can accomplish anything you focus your mind to. Maria is reacting to your thoughts and energy. Think positive about her and around her. That will allow you to do your work while she does hers. You need to change your attitude to bring changes in life."*

Holly: Goodness Rekha, they are beautiful through you! All information I channel is not easy to apply, but I make it a mountain. I feel, at times, there isn't enough time to learn everything, yet the time is slowed for learning. Interesting!

Jesus: *All time is learning. All learning creates time. Each lesson turns hands on the clock of life. Life on earth stands within a master clock, God's clock, which is mandated and run by the White Angel. When you feel as if you have run out of time, it is because **you are not standing within what is to be learned**. Pray to the White Angel and SHE will assist you with what is needed now. She hears and sees all. But it is up to the soul to go to HER, as it is with all Angels.*

MENTAL DISORDER:

Holly: I have much to learn, but my mind is receiving so much information! I am getting something I channeled the other night about Akashic records (past lives reading) because I am being shown souls that have mental disorders. They showed me the word: Disorder. Then my brain started flying: If I can connect to other realms and receive messages, then there are people who can do the same thing and become "stuck" even in previous lifetimes and the mental "disorders" manifest and grow over time, manifesting as a symptom, rather than a true diagnosis. Autism, depression, bi-polar, schizophrenia, ADD, etc. These souls have been "jammed" like a finger gets jammed and this is how we become stuck in time. Our physical bodies just live as a reaction to this life, life-after-life.

This made me think of Akashic records because there is a connection with what I channeled and what I was "seeing" today. Souls are stuck and cannot completely be in a human body because personalities are changing at such a fast pace that the human body could not hold one personality, so they are in limbo. What if this applies to people with mental disorders? It is easier to take control of a body that is in this state. As time passes, the soul becomes weaker and weaker and then possibly ends up short-circuiting and not being able to "stay" in the human body like old batteries.

There are those who have different levels of "disorders" and need deeper work. These souls need Angel's help, combining psychiatry and psychology with spirituality, and requesting Angels to heal, clear, and mend their soul's fragment.

Rekha: It kind of makes sense, but I am not very clear. Maybe Jesus can explain how and why these souls get stuck in other dimensions? There can be many reasons for that.

Holly: Maybe, but there are MANY! The majority of humanity is medicated and many are hospitalized for this reason. I just don't understand certain things. But in the big picture, it doesn't matter. Then when I wrote that last sentence, Jesus said, *"This is the big picture. All humanity is the big picture. All is done for humanity and all is undone by humanity."* So what am I supposed to do? I will just continue writing . . .

AMBER'S HEALING SESSION:

Holly called at night and asked Angel's healing for Amber. She was curled up in bed, feeling sorry for herself. I requested the Angel to show her why people were putting her down at work. It was her father's imprinting. She chose her father because of her past life's treatment of judging others and now she is meeting this within herself. Angels showed her past life, doing the same thing to many souls, and she asked their forgiveness. After healing, she felt free, lighter, and happier. Amen.

October 30, 2009—Rekha: How is Amber doing this morning? And I would like to have more information on how Autistic children's fragments are stuck in other dimensions.

Holly: Amber said she felt "clearer" when you were done. What is interesting is that she couldn't really "see" anything. I held her hand and as you both did what you were doing, I meditated and saw Jesus and Angels had hands over her head and a circle of light from their hands completely covered her. You were also there with your hands on her shoulders. Then Jesus touched His eyes and put His hands on Amber's eyes and forehead. At that moment during the healing, you had asked Amber if she could see the souls she had judged and she said, "Yes."

When you were off the phone, she said to me, "It was so strange. I couldn't see anything, but when Rekha asked me about seeing the souls, I saw many of them walking and they almost had flaming hair." I thought that was interesting.

Some other very strange things happened last night when I was channeling. Something was communicating with me in terms of "we." Not like I talk to Jesus, but some entity. He was not good, but said, "When a level of consciousness is altered, then it is very easy for us to take over. We cannot take control of a soul, but we can enter a body. The soul just gets bumped out of the way, since it is in the altered state. When a soul is not secure within itself, it is easy for us to take over. The soul is off in another realm, a trance state, and we are able to enter—Disorder. We are able to anchor ourselves within the body at the base of the ankles and the base of the head at the neck."

I then began to pray and he did not stay within me, but he was around me all day. I felt breezes at work when there are never breezes. I felt Goosebumps. All is good, though. I was also told last night that "I should turn counter-clockwise to seal the circle of protection."

Rekha: This explains how souls get stuck in other dimensions. Maybe, in some past life, we were alcoholics or drug addicts or depressed or had no desire to live or committed suicide, and in this altered state of mind, our souls wandered off in some lower dimensions and got stuck, allowing spiritless souls to enter our bodies. And when we chose a physical body again in next incarnation, we are born with mental disorder. Please ask Jesus if this is correct.

I also feel that we were trying to run away from life because we didn't want to face our karmic debts, but there is no escape. The possessions are fulfilling their hunger through the host body. Holly, you experienced possession during the healing of a past life when you were a shoe cobbler, crying inside to be free from the possession. And Jesus freed you.

Holly: Yes! You understand so much that most people do not. The way you described drugs and alter state of mind was correct. But I am getting that "just as there are different levels of consciousness and soul awareness, there are different levels of autism." When you spoke of addictions in a past life, I saw myself as a young guy in the 60's who used heroin and other "recreational drugs."

Jesus: *Chemical reactions that take place within the mind as a result of chemicals put into the body alter the psychosis, which changes the level of consciousness—the connection between mind and soul. There are many reasons a mind is Autistic or has another ailment. Not all are easily classifiable within this text now. There is a list that branches off into other lists. There are multiple reasons for these symptoms. They are not easily traceable to one path or consequence. When a soul chooses a body, it is coherent upon entering. Once it is in human form, the soul consciousness can shift and change and this is when symptoms from past life experiences transpire.*

November 2, 2009—Rekha: Holly, I want to share my dream with you. I was staying in a hotel and ready to go out. As I stepped out on a sidewalk, it was covered with white feathers of all shapes, kinds, and sizes. They were so soft and beautiful. I began to pick up a few big ones for Doris. I had never seen these kinds of feathers before and did not see any bird. When I woke up I asked what this dream represents. I heard, "You were in seventh dimension."

Holly: **Jesus says,** *"Rekha, please step softly. Transitioning to next dimension is necessary and appropriate now. However, there is much* *that you must remember—locations to continue to visit, even though you will be evolving. Many dimensions will need you. Feathers represent acknowledgment and light. Hold fast to your dreams because this is where you see!"*

CHANNELING SESSION WITH GINA # 9

Later that day, Gina and I got together at Donna's house. I began with prayer and Gina said, "We are in seventh dimension. We arrived there through a beautiful staircase made of diamonds, like an escalator, everything is very brilliant and bright, yet it doesn't hurt the eyes. There is a tremendous amount of white light. Jesus is here. HE is the overseer of everything."

Collective Consciousness: *There is the energy of Edgar Cayce, energy of Archangels, energy of collective consciousness and you will ask why Jesus is not present, but HE is in the continence of God because WE are love. WE are totally embraced with the vibration of love.*

There are waves and waves of light. If you close your eyes, you will feel the waves of light/love rolling in like a sea of waves, one after another. Feel the love surrounding your Self with each incoming and outgoing wave, allowing you to be centered, totally supporting and embracing you. Knowing your experience and the lessons are illusion, not truth. WE are here for you. You can refer to us as TEAM of LIGHT.

Rekha: What Donna must do?

C. C: *Allow her heart to expand. Remove all those locks, bolts, and blockages that she has put on through eons of time, blocking her energy center. We speak of heart. WE speak that she has so much love to share. Allow your heart to inspire you, your perception will change instantly, your anger will leave and your vibrations will change. WE are speaking of your emotions. Healing fear, doubts, and anger will be beneficial to get in touch with your soul because WE will work to open the bolt of your heart. You will feel pain in your chest; more emotions of anger will manifest. The spectrum of emotions will be from a very deep and dark place. You need to take that step into darkness and emerge into* *light. Honor the process. This darkness is all Self-imposed by you. Our love is so great for you. That's why WE bring the assistance and WE ask: Are you ready to let it go? WE do not separate from you. You are the one who separated from us.*

In the physical dimension, the intensity in your feeling and emotions has a sense of speed, and there is a sense of knowing. Know that in this dimension of consciousness, it is already done; you already are emerged into fifth dimension. The table is set for all of you to join us and break the holy bread and drink the holy water. We are speaking to you in symbols. There is a tremendous gift in sitting at the table, sharing knowledge with you. Each and everyone have a gift; each and everyone have wisdom. We have the entire source of knowledge and wisdom, but you only access the information, knowledge, and wisdom you need. You will be provided for, when your intention is of love and truth. Reason for God and Angelic beings present at the table is also part of teaching. They are there to assist you. WE are always present. WE are always there.

Rekha: How long will Holly and I be at this Metaphysical Center?

C. C: *You both are there for a short period of time. Right now, we are giving you information you need to process. There will be some down time for you when you write. Writing with clarity is very important in what you write, Rekha! Simple writing breaks down the concepts, making them simple to follow and comprehend. Simplicity and clarity brings joy and love.* **Clarity is truth and love.** *We are there with you every step of the way. Remember WE are always there. WE do not walk away. Ask and you shall receive. It is that simple.*

Donna, you have to go through the root of the things. You are like a huge tree. Some roots are very powerful, some are damaged, and some are corroded. The ones that are corroded, let the planet take as nourishment. They are meant to die. Let them go. There is no reason left to hang on to them. Work on these roots that are damaged. They can heal. By healing your "SELF," you are healing your soul family.

Each and every one is on their own path, doing what they need to do. Yes, we want our children to be happy and have no challenges. We want to protect them, but we have to let them grow and fall. No one is getting lost, I know where they are. As I said before, WE do not stop. It doesn't matter how much you separate from us, the moment you call upon us, WE materialize our presence. WE are love. It is a beautiful chain of love and it expands and grows and evolves. It is not a chain that binds.

Rekha: I would like to understand the concept of Soul. I am here as a spark and people out there are praying to Mary and being healed. I have no awareness of that. How does that happen?

Jesus: *Interesting concept of soul. The soul is spurred of the core energy of God, the original soul, which remains in the body of God. For your evolution, each soul was able to fragment into 12 sparks of the same soul. It is really one soul, but these 12 sparks created so many karma with their actions, choices, and dark side that you fragmented these pieces of soul into many, many sparks; a cluster of sparks. These sparks are stuck in the dimension of the lifetime that needed to be healed and integrated with the original soul. By healing, you are integrating of all these 12 fragments and personalities back into that original soul. Each integration of each spark of your soul brings out more love and more joy to the soul. Each integration provides you with more opportunity to clear up lessons because the calling of the original soul starts the process of learning lessons. Ascension is coming home, bringing the nice little solders back into a big one.*

Every consciousness offers healing, realization, shift, and change. That's why all three of you are there. You are already in the fifth dimension. Each fragment of your soul has many, many experiences and has gathered information, knowledge, and karmas. The dark side needed to be fulfilled. Now each of you can enter into my being and be connected to each other. Each and every one goes through this process. It isn't difficult. It is all about intention. The negative energy was sent to me to be transformed into pure love and added to the creative pool of pure energy.

We continue to work with Gina and her with us. We are preparing her physical body. Very soon she will be dematerializing from third dimension into fifth, but she is stubborn. She will be able to materialize and dematerialize soon, and you will be able to do this soon also. It occurs when there is no reservation and doubt. Then it is done in complete and total faith. Continue doing what you need to do and follow your instinct.—Thank you—

I tried to meditate that evening, but couldn't, so I asked if there was a dark past that I need to know. I heard mental disorder being Schizophrenic. So I wrote to Holly about this fear-based lifetime, hoping she could provide more details from Jesus.

November 3, 2009—Jesus through Holly: *A mental disorder was present to confuse the soul. This cannot be within you. You must go back to connect the mind, body, and soul. In that lifetime, you experienced abuse and control, which created fear within. You became afraid of many things and remained inside of closed places as a safety and comfort. Within this solitude, you embraced a mental disorder, which, in turn, hurt you. You carried that confusion over into many lifetimes. Your son was your father in that lifetime and that confusion is still present today.*

November 4, 2009, Holly wrote: Rekha, Maria used to see a little boy when she was two years old. She would cry because she was afraid. Lately, she has been seeing sprits. I am concerned and very interested in your children's class.

Jesus wants to tell you that Sarah is supposed to be there because she is paying Karmic dues regarding her children. All children are her children! Here He comes, *"Amen! Amen! Hallelujah to all! These words fall on very special ears, as does the breeze that comes from the Heavens! God speaks through the work done with children! This is important because you are laying down the foundation of their paths! It is important, as I am placing you on their paths because they need you. They will look up to and rely on you. Sarah, you bring MUCH love, joy, and comfort to all children and this class is an opening within you. I am placing you in front of them as a mother with my mother! This MUST BE. More children are coming. Sarah, you must not stray. There are BIG plans for you through this. This is only the beginning."*

"The classes are being offered to enrich children and provide the spiritual nourishment, which the natural, outside world cannot provide at this stage. They

will be surrounded by like-minded and similarly-aged peers. They will be taught how to connect to their inner-selves at this age. This is important because this is the age that adults must return to in order to begin their own healing. Children will be able to connect now and move forward appropriately as a whole."

November 5, 2009—Sarah wrote: Rekha, I wanted to give you the heads up that last night a lot happened with me and my family and I feel completely broken, more broken than I ever have before. I just really need your help and I don't know what to do anymore. I am very anxious to heal. I need it so much. I will see you. I love you, and I will be saying the prayer that you had sent.

Rekha: It's happening for a reason. We have been carrying these emotions life-after-life. It is about time that you clear negative feelings and bring clarity so you will know your purpose. Prayer will clear your negative thought patterns. Angels will heal tonight.

SARAH'S HEALING SESSION # 1

I began with prayer. Sarah informed us that she's having hard time with her stepmother and there is too much tension and negativity in the house. I requested the Angel to show her why. Sarah saw a past life and described a woman spinning cotton into a ball. She was miserable and very angry. Her husband had left her and her only daughter had died. She had adopted orphan girl about seven years of age, named Cynthia. Sarah recognized that Cynthia is her stepmother now, but then, Sarah, as her stepmother, was very mean, cruel, and angry at her. She left her sitting out in the rain and Cynthia got sick, but the stepmother didn't care and did nothing.

I told Sarah to approach this woman at the spinning wheel and tell her that you and her are sparks of the same soul and are here to heal this lifetime. Tell her that Angels are helping you to accept your negative behavior and actions because of your own anger. You are so bitter and miserable that you can't experience love from souls around you. Your daughter died and God gave you another opportunity to raise Cynthia to experience love as your own daughter, but you poured all your anger and hate onto little girl. She is your lesson so you can learn to create love in your heart and in life.

I asked if she understood this. Sarah said, "Yes."

I said, "Then you must ask Cynthia to forgive you." She did by giving her ball of yarn. Then they hugged each other and changed into white light.

Next, she saw herself as a ship captain. His ship was sinking in shark-infested waters. There was much chaos and she was afraid that the approaching shark would bite her. I said, "Take a deep breath and move into your soul, knowing it is an illusion."

She felt no pain and asked, "What about all my friends?"

I told them to do the same and they all turned into white lights, as I continued the healing prayer.

Then she saw Jesus' life and became very agitated saying, "I don't want to see because it makes me very angry."

I asked, "Why?"

She said, "They are whipping him and the whip had a hook at the end of the rope that locks on his flesh, wounding him. He is bleeding and it is very difficult to watch. They whipped him many times. Mary Magdalene hated them, not understanding why they would do that to him.

Jesus is asking, "Is hate more powerful than Love?"

She said, "No."

I told her to forgive them, as Jesus had forgiven everyone. He had never left you and he will come down from the cross to free you from this pain. Jesus did and Mary Magdalene made peace with Jesus' death and with others. I finished healing by cleansing everything, including the whip, hook, Jesus' blood, soldiers, earth etc. Amen.

Sarah later told me, after her session that night, around 10:00 p.m. she was laying in her bed and her stepmother walked in, sat on her bed and apologized to her saying, "I should have been a better mother by giving you love and care." They made peace and after that the relationship between her and her stepmother changed. I said, "It wasn't your stepmother's fault. It was you, holding the negative energy from the past. When that was resolved, only love is left. And after healing with Jesus, she began channeling Jesus—a beautiful instant connection!

Holly Wrote Answers From Jesus:

Rekha: What karmic debts do Holly and I have with Lorna?

Jesus: *In two lifetimes Lorna was a child and a sister. She was your child, Rekha, and a sister of both. All three of you were sisters. This life is her "Karmic debt" due to her past experiences. She poisoned Rekha as a sister, and was cruel and mean to the other. She was the eldest. In the other life, she was a child of yours who died at a very young age. It was crib death. You did not have her long and she was a very difficult pregnancy, as is the relationship now. Make peace with her as best as you can for your "soul journey," but many lessons are hers to learn.*

Rekha: I would like to know more about twin flames and original soul, spurring into 12 sparks.

Jesus: *Spurred Souls are one immediately before they are even conjoined. No matter the time nor the distance, they will always remain close together. The sparks are sparks of light that each individual soul gains as lessons are learned. The soul begins as a dim, yet complete, globe. Over lifetimes, it becomes brighter and yet fractured; pieces remain behind as lessons not learned and this is where healing in connection with the lesson is necessary. The soul always knows where its sparks remain and where it is going. As it learns, it becomes brighter and brighter, shining, and gaining speed in sync, so does its counterpart, the connected soul. The **umbilical cord** keeps them connected with all their fractured sparks. The lessons learned are always greater than the pieces left behind. These pieces are left for remembering. Something within will "spark" and remind you where it is you need to go and to which dimension to collect this piece. Some sparks are automatically* *connected to others and several can be healed and integrated at one time.*

Rekha: Are these sparks all on the earth at the same time or in other dimensions?

Jesus: *No. They are within sections of time. One large spark is at the end, the main spark (original soul), to collect all the other sparks.*

Rekha: Can one spark do bad things to its own spark?

Jesus: *No. Sparks do unto others as they would have done unto themselves. Learning . . .*

Rekha: Can more than one spark of the same soul have a physical body at the same time?

Jesus: *Yes. These souls are more fractured and more scattered in number. They have to learn many lessons.*

Rekha: Why do I need sleep after healing?

Jesus: *Losing sleep is not optional at this point in the process. Physical body needs much rest, as it is being reprogrammed after one heals. During reprogramming, the soul/mind receives messages that are mandatory to the continuation of one's journey.*

November 6, 2009—Holly: I have MANY issues with my mom and I feel I have to justify EVERYTHING. In any event, she has much guilt in how she raised us. I feel confident in how I am raising Maria. My mother is never proud of me because she is never proud of herself and it hurts me so deeply.

Rekha: Holly, the last sentence you wrote that it hurts you deeply, go into these hurt feelings and you will see your past life or these feelings will lead you to your issues. Your mother is only a trigger for your emotional issues and past life to resurface, and more so, you chose her because of your karmic debts to her. It is good that all is happening now, so you can heal. Do not see what she does, for that is judgment. Only see how you feel. It is your mirror that you are seeing in her; your personality from another life. But now the tables are turned, so you are meeting within.

Holly: Hurt feelings of Anger, upset, feelings of "not proud of me and truly supporting me." An ex once told me that I have approval-seeking behavior. I really have that with my mother.

In any event, I feel like I have betrayed her. I also see my mother and I as having been brothers in the 1920's and having issues then, too. We were teenagers. She was more like me and I was very mean to her. I was abusive and we fought a lot.

Angels keep showing me the movie "Dolores Claiborne" of Stephen King and the scene where she ties the guy to the bed and puts his foot on a cinder block and whacks it and breaks his ankle. Maybe I did something to her. Almost like she knew something I did and I had to cover it up? How horrible! I don't want to see these things. But I understand the process. I may need you for this one.

November 7, 2009 CHILDREN'S CLASS:

In the children's class, Maria, Holly, and Sara joined me. I began with prayer and followed Jesus' instructions, asking Maria to deep breath by putting her attention gently between her eyebrows and tell me if she could see her Angel. She nodded. Then I asked her Angel's name she replied, "Angelina" and named mine, Sarah's and Holly's Angels. She wrote her Angel's name. Then Maria talked about her school, where she had learned about Amelia Earhart, saying she wanted to be a storm chaser when she grows up. All three of us looked at each other knowing that Amelia was her past life. Holly said she has fears of flying.

I asked her to close her eyes and tell us what Angelina is showing her. "I see Amelia flying a plane. It hit the storm and went under the water. Amelia swam to an island and ate small fish and crabs. She is lonely and alone."

I asked what happened next. "Now Amelia and I had put on water goggles and swam in the ocean. We collected all parts of the plane, put them together and flew home!"

We asked, "Where is home?"

She answered, "Home!"

A week later, Holly said, "Maria is getting daily messages from Angelina and progressing. I thought she always saw her Angel and asked. Maria replied, 'No, Rekha taught me how to see her.' Rekha, your persistence in assisting others is paying off, but with a dual purpose. Persistence in you, brings persistence in others."

November 13, 2009—Jesus' Outline/Process of Completeness and Growth—Foundation of Life on Earth:

To heal thy Self is a PROCESS. It does not just come, nor is it a miracle. It is a process that one must complete step-by-step through learning. *Each* step is as important as the previous and the next to create a *whole* process.

1. **Journaling** opens the Awareness and creates humbleness within your Self. It "opens" your internal eyes so that you can begin seeing and feeling and hearing. Without this first step (which includes many smaller steps—thus the Journaling class) you cannot truly grasp and understand the next step.
2. **Meditation:** This goes hand-in-hand with step one and must be practiced together. These steps may take days, weeks or months, but they will be achieved and the rewards are limitless. Meditation takes journaling to the next level by taking your Awareness of Self and transitioning it to Awareness of Higher Self.
3. **Welcome to Higher Self.** This is your inner child. This is where "Healing with the Angels" begins. This step opens MANY further levels and this, too, is a mandatory part of the whole process. It is important to note that within this step, there is *much* patience needed. This step, as with all steps, is a process within the process and *takes time.* There are "Higher" sources orchestrating the healing processes and you must have patience and awareness within yourself to allow this to happen. Remember this is also a process, with practice and patience required, but the rewards do come.

This step is beautiful because, as the Angels assisted you in the other beginning steps where you do the work and GO TO them, in this step they come TO you. They speak THROUGH **your emotions** and through this step you speak back to them.

Prayer is a MUST within all steps and is defined here. There is one prayer of bubbling that is to be learned and used as it is important in this process WITH the Angels. This creates a connection between you and US and a level of trust and faith. You do your job and WE will do OURS.

4. **Connection of all within, above, and without:** This step is a *combination* of the above three and elevates you to other levels of consciousness and Awareness. This step allows you to begin healing others, seeing Higher Beings and communicating beyond the physical realm.

5. **This step continues the connection and combination and brings you closer to God—all steps are the goal of just that: To bring you closer and closer to God.** Through healing yourself, you heal others. **Through ALL healing, you see and begin to know God.** You continue elevating to other dimensions, while ALWAYS repeating above steps. This continues the communications and healings universally, spiritually and intellectually.

6. **This step is the "above all" that ends and begins again.** This is a circle of life; through this step you transition to the soul "Self" and leave your earth body. You continue your journey through death of the human body and enter into the life of the Spirit. Here you begin again, but on OUR plane to journal and "take notes" to continue on your path. We are ALWAYS here to assist, guide, heal, love, protect, enlighten, educate, and walk with you.

As all steps are important, you cannot get to the next without taking the first. There must be trust and faith within all of these, which is where the first step begins: Yourself WITHIN. Only from within can you journey outward. Each step has processes within them. These are also important. Steps within steps; all steps lead up. And **ALL steps are to include prayer.** Prayer is what will keep you diligent and honest, it will continue keeping you focused and open. Prayer is constant communication *with*

US. What steps can you take without knowing how to take them? Your parents nurtured and supported you when you began to crawl, then walk, and run. We are no different. AMEN!"

Rekha: It is important for people to know how to connect with God within and get their own guidance. They do not need to depend on others. This "Movement" will bring them to their own individual Paths with their Angels. Believing in 'Self' is a hard lesson that I struggled with for a long time and now I see Cathy is struggling. This is a big and complete project of life.

Jesus: *Projects, yes, but projects are the "outward" process, as you continue facilitating the steps and the healing process. This **"process"** is **the foundation of life on Earth**—to look at life in retrospect and move forward now, in this time scope. You facilitate this and we work through you to do this. This Movement is much of your Karmic credit.*

November 17, 2009—Holly: This story has to do with you. My friend, Tanya, at work, was telling us about being at Marshall's this past weekend and the whole time she kept hearing someone calling "Rekha." Finally, at the end, she saw that Rekha was a little girl, screaming and crying because her parents were not buying her a book. The book she wanted was "The Holy Grail." Tanya paid and left and as she got into her car, she saw the father go back into Marshall's and buy the book for Rekha. Rekha stopped crying.

So what is the message? You are crying for the Holy Grail, but it has been within you the whole time. You carried blood of Christ, as did His bloodline and all of us, as we accept His will and Grace, and carry on His message.

EARTH IS THE HOLY GRAIL. This message has "dual purpose" as all do. I feel there is much symbolism in it with your childhood and wisdom of the Grail in you. I also feel there is symbolism with this with your father bringing Christ to you. There is healing that must be done between your father and yourself with something that took place in childhood. This is the same situation as it presents itself in your daughter. Look within, into the Grail, and you will see Christ.

Rekha: This is interesting and the little girl's name happened to be Rekha. I am trying to think, but I can't figure it out. Thank you for sharing the story.

Jesus: *Child! There is meaning in this story and your story with your father, which will help children that are coming to you. This is the next level of learning for you.*

Rekha: Could you please explain more? Is it that I didn't get what I asked from my parents? I am totally lost and can't even think! Maybe that is my issue!

Jesus: *Do not look so deep. Sometimes the seeds lie just under the surface of the soil. There was much love within some of the dark lessons of your childhood. There were moments of very good lessons with your father; father from the father to the Father (God).*

From a child, you are now an adult, full circle. Children will be coming to you! Glory! We are to learn from the basic lessons of our parents; nourishment, love, care, neglect, contentment, wishing, hoping, joy, celebration. Today is a day of celebration, as you will see later on and you must know that your father brought celebration into your heart. You shall teach new children the same. From your father on earth and your Father in Spirit—I AM and you are. Repeat what is good. Do not repeat what was hurtful: Basics.

[I remember my earthly father taught me to focus on whatever I wanted to achieve in my life. Thinking of this, I asked God, "Out of so many Gods, who is the real God? So I can focus on one." And God showed up as a very bright beam of white light. So my father led me to come face-to-face with my Father in heaven. I wrote this experience in my first book. This experience led me to search for Truth and answers later in my life and brought me to where I am today. Now I bow in gratitude to both my fathers, as I am able to understand how my earthly father brought celebration into my heart. Amen.]

During Holly's class, Sarah drew a beautiful drawing for me—a lady being held by a hand and her face was glowing with blue flame. She is being wrapped with white and golden Divine light. Sarah said, "I am glad Jesus asked me to make my first drawing for you." She wrote a message: "Michael's flame in you will light the way in darkness for many souls to follow the light."

I asked Sarah if she could ask Jesus why I don't see. She said, "It is not time yet to see." I asked, "Why? Is it karmic?"

Jesus: *No, not your karmas. If everything happened sooner than it was supposed to, it would not be appreciated. [He says not to worry mother.] I will provide in one way or the other. I want you to trust that everything will come in due time.*

Message from Jesus through Holly: *"You stand tall: Your healing and helping others have reached a very pivotal step. Why do you keep wanting to see when you see through their eyes? You have bigger things to do."*

HOLLY'S SESSION:

Holly was having a hard time doing Angel's healing on her own. I begin with prayer, and then asked what Angel brings to her mind. She replied, "Movie scene of Robin Williams *What Dreams May Come*. His wife committed suicide and he cannot get close to her. Now I realize this was my past life and I am her husband and reaching out to my wife (mother now) but can't get to her because she won't allow me to get close to her."

I told Holly to take a deep breath, "Imagine that you are at the beach and let this perception of yours washes away changing into 'I can get to her.' Now look right into her eyes and talk to her."

Holly replied, "It is so dark and she is attached to a wall with dark roots coming out of her body. She is closing her eyes and won't allow me to look in her eyes."

I told her to keep talking to her and tell her what she must do to free herself from her darkness. Tell her she can do it because Angels are helping her, through us.

Holly saw her color begin to change and the roots disappeared. After that, Holly saw her mother walking on beach with her grandmother, who came to comfort her, saying, "I committed suicide, leaving a lesson for you to learn." Then Holly saw pelicans flying, her mother's favorite bird. She was very happy. I closed the session with gratitude.

November 18, 2009—Sarah channeled message of Love: *"Simplicity is a virtue. We need you to know that with all these gifts you possess, it is easy to magnify and be curious about all the splendors of our universe. But a word of wisdom: The greatest thing you will ever learn is just to love and be loved in return. This must be taught. LOVE is all we will ever need. You and your students spend much effort trying to understand the Angels or God or spirit guides. This is impossible. We are infinity. You already know every answer. We urge you to tell Rekha, the answer to everything is simple, love. The real lesson God is teaching is to love. Not complicating. Therefore, search no further or no less. We love you, child of the stars. Namaste."*

November 19, 2009—Holly: Jesus wants you to know the meaning of Grace:

"Grace is the state in which we approach life, not the state in which life approaches us. *When we are IN Grace, then, and ONLY then, we will be able to control life around us. When we are OUT of Grace, then life controls us.*

"Grace is not that which you fall upon and hang onto tightly. It is not something that slips in and out of your life like a cold ice cube on its own. It is that which you come to, that which exists already, all around you, always. The difference lies in the recognition. When you recognize that Grace is a permanent continuity of life and of earth from Heaven . . . the forever dimension, then, and only then, can you realize that you can choose to dress in it each day.

"Grace is what changes us inside so we can approach life, mind, body, and soul with love. Without Grace, we approach life with only mind and body. Grace envelopes us so that we develop. Grace burns through us so that we can burn for others. Grace is the Breath of God on Earth for us to breathe in, so that we can exhale again and grow. Grace allows us to be calm and wise. Grace allows us to be. Without Grace we are not. We just are. Breathe deep and envision a white

bird flying free as the sun has just risen . . . early, quiet and bright. This bird is flying slow and peacefully against the new sky over a crisp and smooth body of water. No chaos or confusion. This is life upon life. This is Grace."

November 20, 2009—I was reading book on well-known people in history and an Angel told me about one of the personalities that was Holly's spark. After waiting for a while, Holly finally said, "You haven't shared Angel's information with me." I told her, "I wanted you to be ready to hear it because it is hard to accept what I am about to say."

Holly wanted to hear it, so I said, "It is your past life—a very dark spark of Adolph Hitler." She was not happy, but said that she had been attracted to Hitler's time when she was a teenager and knew within that it was true.

November 21, 2009—SARAH'S HEALING SESSION # 2

I was told that I had karmic debts with Sarah. I began with prayer and asked Sarah what the Angel was showing her. She replied, "I see myself as seven years old—A white girl with blonde hair, living on a cotton farm in North Carolina. You are a black man, a slave working for my father, but you were very kind, giving me support and courage, which my father did not give me. My father put me down a lot. I liked talking to you, but there was something very evil in you. One day you molested me and my father and two other men beat you to death."

I told the black man to ask the little girl's forgiveness and little girl had no problem forgiving him. Then I told him to ask forgiveness from her father and the other two men, and he did. I finished the process of healing and clearing.

Sarah saw her grandfather was her father in that lifetime. He is still very controlling and puts her down all the time. He had been doing this to all slaves and being very cruel to them, life after life. He showed up, asking to be cleansed and released from his karmas. At the same time, I was given the words "mental disorder" and realized that I (black man) was possessed, and possession molested the little girl.

I requested Angels to bring all souls from every dimension and asked Sarah's father to kneel and ask forgiveness to free each other from this karmic bond. Then I requested Jesus and Angels to cleanse him. Sarah said, "I can't believe the number of slaves pouring in. They are countless. Then Jesus began to clean him and a thick layer of gooey tar and dirt came out of him (negative energy of many lives) until he got cleared."

I requested to bring in the black man and asked Sarah to look into his eyes. She replied, "Oh my God, they are pitch black and he is convulsing, like having seizures and possession is telling me that it was very easy to get in his body."

I requested Jesus and Arch Angels to remove this possession and clear him. He changed to himself and asked forgiveness from every soul he hurt. Then the Angels changed it so that it never took place, as I recited rest of the healing prayer, releasing and freeing all souls by closing off the dimension. They all became white lights and left. We thanked Jesus and His Angels. Amen!

Sarah checked the accuracy of the session and wrote: Rekha that was very well written! It's so funny hearing my own story told by someone else because I can still see and picture all of the events that happened during that healing, but it no longer hurts. It's like all of the cotton fields are just left with flowers. SO MANY FLOWERS!

November 24, 2009—Rekha: Holly, my daughter, Sheila, is visiting and there is a lot of learning going on. Does Jesus have any message for me!

Jesus: *Aw! I am SO proud of you! Sheila, Sheila means Love and slow growth, but growth nonetheless. She is a piercing light that outshines others, yet she is to learn. This light is a light of guidance, not competition. You are her light and she is yours. Enjoy the combining of both lights this trip.*

All of life is a staircase. Yours has been happening a long time. You have been climbing a long time. Everyone needs joy and rest. Sometimes, when you are not doing what you always do, there is a reason. The car runs out of gas to stop. Take time to refuel. Do not try to jump start your engine.

Everything in life that is important is within education. Within education, you learn about yourselves, which is "The Movement"! Anything that continues The Movement is considered granted because this Movement MUST proceed.

November 25, 2009—Grace wrote: I was journaling and your name came up; yours, Holly's, and Cathy's. So I thought I would share what came to me about you.

"Dealer in dead, enlightened with hope, choices are made. Jesus transcends light and energy is made! Life is the past and dreams are abundant."

I wrote to Holly about the message and told her, "I am not sure what to think of it. See what you get from Jesus! Thanks."

Holly: I get several things:

1. You have been "A dealer of dead" in MANY lifetimes and you are now enlightened with hope. You have made choices and choices have been made with you; future that is not yet revealed. You must not seek the future. Go with the flow . . .
2. You walk with the Angels, but ALL Angels walk with Jesus! Jesus = Universe. Universe = energy. Energy = Healing. Healing = Hope.
3. Life is the past—Yes. We, technically, are already what we were and we are aspiring to live up to the abundance that is rightfully ours. All of this comes through patience and release of ego. Ego is still the main problem with everyone, including myself.

Rekha: Are these similar lifetimes, as we were dark priests and repeated many lives with the same issues, created clusters of dark sparks that had to be cleared. Please ask Jesus.

Holly: Rekha as a response from Jesus to you: You are asking questions of purity and clarity, so your answers will be just of that. I don't want you to become frustrated and tired with your Self. We never stop learning . . .

Jesus: *Each lifetime creates new windows of "opportunity" to go back and heal. But you are still not applying this healing and its lessons to that of your current life. When you heal and then the application is neglected, the healing is nothing more than a trophy on a wall. You must look at each healing, take the lessons and APPLY them to your current tribe (family). This is where all lifetimes come together now; in here and now. You have spent a great deal healing yourself and your lifetimes, and you have spent a great deal applying these lessons to other people's paths (necessary), however you must do the same for you. This has been Mary's human issues her whole life and each lifetime thereafter—application on Self.*

Rekha: It is hard to figure out. I can only know what I feel and apply within my tribe, but I am overwhelmed and confused. I don't know what is chosen for me. Maybe when I had so much karma that I had no choice but to choose what was chosen for my growth. I don't understand much, but I will figure it out by myself—if not now, maybe someday! I really do not know much, but thanks to both of you.

Jesus: *Oh you know more than you think you do. It's not a riddle at all! Give the stuff back and let it be. You are so very much loved and I will say one thing: You and your husband may look at things from different angles, but you both stand on the same stone of stubbornness. So much so that you are back to back and you don't see it. You are good. Very good! Beautiful! Smile! Joy! This lifetime is of much hard work and Joy and you have to let the joy in . . .*

[I did realize my patterns few days later and Angel cleared it on my level of acceptance. Now, a year later (Jan. 20, 2011), I see clearly that I was overwhelmed with my emotional garbage and my ego was blocking me from seeing with clarity. I was frustrated, sad, angry, defensive, and insecure. I finally gave up on myself because anger creates stubbornness and I refused to accept it. Thank you, Jesus for your continuous support, teaching, and advance clearing prayer. Now I am able to clear all karmic bonds. Amen.]

["Dealers of dead" were my dark sparks of past lives. They are described and healed, as Jesus continues to teach, show, and heal these lives by giving new methods of clearing through Jill. They will be written in

"Book 2." In Book 2, we are taught to clear personal, as well as the planet's dark energy.]

December 1, 2009—CATHY'S HEALING SESSION # 2

Cathy called and said, "I was pain free for a while, but now my neck, lower back, legs and foot are in so much pain that I can hardly walk. I had been trying to heal myself with Jesus and the Angels, but I'm not getting any answers."

I told her, "All I am getting is another level of awareness is opening up for you."

We began with prayer, asking Angels to show her why the pain is still there. The first thing she saw was her little girl jumping on the bed and falling, hurting her neck. I was told that her little girl's perception needs to change. She is associating pain with negative things and creating more of it. I said to her little girl that she needs to look at pain as lesson for her soul's growth. She understood. Then I requested Angels to clear her old mindset, replacing with new perception.

Next, Cathy asked about pain in her lower back. I told her to take few deep breaths and tell me what the Angel is showing you. She saw a young woman, filthy, in a cell, being sexually assaulted by a man causing a lot of pain. I told Cathy to talk to this girl and tell her it was her past life's karmic debts meeting within and asked her if she understands this.

Cathy said, "Yes."

"So tell her to ask forgiveness."

Then Angels changed the life prior to this and this never took place. I requested the rest of her clearing releasing all into Divine light. Thanking Angels.
I asked Cathy if she had a relationship in which she had a painful sex. She told me with one particular boyfriend. I told her he was the soul who was assaulting you.

Cathy said, "No wonder why I was given his name when I asked about my pain during meditation, but I could not have figured it out on my own." Cathy's pain became from intense to mild. Then she said, "Now that other pain in my neck and back is not so intense, pain in my foot and thighs are killing me."

I said, "Let's ask the Angels." She took a few deep breaths and saw a guillotine blade coming down on her foot. A man put a cloth mask on her and chopped her feet then thighs then torso and neck. I told her it was during French Revolution and requested the Angel to show her what was happening prior to going under the guillotine. She saw they were a bunch of men fighting for freedom.

"We were all caught and hurdled in a cell. We are very fearful."

I told her to tell them that you are there with the Angels and they do not need to fear because the soul lives on. There is no death to soul. They have to get in touch within and will not feel any pain. Cathy said they have calmed down. Then I recited the clearing prayer. She felt no pain going under guillotine. We finish healing with gratitude.

Two days later Cathy told me, she was shown more past lives of being painfully killed, and healed them. She is practicing not to associate pain with suffering or fear but as karmic lesson and positive growth.

November 30, 2009—Holly: I got the "ok" from my boss to work part time, but I need some help/guidance on a medical issue for myself. If I go part time, I lose my insurance. This is fine. However, the only monthly medical expense I have is medicine. I am on mood disorder and antidepressant. Next month, I will see my psychiatrist again to readdress the medicine because I don't feel I need it. Do I need this medicine? I have been on antidepressants since 2001, after I had Maria. I don't want to take it if I don't need it. I also don't want to hurt myself if I do need it. What do the Angels say? Anything! Maybe?

Rekha: This is what I think: The medicine is only masking the cause and you need them until you clear your emotional trauma. It is all happening for a reason. There is much fear and learning and you must ask yourself if you are ready to do this. I feel you will wean off the medication eventually, as you heal, but it takes time. You have to feel and see how you want to do it. Your depression is from Hitler's life. Deep sadness and guilt set in after that life's review. If you don't heal in this life, it will carry forward into next.

December 2, 2009—Holly: Not a good day at all! I have major issues with ego and blame and injustice. The medicine has only been blocking these feelings, but wow! I am filled with anger, hateful feelings, and much, much anger!

Rekha: We carry these feelings life after life because we didn't know how to work on them. I am still working on myself because learning never ends. It is good that I have days off, so I can work on myself. Maybe it is time to work on yourself. When you have time off you can focus better, channel better, and ask which lifetime they are coming from.

Holly: And the lifetime where all of this is coming from is Hitler. It is time to face it. Good, yet much pain. I am about to read the book you lent me. Boy, do I have many questions! My path now is the opposite of Hitler's. I want to succeed on this path of bringing hope and enlightenment to others. I want everyone to know that love conquers all, not hate and violence. So I am questioning myself now a lot because I mean well at my most basic core. I don't wish to hurt anyone and mostly I don't wish to hurt myself or my path. Jesus hasn't stepped in to say anything.

Rekha: Mostly, our dark lives are about control and power, creating fear and terror in others. Healing will bring clarity and clearing to free you. Jesus is saying, "All you have to do is ask." Healing Hitler's life will need at least 2-3 sessions. It will be done in layers, as the levels unfold. You will succeed because in the end, everything balances out on its own. Don't worry! Look forward to healing and learning, so you can have positive thoughts. As long you remain in learning mode, Jesus will always answer you. If you get in negative mode, He won't.

Holly: I am so excited about learning mode. It is a MUST if I am to succeed on this path. I channeled a lot of info about me and Hitler. I am another spark of my original soul. I must follow this path to bring hope and awareness to humanity, which is where he took it away. I am very ready for all of this.

In this channeled book, the section about Hitler returning to Earth confuses me. If I am him, I am here and author says Hitler is not returning to Earth soon—in 1999—so he answered as if he wasn't sure when I am already here?

Rekha: Maybe one fragment of the same soul doesn't know the existence of its other fragments. More than one fragment can take body at the same time. This fragment probably is still possessed and giving wrong information. Do you think he was possessed? Because I feel this strongly!

Holly: Yes. He was. But he chose it by choosing to live a spiritless life. When we are spiritually vacant, we allow possession to take over our body and mind. I almost see that because of his soul's decision prior to birth, the soul sat in a cocoon state "charging" for future lifetimes and ready to activate again when he died.

December 4, 2009—Holly: I am at work and there is MUCH distraction and issues here. While I am still full-time, it seems there are going to be MANY lessons, right up to the point when I go part-time. I got four tickets this morning dropping Maria off at school. It was good because I need to fix my driver seat belt and just haven't done it. Then I made a right turn into school (the same turn I have made for the last three years) and a cop pulled me over in front of everyone. I got two tickets for the seatbelt, one for the right turn and one for not having the registration in my car (Amber just cleaned out the glove box and it's in the bedroom). I was so angry! The only lessons I got were fix the belt soon—overdue, learn about the right turn now because it is catastrophic in the future if I don't, and I need to learn how to stay calm in these situations. I am super emotional, irritated, and angry almost all the time now. I want to be left alone and I feel like just staying in bed, crying!

Even with work, the daily injustices that take place are amazing. I feel like the world has ripped off my shoes and thrown me right out onto fire. I don't like feeling angry, defensive and explosive. Even when I calm down, I don't like some people's behavior. And I think, "How can they be allowed to work here?" I realize this is judgment and ego, but I still want to cry.

Rekha: *"You wrote what Jesus said about anger: Hate and anger plague all souls like a spider web, unseen, but clinging to every part of your body. Do not go where there are spiders."* You must know that, behind your anger, there is much hurt, pain, fear, guilt, shame, helplessness, and sadness. In God's creation, there is absolute perfection in every situation in life. Everyone goes through what they have chosen to learn for their growth. Lessons are karmic and we create them. We all pay one way or another to learn our lesson. There are many lessons that the Angels are showing you. If you feel sorry for yourself, then you will cry and you have lost your lesson, but the lesson will repeat. It is a vicious cycle until you face it head on! I will pray for your healing, peace and release. Amen.

Holly: I think I have felt the release of your prayer! I pulled a card last night "Release" and I need to give it all to God and do what I am supposed to do with what I have. I prayed and channeled some last night and wrote a poem. I then awoke this morning and felt amazing! With God, anything is possible and workable. My issues are leading me to your table and under Angel's hands. These are all symptoms form Hitler's life. The sadness and helplessness is beyond explainable and there is much more that will open up once I begin releasing him and the others who are tied to this.

Amen to your prayer Rekha! Thank you for Angel's guidance and your support! I am filled with so much light and happiness and positivity today! I don't know what it is! But it's wonderful!

Someone sent me pictures from the Holocaust. Rekha, this is horrible, yet it is a STRONG reminder of what took place. History not only has scars and shame, but it has PROOF that humanity is NOT perfect. We choose imperfection for others' growth.

Rekha: Truly, I think there is a reason for receiving these pictures. I feel there is God's hand behind it. I saw them, but it does not hurt, although I was one of them. Just take a note of your feelings and what you need to work on.

Holly: I received pictures of Hitler and his wife, Eva. Rekha! His wife is my mom! Her picture is the same woman—I saw her face in the healing session with you as my wife, committing suicide. But yes, God has a BIG hand in all of this. I must heal this for MANY reasons. God has much purpose in me seeing all of this and putting it together. Hitler took hope. I offer hope. I have MUCH to do for humanity that I took away.

Holly's Healing Session (Hitler)

Before we began the session Holly got a message: *"The souls will be returning back to their Higher Selves. Masses of souls died. They have been stuck through all of the creation until now. Bodies have been living, while the souls have been existing only partially in the bodies. Now, because of the massive number of souls that are going to be set free and reconnecting to their bodies wherever they are now, there is going to be a physical shift taking place on the Earth. Humanity is going to feel it. People are going to feel themselves becoming more complete. Therefore, the positive energy is going to start rising above and it is going to be pushing the negative out. That is going to create a physical shift on the earth because it is not one family/one tribe; millions of tribes are involved. It is like one pebble in the river creating a small wave, as opposed to a huge bolder in the river creating a tidal wave."*

I began the session with prayer, asking Jesus and Archangels to assist Holly. Holly saw her little girl was happily playing with an orange cat, but soon she turned into a little boy and started kicking the cat and became very abusive. His room was full of dead bugs, butterflies pinned with needles posted on the wall. I told Holly to look into his eyes, she said, "He has a blank/vacant look as if he is not there. He is lonely and not being treated with kindness by his parents and now he is writing that he wants to be a leader."

I told her to talk to him and tell him that you are there to heal this life and feel love. Give him a hug and as Holly went to hug him, he stabbed her and took off on a boat, but when he returned, his stomach was bleeding. He realized that he stabbed himself and he broke down crying.

Holly saw adult Hitler in the corner of the room standing. He opened his jacket and there were so many human heads that filled his chest. His eyes were black. I recited Jesus' clearing prayer to clear his possessions and thanked him. Then I told Hitler to touch his heart and feel his feelings returning. Holly said, "He never felt love or joy in his life. Eva was beautiful and she was the only one who brought moments of joy in his life. His relationship with Eva was beautiful from the outside, but it was a complete chaotic sewage inside. She was pure. That's why he was attracted to her—it was a natural soul attraction."

The room's wall disappeared and became a huge field with piles and piles of naked bodies. I told Holly to tell him what he had done and that he must ask forgiveness. "You are going to teach him how to ask forgiveness for creating genocide. Hold his hand and ask him to kneel."

Holly said, "It is interesting that he is very willing, but he does not understand how. So now we are doing it together. We are kneeling down and I am telling him to touch his chest with his hand and that I am bringing HOPE TO ALL NOW, as I took away hope from them then. We are hugging now and he is almost feeling the opposite of the vacant. It feels very good, but it is foreign to him."

I told him, "It was your choice. You did not want to be in your body and allowed possession to take over."

Holly replied, "His true soul lay dormant, while he led his entire life. What is happening to him now is that his soul is connecting to his physical mind for the first time. His eyes are opening up for the first time and he sees what he has done."

I said, "It is a very good sign because he will be able to accept this for the first time and that will lead to his healing."

Holly said, "He is walking through the piles of bodies and totally shocked."

I told him that all this was done by his choosing through ego, but there was a Divine purpose. All these souls had to go through this to meet their karmic debts.

Holly said, "He was driven by his ego, control, and greed. He threatened his commanders to follow his orders. I see thousands of soldiers and Amber is standing on his left side. They all have black masking tape on their mouths, meaning: You are not to speak anything that you have witnessed. You are allowed to feel, but you are to keep it to yourself and continue to do what I tell you to do. That is why Amber has the issue of not being able to speak her truth."

"Now he is walking over to soldiers because he can't ask forgiveness from the masses without making amends first with his soldiers, as they originally helped him kill the masses, so it's like a backward rewind. I told him that he had to change the mental recording of these soldiers, as he brain washed them and now must reverse it by telling them they can speak their truth and have total freedom to choose what they want."

Holly said, "There is a big black hole in the back and there are bunch of soldiers choosing to walk back in the hole because they are not ready to accept responsibility and they will do this in their own terms in some other time." Then I prayed for remaining soldiers to be cleared from possessions.

Holly said, "Now the black tape was removed from their mouths. They are beginning to set down their guns and rip off white band with swastika from their arms. Hitler was ripping it off for them as well, but he was still stern. He is speaking German, asking them to bow their heads so he can pray, but saying, "I don't know how to pray.""

I told Holly to teach him how to say a prayer of forgiveness. Then I requested Jesus and Archangels to bring in every single soul from all dimensions to forgive each other. I requested everyone's healing and clearing, including Earth, with gratitude. Amen.

Holly said, "Wow, there is a very deep silence. I can't put it in words. There is a massive silence that just took place. There is a presence coming from over the piles and piles and piles of bodies. Angels are bringing LIGHT to clear old energy. This silence and peace is like a humming sound. There are miles upon miles upon miles to the naked eye of human bodies and on top of all of them it is almost like a huge hush of Angels hovering and nothing is happening. It's going to be a while, as if it is a process."

"Now the bodies are coming alive and they are screaming very loud. He is holding his ears with his hands. It's the first time he has witnessed the devastation of so many human lives."

I told him that he needed to go through this in order to heal.

Holly: But the screaming is so loud it is hard to take.

I told him the only way to stop this screaming is if all souls look within and he asks their forgiveness.

"By this time, Hitler removed his uniform completely and said, 'For me to have their attention and have them believe me I had to be without my uniform.' He only had blue boxers with suspenders attached to his socks. This was necessary because this makes him look as human as they are."

I said, "Now he is ready to ask forgiveness and tell him so."

Holly: He is screaming on top of his lungs in the silence saying to all of them. 'Please heal me!' and it is so loud and peaceful that it echoes and it is very clear. He had to say it so loud because he needed to hear it too.

Holly saw a lot of Angels showing up in between bodies. Bodies in some patches, not all of them, are starting to put weight back on. He has a big pile of clothing and he was giving all back to them. Then Holly begins to cry, saying, "There is a little girl standing looking at me, tapping with her boney hands on Hitler's thigh. He cut her hair off when she was alive. It is you, you were very little and so, so skinny and hungry. Oh my God, you were so emaciated, but he is picking you up and he is giving you a banana. He is putting you on his lap, looking at you and rubbing your face and he is just amazed that he had life put back by his hands so easily.

You have a little toy in your hand and you are rubbing his face with your little fingers. Her cheeks are turning rosier and her hair is growing. She is saying her name is Mary Beth and showing seven fingers for her age. She is so pretty, wearing a long sleeve nightgown and spinning around saying, "Look how pretty I am!"

Hitler is looking down to her, giving her a baby doll. They took everything away. Children had no toys, clothes, food, parents, brother, sisters, or anyone. In fact, he has piles of toys for them. They are lining up, as they used to line up for food, and he is giving them toys. He is saying, "I want to bring children first." All boys, they are back in pajamas and clothes. Some of them had their hats back because he took them away. Their hats were the most prized possession. They got their harmonicas and there is lot of giggling, joy, and happiness as if they are free."

"He is going to have very hard time with older boys because they do not forgive as easily as children do. He lured these teenage boys by promising things, to get them to come in masses, telling them if you come, bring your family. This is how it began. Then women, men, boys, and children were separated and boys were dismayed, but they were told not to worry, 'We are going to give you education' and they freely came. Now they are full of mistrust."

I told him that he has to gain their trust by asking for forgiveness and giving them back what he took away from them. The boys replied, "We are happy that you recognize your act, but look at our bodies, you took our souls from us and all of these lifetimes we have been lying here dead in a mass of flesh and bones because you did not have a soul."

I told them that now Jesus and Angels are here to release them from this dimension. Holly said, "Hitler is giving clothes to boys standing in a long line saying, 'I am not giving you money or food, you already have that. I want to give you a pen and paper because I want you to write how you feel and I want to hear it. I took away your opinion and I want to give you back your freedom of speech.' They are accepting that. Hitler was shaking their hands and they were taking their pen and paper and walking away poof in the air—free at last from earthly dimension."

Holly: The Angels are still healing. Children are playing, but they are waiting for their mothers to pick them up. Women are coming—there are lots and lots—millions of them. They have been raped and killed. When soldiers asked what to do with them, Hitler said, "Do what thy wilt, but I don't want to know." Hitler did not want to know the ugliness of their acts, thrown in his face to deal with, so he gave them a green light. They raped children, teenagers, mothers, and grandmothers, then killed them. They had no respect for the bodies when it was over. Hitler had no love or respect for life, so any feelings of immediate self-gratification was welcomed, for it gave him control and power over others that he did not have within. Control over people was the love of his life. Greed was an addition, but in the end, he lost it all.

The women want their hearts back. I told Hitler that he has to ask forgiveness, along with all of his soldiers, by kneeling because they feel destroyed by his hands.

Holly: This is where all Angels came in and the hush of Angels was hovering over the women, but the women were also kneeling and praying.

I said, "They also are asking forgiveness from soldiers because they did the same to them in another life and wanted to free each other from this karmic cycle."

Holly said, "Lucifer turned around and left and you can feel a huge vibration lifted on the land where he was standing. I see the people, the bodies are all now standing and Hitler and all his soldiers are kneeling. It's a complete opposite and Angels are turning them into light by healing them. Now it is almost like a sound of wind chimes and very pure energy. They are raising everybody and the bodies, all of a sudden, are turning into tiny beads of light going pew, pew and pew shooting back to heaven. They are flying back into their higher Self in the body of God.

"Hitler is kneeling and looking at me. He is taking my hands and putting them on his eyes and saying, 'I could feel and I could see.' His eyes have color and he is putting his arms around me and his head on my chest, crying and sobbing like a child. He is ready for me to take him. But Angels are doing more healing. There are little boys that came to claim soldiers. They are their inner children. Amber's (soldier) little girl came to claim him and they all integrate into their hearts. The land is gone. It is like after the huge war. It is a land with gas chambers. I see when we do another healing, we have to come back and cleanse. It is like the land has been completely molested, abused and barren. This is where all the action took place."

"The Angels needed to do this healing were from different dimensions. Although Hitler is within, I see him externally, as if he still needs more healing with his garbage in our next session. I see out of this empty land there is a man walking towards us. Now he is standing in front of both of us. Hitler is holding onto me for dear life, as the man is tapping on his shoulder saying, 'Excuse me, just what do you think you are doing? You are wasting your strong and smart mental ability.' He is his father and he has a huge garbage bag on his shoulder—the whole land that was dry, smoky, and abused. His garbage bag filled the entire land as if it belonged to him and he is saying to Hitler, 'You expected me to carry it on my shoulders?' Hitler was telling him that it isn't mine anymore."

I said, "His father has a choice to release it into Divine light and it won't be his anymore. Or he can keep it." He wanted to release it because it was too heavy for him to carry. I requested this through prayer and gratitude.

Holly said, "They are shaking hands and hugging each other. Hitler's father is my father now. His dad always called him Adolph and he is holding his face and saying that you need a pat on your back for healing this life. Hitler is feeling very satisfied because this is the first time he has been approved and appreciated. He is standing in a kitchen with his father and still wearing boxers and socks. Although he is a grown man, he is so excited, like a little boy."

I told her that this is the first time he has ever experienced anything positive.

Holly: Now his dad is saying he has to go and he turned around and jumped into the ocean. I see Hitler as a grown man, but happily skipping around with my little girl.

I said, "Bring your little girl into your heart and request angels to integrate Hitler's fragment into her higher Self. Then, finally, we ended the session with gratitude to God, Jesus, and Angels. Amen.

December 5, 2009—Rekha: I had a dream: I was with Jesus, but I don't remember all that He told me. I only remember Him saying that gifts are pre-programmed in the beginning of our first incarnation.

Holly: Yes, the gifts are pre-programmed. This is what I channeled a few months ago.

Jesus: *When your soul spurs at that moment, you are connected with your total soul essence; all that is needed, ever, in all lengths of one entire soul's life. You must learn through each lifetime how to use these gifts. You do this through each lesson in each lifetime. They are pre-programmed and activated as you learn. As a flower grows from seed, plant, stem, then develops petals, so do all souls. The problem is that most souls on earth are at seed stage. There is much growth to be achieved. Flowers grow WITHOUT worry. They grow bright and beautiful. They didn't create themselves before they began. God creates and they trust in that.*

Your dream last night, Rekha—I am always with you when you sleep because of your soul. I am connected in areas of interest where you are not looking. We discuss this on many planes because of your soul's evolution. It is easy to communicate with you when you leave your body. However, the difficulty is that your physical mind is not grasping all that the soul is consuming. You are very wise and I have been giving you areas of interest where you will be able to connect the wisdom of your soul to wisdom of your mind. You are close to two becoming one. This is much enlightenment of fifth dimension. The linear disadvantage is that you are still hanging onto certain aspects of physical darkness. This world, this earth, this lifetime has much awareness rising; at the same time, darkness is rising too. Focus on the light and listen. You can see the light. You are aware of light on earth, but there are times in this lifetime, Rekha, as a human, that you do not "listen."

Rekha: Thank you Jesus and Holly. I understand it is my ego that overrides my listening and I am working on my fear, anger, defensiveness, stubbornness, and non-acceptance. Please help me. Thank you.

Jesus: *You are wise. You have worked hard to become as wise as you are. But in this lifetime, you are still human. Learning does not end. You have healed many, many lifetimes and are close to being complete. Yet, as much as you heal, you are left to one thing: this lifetime. During this lifetime, you still can create Karma—debits and credits. You cannot heal this lifetime until the next, so be calm and listen to now.*

So in life, your life, you have a choice. In all previous lifetimes, most souls were unaware that negativity would prolong their individual advancement in the next lifetime. In this lifetime, most souls are aware of this and it is possible to go back to negative lifetimes to heal and collect all that was "lost" when you were not learning. You always can learn. That is why you are here. Fear traps your thought system. FEAR TRAPS YOUR THOUGHTS and PARALIZES YOU. You must live as simple as a finch life—tiny, but possible. Every morning fluttering, breathing and just being. That is all asked of you. All that is happy and of love is simple; anything in addition, any negativity, is where fear is created and you are no longer a finch. You become one who is fearful of life.

SARAH'S HEALING SESSION # 3

I began with prayer. Sarah saw a past life as young girl, praying in church, and knew that the priest was watching her. She said, "I just wanted to learn from him, nothing more, but his eyes were seeking more from me and he is staring at me." I told him that the love you are seeking in Sarah will not be found, for you need to seek self-love within.

He disagreed and said, "Being a priest, I can't have a relationship."

I told him, "You chose to become a priest, so you could find God within and you must look within."

Finally, he understood and went to play piano. He then disappeared into the sound within the pipes and smoke came out of the pipes. Then he became a person who is doing the same thing to Sarah again, except the priest had a nicer side, but this was his dark fragment. I told him the same thing, asking him to seek love within and not from his ego. He did not want to hear us, so he put up a wall around himself as I was speaking to him.

Sarah said, "Jesus is saying, 'A wall may stop the touch but cannot stop sound. He is listening and the bricks of his ego will come down one by one in time.'" Then we finished the session with Sarah's healing and clearing of fear, with gratitude to Jesus and Angels.

December 16, 2009—CATHY'S HEALING SESSION # 3

Cathy called and said, "I am in much pain again from neck, lower back to legs." I didn't believe it and asked what she was going through. She told me that she was worried about her husband's health and afraid that he is going to die (holding her tears back.).

I told her, "Maybe that is your issue. Your fears, worries, and concerns are causing negative energies and your body reacts with pain, triggering another memory of a past to heal." Next day, she returned for Angels' healing session.

Cathy wrote her session: Although I had been healing myself of many situations with Angels and Jesus, I became stuck. In my meditations, I would ask why I had this excruciating, debilitating pain in my back and I felt a surge of fear. I couldn't understand this because Angels had already healed this many times (not knowing that there are many past lives and many levels of anger and fear). Also, in a previous session, Rekha addressed this pain in my back and neck and it was healed! Well, something else was arising to the conscious level and I couldn't figure it out after three days of working on myself, so I had to seek assistance with Rekha.

The session began with prayer to invite Angels for healing. I felt their presence immediately and a beautiful blue and green light was flowing from Rekah's hands. Angel showed me a young girl in a prison camp. It was cold and prisoners were barely dressed. They were all starving and very thin. I then realized that it was a Nazi camp. I saw German guards who were just as cold as the weather.

Prior to this session, during my daily activities and meditation, I would hear the name "Ann Frank." I knew that Ann Frank was a prisoner in Nazi camp during World War II. She wrote in her diary about being in hiding before her family was found by soldiers. Her name came to me periodically for about four months. I thought the message to me was to continue Journaling. Now, continuing my session with Rekha, I see a Nazi camp, people freezing, starving, abused beyond repair, and I see a young teenager. I then realized that I was Ann Frank. All emotions started to arise from core of my being. I had immense fear. In the camp, I could smell death and fear, it was so potent. I also felt very angry, thinking, "How could they do that to us?" but I always had to be quiet, keeping my mouth shut. I was cold and dying, with hunger.

Rekha began to pray for healing my fear and anger. I forgave Hitler and Guards for their abuse, starvation, power, and control because I must have created this karma in another life. Wow! I felt such a relief. The sun began to shine and coldness of the camp started to dissipate.

Then I heard a strong, but a gentle voice say, "fear of Collective Consciousness." Rekha was told that it was the whole camp and all souls needed to be healed from fear. Angels began healing all men, women, then all children appear, happily saying "Don't forget us" and Rekha requested their healing, cleansing of the whole camp, gas chambers furnaces, earth, and freeing all souls from that dimension. Sun became very bright. Off to the side, I saw a German soldier kneeling on one knee. He bowed his head and placed his firearms on the ground. I forgave him. The pain in my back and feet disappeared. I felt a warm wave of love passed through my body.

I thought it was the end of my session, when all of a sudden, Angel showed me as young adult, running across the train track, constantly looking behind, filled with fear. I was running, escaping from someone and was so afraid. Bam! I got hit by the train. I saw my head snap back and I witnessed my life force leave my body. Again, Rekha requested healing of fear and pain, releasing it from cellular memory. Again, the warm wave of love was gently flowing through my body. We thanked God, Jesus, and Angels.

When I was driving home from my session, I heard quite clearly, "Now you can ski and dance." I cried so hard that I had to pull over into a parking lot, so I could cry freely. I have missed being physically active for 12 years. My heart and spirit smile when I am dancing.

December 17, 2009—Holly: I am so upset, anxious, scared, and defensive at work, and I am wrong. How do I not allow others to bother me when what they are doing is incredibly bold, selfish, ego-driven, and it's hurting me? So the answer came:

Jesus: *You do not take everything as is. You try to simplify mountains when you shouldn't be on the mountain at all! Why are you on the mountain when you are supposed to be in your meadow? Refocus and be quiet! Listen. Your boss will deliver some information that will upset you if you let it. All is going on as it should. Leave your weapons and ego at door. Bow your head and move on. Heal! The world will open up to you when you open up to it. Be calm in the center of the storm. Please stop trying to be the storm. This is not your weather to be in, this is theirs. Please stop trying to make it yours. Simply pick up your belonging and sit waiting for the bus. It is time to let our bus come to get you. Relax and trust US! Many beautiful things are around the corner, but you cannot see them as you try to fight this mountain. Little, little child; big, big mountain.*

Thank you. I am all yours, forever—Amen.

Holly's Second Healing Session (Hitler)

This session was all about removing possession from Rosario and Hitler's lifetimes. Jesus and Archangel Michael worked to fill the deep black hole in her body with blue shimmering light. In the end, Jesus was saying all negativity goes through my body to become pure love once again. I felt a deep gratitude and kind of bad, knowing how much He does for us out of love. Jesus came around and put his hands on my shoulders to comfort me, saying, *"It is ok to heal souls like this. They all get healed through ME."* Amen!

December 20, 2009—During my morning prayer, I felt cold and starving to death (Holocaust). I was healing myself and all souls who went through the same experience. My daughter's green budgie flew in, asking to be healed with the same issue. His story took place back in Canada. In November 2003, he flew away. Next day, my daughter called the Humane Society. They told her someone found a green budgie with a broken beak near our house and brought him in. That evening after work, we rushed to Humane Society to see the bird. Seeing his condition broke our hearts, as he was frantically dipping his head over and over in a seed bowl trying to eat, but could not because he had lost the upper part of his beak to peel seeds. He had been starving for two days. We brought him home and begin feeding him peeled millet by hand. In six months, the top part of his beak grew long enough to peel seeds. It never looked the same, but it did its job for what we prayed for. I realized I will have to heal the whole animal world that had ever been starved and killed by human hands. I did a prayer, requesting Angel's healing and clearing in all dimensions for everyone, with gratitude. Amen.

A few weeks later, on January 5, 2010, my daughter told me, "Minty, the green budgie has gained weight. He feels heavier and looks very big." All of a sudden, I remembered how he showed up for his healing and all animals' healing. Then I shared this experience with my daughter, telling her Angels always heal collectively, so he brought in all animals to be healed.

December 21, 2009—Holly wrote about future changes/growth: I want to let you know that things are happening and changing, as we have been doing our work on those who needed it because their souls are being set in motion to come to us. Now, with this taking place and while they are out in the world doing what it is they are supposed to do, the flow of the universe will be sending back MANY people to us for continued and mandatory learning and healing. I also know that you have some questions for Jesus. Ask away!

Rekha: Is there any guidance for me and Holly?

Jesus: *You both are already being guided. You know exactly what to do and you are following that.*

Rekha: Is it true that a highly evolved spark of soul collects rest of the sparks?

Jesus: *No. It is not always necessarily adequate to collect all sparks when the Higher Self is motivating the individual life. When one being is not in connection with the Higher Self, collections of the spark are necessary in order to move forward. All sparks gravitate towards each other and become the One Higher Self, only then can a soul transcend as a part of the collective consciousness.*

Rekha: Does that mean the more past lives we heal, the more sparks we can integrate into our Higher Self?

Jesus: *You are focusing too deeply into the general structure of soul "recipe." Please continue healing and bringing souls back where they need to go to heal the emotion/hole. You bring souls to US. The in-depth dynamics of soul structure will be understood when you are on OUR side. It is not necessary to know for your path now.*

Rekha: How is it that in some cases, possession is temporary and the soul is fighting to be free? And in some cases it is permanent?

Jesus: *Ok, this is more of a clear question because it does pertain to your path now. The agreement is made at both times. When possession is chosen as a lesson for the soul, of the soul, and for other souls, it is made prior to entering body. However, when possession takes place on earth at a pivotal time, it is a symptom of human condition. The soul becomes weak confused and then opens the body and possession takes place. Low level beings (soul and soulless) are waiting at any moment to take over. But as all lessons are pre-planned, these entities are placed strategically here on earth FOR the lessons of others and the primary soul, as they are taking body form. The soul, at all moments, has true choice, but when a soul is weak, they turn all choices over to the earth dimension.*

Rekha: Are we all possessed in one or many past lives?

Jesus: *The reason for possession is negativity. It is in everybody's past life.*

Rekha: I would like to clear my overwhelming feeling of "having given up" on myself. I have worked to heal, but it is still there.

Jesus: *Your mind goes in circles. This is good and this is also restrictive. You have healed many of your lifetimes and issues. However, you cannot heal the present moment in which you are standing. Now, that moment has just passed and it is able to be healed. But all moments as we stand in them, current moments, are not for healing because they are active. We speak primarily on healing of the soul. There are opportunities presented for healing other levels, but in soul healing, this moment has the answer. **The only healing that is done presently is through the active decisions that souls make.** This then creates the past and an open opportunity for soul healing. Because the next moment is not here yet (now it is and there it goes) you are not able to "see" the lessons at hand within that moment.*

It is like a car traveling, you see it coming, but you cannot read the license plate until after it passes. The soul is exactly that: YOUR license plate gets registered and becomes valid on your body (vehicle). Because your personal soul is primarily on a higher vibration than most, it is used to moving at a higher speed, thus creating frustration within your human body, which does not operate at the speed of your soul consciousness. You must remember and realize that this lifetime is important because you are human and that, alone, presents the lesson. If you were able to be on the soul level purely (on other dimensions, which would be comfortable to you) you would be able to think and receive answers simultaneously. On earth, this is not the case.

On earth, YOU are human and this is difficult for you because of the ascended state of your soul. This is also why you are almost at the end of your lifetimes. Be in the moment you are in. Heal the moments that have passed and know that the future holds many additional lessons that will then open recollections of past lives that need healing. No more. No less. Take the ingredients and make a cake. Do not make a cake first without the ingredients. Problem = Lesson. They are interchangeable words.

Rekha: Thank you, Jesus for placing Holly in my path for my learning. I appreciate her gift. Amen.

December 29, 2009—In Holly's class "Journaling from Within"

Jesus: *Rekha, joy is on your feet. It is time that you run with it. All WE can provide is the road. Smiling is beautiful and you bring much of it to the world; it is karmic credit. Yet, what is it that makes you smile? Do not consume yourself at all moments with "What else must I do for humanity?" Rather, step back and say, "Welcome, I am human; what must I do for me?" When you can climb back onto your own rock, your vision will change: The higher the rock, the wider the scenery.*

January 2, 2010—Holly's Healing Session:

I began with prayer, requesting Angels to show Holly what she needs to heal. Holly saw her little girl and Rosario from lifetime in Greece, but his eyes were red, not blue, and he was saying, "Get out of my way because you don't know what you are doing!" by waving a spear in his hand. Holly was telling him, "Put that thing down!"

I told Holly, "He is not going to listen to you because he is possessed" and I began praying to Jesus to clear him.

Holly described, "It is really ugly. Archangel Michael had to wrap his arms around him to hold him. There is a lot of demonic screaming coming out of his mouth and his chest is shaking and rising off the ground, so Michael and Jesus had to contain him. Now he is lying on the ground crying because he is himself again, feeling helpless."

I told Holly that this is the right moment to give him all strength, support and energy that you have by telling him that you will support him because you and he are same soul. Holly replied, "He is not trusting me and I think he is trying to stab me or hit me."

"Ok, then I will have to request Jesus to clear him again." His eyes became normal and I told her, "Now it is your job, you must make him believe in you. Why does he not trust you? Do you trust yourself?"

Holly replied, "No. I don't."

I told her, "You must learn to trust yourself and go with all the trust and faith you have, remembering how Jesus helped you and you know how to do the rest."

Holly said, "Jesus is standing there, holding my hand and I am telling Rosario that I trust him, but he is saying that he doesn't trust himself and is threatened by me."

I asked, "Why?" He replied that it was because he had no guidance. All he had was his old, blind mom. I told him that Holly is here to give you guidance.

Holly said, "He is looking at me. My little girl is talking to him and he does not understand how so much guidance can come from such a little person." At this point, I needed to give him understanding. I told him to take a deep breath and look within, see how big and pure his soul is and how he is connected to this little girl's energy. "Look into little girl's eyes. Only then you will see how little girl can give you so much guidance and understanding."

Holly said, "His heart is beating hard as he took a deep breath. His feelings are alive now and he wants to cry. He is shaking his head, saying, 'I am so sorry. I never had to do anything for myself.' I told him, 'Now you have learned that it is never too late to accept your mistakes and lessons, and make changes.'"

Holly said, "He wants my little girl to sit on his lap and put my ear on his chest to listen, saying, 'Do you see it is a big chest with such a little heart inside.' I told him, 'you made it little by your perceptions and you can make it bigger by changing them.' He said, 'How? No one ever loved me, including my mom.'"

I told Holly to give him a hug and tell him that you love him. He should feel your love and you should feel his because both of you are one soul and the same energy and want to love your "Self."

Holly saw his wife walk in and something was not right with her. It feels very negative. Archangel Michael is standing between her and me. I told her that she is possessed and she is your boss in this life. Then I requested Jesus' help through prayer to clear her possession and connect her mind to her heart.

Holly said, "Oh my! She has the same personality as my boss has and her possession feels the same as Hitler's. She always told Rosario, "You are no good. You are not even a man" and put him down constantly. There was absolutely no love. His mother always told him how good he was, although she was old and blind. She always tried to give him hope, but his wife counteracted. Is there any lifetime when I did the same to my boss, so every lifetime she is doing this to me?"

I said, "Ok. Let's see . . . She was your mother in Hitler's lifetime, wife in Rosario's and now, as your boss, doing the same. So I requested healing and clearing for this life first, then requested to show what Holly did to her, prior to these lives.

Holly saw Michael zip through every lifetime with her and ripped through blue light, right in her being. Then HE grabbed her and Hitler's mother and few other women (same soul) put them in a pile and connected their soul to their minds and hearts. He cleansed all of them at one time with blue and white light shooting up from the middle of them. He zips through all dimensions without going up or down, as if they were all at the same level. We thanked Him.

Then Michael showed Holly's past life: I see bunch of human heads on wooden beams like decapitated heads. I am doing black magic, but I see her as my servant (a little boy). I belittled her completely. I let Holly know that I needed to do Jesus' clearing to remove his possession before we can approach him, and prayed for it. The little boy was hiding in fear.

I told Holly, "Tell your spark that you come with Jesus and Angels to heal this life. You must ask for forgiveness from the little boy and from all souls you killed."

Holly said, "He is saying the same thing as Rosario was saying, 'No one ever loved me. This treatment was the closest thing that I knew being loved.'"

I told him, "After going through all these lifetimes in darkness with possessions, you, as Holly, have learned the value of light. I want you to learn the value of 'Self Love' by loving your Self, so you can grow, heal, cleanse, and free yourself."

Holly said, "Wow, all heads that were on the wooden beams are growing back in their human bodies with their arms and hands and the rest. Now, they are lifting towards heaven. I prayed for all souls healing, cleansing, and releasing in all dimensions. Then Holly saw her little girl and her boss's little girl were playing, hugging each other, and made peace. I requested cleansing for earth and thanked Jesus and his team of light. Amen.

Jan 2, 2010—CHILDREN'S CLASS: Children were so happy that they can freely talk about their experiences. Cathy's daughter, Alice, saw Jesus conducting the class and said, "He is whispering in your ear, Rekha, and I see a female soul present in the class." I showed her how to cross her over into the light. Children got a lot out of it. They were very happy and looked forward for next meeting.

Holly channeled message from Jesus: *"Each Crystal child is given a direct badge of Divine power of light. They were born ignited, as opposed to adults, who have to work to ignite their power within. All humans have guides and Angels. Yet, Crystal children have direct guidance from Angels always. They are Divine angels on earth and the channel through them is Divine, pure, and open."*

Jesus is sitting in the middle of the circle with doves. His Angels are in a circle around us— *"Predominance has creatively been revealed. Allow them to do as they are to do; encourage their creativeness. Do not hinder this by injecting your own failures. They have chosen you for a pristine guidance that you are to offer, that you can offer because of your own universes and Divine right."*—Thank you—

CHAPTER 10

HEALING PAST LIVES # 3

January 6, 2010—CATHY'S HEALING SESSION # 4

I begin with prayer and placed my hands on Cathy's forehead. I felt much activity going in her mind and asked, "Do you think like your parents?" Cathy replied, "Yes."

Then Angel showed her little girl talking with her both hands moving with her fingers tapping onto her thumbs saying to each other . . . tha, tha, tha (like verbally abusive) and her mother was pointing finger at her in anger. I said, "You must have done this to your mother in a past life and I requested Angels to bring Cathy to a life when she was verbally demeaning to her mother."

Angel showed Cathy in a Chinese dynasty, a king dressed in military attire. Then she felt his wife standing next to him and sensed her unworthiness. I told her, "She is your mother now and you made her feel unworthy." Then I asked her to look into king's eyes. Cathy found his eyes were completely black and empty.

I requested Jesus to clear his possession, but it didn't happen because king was very stubborn; he wouldn't let go of his power. His ego wanted control. I told him love has more power and freedom than your ego's control. Look for love within. Cathy saw a beautiful shiny diamond in the middle of his chest. Then she placed her hands on his chest to send him love. She simultaneously felt a warmth and loving feeling in her chest and upper back releasing pain. Cathy sensed he was very talented with his sword and he refused to let it go.

I told him, talent comes from soul's creative aspect. However, your ego used it in a negative way causing pain and suffering to others. You need to learn to use it in a positive way as an art. Angels are with you, giving you an opportunity to make a different choice. There are many souls waiting to hear your prayer of forgiveness. He then knelt down on one knee, bowed his head and placed his hand on his heart.

I prayed to free all souls in every dimensions and from his karmic ties. At this point, Cathy saw two beams of white light shooting out of his eyes. He then asked for forgiveness. All souls became white doves and flew to heaven. They were the souls who were freed from his tyranny. Then he was standing with his open arms receiving Divine light from the heaven.

Cathy heard unworthiness and saw his wife saying by moving her hand that this issue has been repeated many lifetimes. I told Cathy that the king must ask his wife's forgiveness. As he did, Cathy's little girl appeared and was hugging both of them. They were hugging and smiling. Then little girl blew them a kiss as the king and his wife integrated into their original souls. Then with Angel's help, I worked on her parental imprinting by giving her two garbage bags. Cathy filled these bags with anger, unworthiness, and mental chatter. I requested healing and clearing with gratitude. Her little girl was happy and ready to integrate into her heart.

November 3, 2009—AMY'S HEALING SESSION # 1

Amy had attended **Angels'** workshop in September and had a private session, but this time she asked for Reiki session. After the session, Amy told me that the Angels never stopped showing and healing her past lives, one after another. There was one with her late-husband, making peace with him and he told her, "I am going to help you with our children." In another life, falling from a height to death, and in another, she drowned and was healed from her fears. Then she asked if I would teach Reiki classes. I told her that I can.

I wrote to Holly asking what Jesus would say about teaching Reiki classes.

Holly: Interesting because I also would love to learn Reiki. Who better than you to teach it?

REIKI

Jesus: *Any teachings are worth reviewing. In any teaching, you are able to advise others of The Movement. All doors lead to ME—**Healing Hands of Jesus.***

Teaching Reiki 1, 2, and 3 . . . this is necessary as it will bring in more people and paths will cross. This is the way we have created for others to come to you. You teach and heal in many aspects. Do not seclude yourself to just one way. You have been given many seashells, no need to use just one. All are purposeful in showing the beauty of what God can do.

Reorganize what you already have (knowledge). What you threw away (Reiki material) has been soaked into your existence. You know all of it already; rewrite data. Information is the same; flow is different. It is polar opposite. You are already born of it. You have the shift in energy and this makes the difference in its flow.

January 22, 2010 AMY'S SESSION # 2

Amy had been working on her own with her Angels all this time and we kept in touch. She wrote and asked if we may have had a past life together. I asked Jesus about our past lives and heard that she was Mary's Mother, your mother. I wrote her what Jesus said.

When Amy arrived, she said, "I asked about a possible past life because I was looking to buy a house two hours away from Fort Lauderdale and felt pain in my heart thinking, 'I am going to leave Rekha, as if I am leaving my daughter behind.'" Upon hearing this, it confirmed our past life connection.

I began the session with prayer, requesting Angels to bring her into a past life. Amy said, "I am in a house made of clay and Mary is about ten years old playing on the floor. I am watching her. I am very attached to Mary."

I said, "No wonder why I became very attached to Jesus and we both have this issue now." Amy agreed and said, "You use to play with Elizabeth, your cousin. You were very good friends." I requested Angels to clear mother's and daughter's attachment from core of our being and free us from this illusion. Then I finished the session with Reiki, thanking Angels. Amy felt relieved.

August 11, 2010—AMY'S SESSION # 3

Amy had severe pain in her right foot for several weeks that restricted her from walking. I began the session with prayer asking Angels for the reason of her foot pain. Amy saw herself as a ten-year-old, male, black slave, wearing a heavy iron shekel on his right foot. He was in so much pain, as he grew in it. It rubbed against his skin and bones while he walked.

I requested the Angels to show her a lifetime before that and what she did to cause this experience. Amy saw a man in the Middle East wearing colorful clothes. He had a kind of machete in his hand, chopping people's foot as punishment. I told her to ask this man why he was doing that, causing his soul much suffering and karmas. He replied that he was following the order of his rich and powerful boss.

I asked, "Why does he work for him doing such a gruesome job, harming other souls?" The man replied, "This man had taken my wife for his pleasure and threatening me to take my children away if I don't do this work."

I told Amy, "You had much fear in this life and carried forward in the present life. The man you worked for must have been in your present life."

Amy said, "Yes, but he is dead now."

I told her, "It doesn't matter. The soul lives on and creates the same experiences over and over unless you heal these emotions."

Amy said, "He was my ex-husband. He was very abusive, controlling, alcoholic, and cheated on me."

I told her that he is possessed and requested Jesus to clear him. Then I told the man, "You no longer need to fear because Jesus has cleared your boss. Angels are helping you to change this life, so go to the rich man and tell him you no longer work for him." He dropped his machete and knelt down to ask forgiveness from all those souls to whom he was causing pain and suffering.

I prayed for everyone's healing and clearing. Then I told him, "Now your wife is free and will come back." Amy saw his whole family hugging each other. They were happy. The slave boy hugged this man, thanked him for freeing him, and happily returned to his family. Amy's little girl was much relieved, peaceful, happy, and integrated in her heart. We thanked God, Jesus, and the Angels. Amy walked away without limping. A week later, she was walking normally.

MIGRAINE:

I asked Holly to find out the reason for a client's migraine headaches and what Jesus wants me to do.

Jesus: *She has many issues and struggles, not comprehending in the past. She had a lot of blame in prior lifetimes. Nothing is her fault. She is much of a victim in this lifetime because she victimized others in her past lives. It seems like she has quietly accepted the victim role and must give it back (parental imprinting). She needs both Reiki and Angels' process of healing. Reiki will work as the energy relieves and lessens negativity that has been physically situated within her mind, behind her eyes, and at the crown of her head. There is much swelling in that area.*

Bring her to ME. Through you and your faith, I will heal. She must believe that I run through your will. Her belief has been damaged. This is what renders her from healing. She must also learn to rely on herself and on her own will, rather than that of others. That is where I AM and only I can heal her completely. [I did exactly what Jesus instructed me to do.]

January 21, 2010—CATHY'S SESSION # 5

Cathy was still dealing with great amount of pain in her feet. In one of Holly's classes, she was given a message that her little girl was dancing on broken glass. So she asked if she is still doing that. Jesus said, "Most of it is gone, but there still a little bit left in a dust pan that her little girl wants to keep."

After the class, we did Angel's session with prayer. Angel brought Cathy to meet her little girl and showed a past life. Cathy said, "I am in a dungeon and a man was shoving an iron rod into my left foot. He was screaming, and yelling curse words."

I requested Angel to show her what she did to him prior to this life. Cathy saw she was whipping him with such anger and hate on a farm and realized her issue of anger and rage. I told her to kneel and ask his forgiveness.

Cathy said, "He is hesitating, but then he forgave me. Now he is kneeling down on both of his knees and asking me to forgive him. I placed my head on his chest and hugged him with such a genuine love and we both integrated into our original souls. I feel my little girl, all of a sudden, got so mature in her being, not in her body. She gave me a feeling that her hands are on her waist saying, 'It's time that you understand' and kicked the dustpan with one foot."

On February 21, 2010, I called **Sherry** and she channeled answers for Cathy and her daughter. I passed it to Cathy so she can heal herself.

Rekha: Why is the pain of Cathy's daughter, Alice, not leaving? Is it from many past lives?

Angel: *She attaches to the pain. It is deeply ingrained into her cellular body. She must be getting payoff. It is going to take few months of work. She needs to let it go.*

Rekha: Why does Cathy still have foot pain?

Angel: *It is her past life. She jumped to save a young girl (her daughter now) from a stray bullet and fell into a muddy hole. Her left foot flew up* *and the bullet went through, making a hole in her sole. She was a 15 year old boy, her brother. He was in horrible pain, trying to walk on his right foot.*

August 9, 2010—CATHY'S SESSION # 6

Cathy called. She was still in pain, asking what had transpired while she was away on holidays. I told her, Jesus had taught us (Jill and I) through His advanced clearing, how to clear residual energy at the DNA level from the core of one's being, in all dimensions, on all healing we have done so far. Maybe you need this now.

I began the session with prayer, requesting the Angels to bring her in fetus' awareness and asked, "How does she feel?" Cathy told me that she felt fear and anxiety. I heard "mindset," so I put my hands over her forehead and felt energy buzzing in her head. I asked, "What was going on before coming here?"

Cathy told me there were ten million things because her mind never stops. She said that her systems were not working properly, she felt bloated, swelled up, gained weight, and had neck, back, and foot pain. I requested to balance her left and right brain, aligning all her systems; nervous, circulatory, digestive, glandular, and respiratory to work in their optimum vibrations and harmony with each other. Then I requested to clear all residual energy from the core of her being and DNA, from all past lives and emotions that we have worked on so far, thanking Angels.

Then Angel brought her back to meet her little girl, but she wouldn't talk to Cathy. Cathy said, "She is shy and closing off." I told her, "Shyness comes from guilt and fear, but I feel she is very angry. Anger originates from fear."

Cathy tried to get her attention, but she wouldn't give in. In frustration, she implored Jesus' help. I told her, "It is not Jesus' job, but your job because you created this stubbornness by giving in to your ego and you must resolve it. Jesus is doing His job by showing you your anger.

Your little girl is telling you to leave her alone because she wants to stay this way."

Cathy agreed and said, "I can't get her to budge."

I told little girl that she can keep this behavior life-after-life and relive it over and over. It isn't going to change unless she looks at it and works to heal.

Cathy said, "You got her attention. She got up and looked right into my eyes, taking me back again to my Chinese Dynasty lifetime. I was a tyrant king and brought about horrible manslaughter."

I asked Cathy to look into his eyes. Cathy replied, "They are empty and distant."

I requested Jesus' clearing and the king changed. I told the king to ask everyone's forgiveness and to change this life by opening doors of his prison to free them and give them back what he took away from them. Cathy saw white light pour out of doors and he felt free and joyful. Then he integrated into her higher Self. Her little girl was jumping with joy and clapping her hands saying, "I am free! I am free!" And she integrated into Cathy's heart. We thanked Angels.

August 24, 2010—CATHY'S SESSION # 7

Cathy returned because her pain was back with a vengeance. This time, I noticed a lot of anger in her voice as she was telling me how she was asking Jesus' and Angels' help. Cathy had never identified the connection between her pain and her anger. I told her that she was angry at God in many lifetimes, including this morning when she was asking for help. At first, she denied it, saying she can't be angry at God. She then quickly admitted it by saying, "I was angry at God because I have done so much work on myself."

I told her, all work goes to waste if you don't learn the lesson and apply in life's experiences. You are not aware of your anger and how it sneaks up on you. She questioned, "Am I not supposed to have any anger?"

I said, "Absolutely not because your anger is a weapon used by your ego against you by creating negative energy, hence, pain. You need to accept that you created this experience in the first place."

She said, "I am not angry at others, but when I get angry, I keep it inside and do not say anything."

"So, you are angry at yourself. Inverted anger is still anger and the same energy that causes sadness, feeling sorry, and depression."

We began the session with prayer and Angel brought her little girl. Cathy said, "She is very angry and stomping her foot on the ground."

I told her to ask if she is angry at God. She replied, "No." I told Cathy, she is not telling you truth because she is possessed, and requested Jesus to clear through prayer.

After that, Cathy said, "She is crying and feeling guilty for being angry for so long in many lives."

I told her that she needs to look at why she created these feelings. I requested Angels to show her where this anger and pain was coming from. Cathy saw a primitive life as a young male, being imprisoned in a bamboo enclosure and people were making fun of him and not giving anything to eat. He was very thin and dying from hunger. She felt a headache and pains in her entire body. He was too embarrassed and ashamed to tell us details of his crime. He only said that he was a thief. He was very angry at people for what they were doing to him. I requested Angel to show him what he did to all these people prior to this life. Cathy saw he was an army commander and these people were his prisoners. He laughed at them, mistreated them, and did not give them food. He understood and asked everyone's forgiveness.

Then I requested healing and clearing for everyone's hunger, pain, humiliation, anger, and karmic release, with gratitude. Cathy saw he had put on weight and looked healthy. He thanked her and then integrated into Cathy's original soul.

I requested White Angel to show Cathy what she needs to learn from her book of life. Cathy said, "I see a big White Angel with a wand made of light in his hand and a big white book of life. In this book everything is written in golden light, like a hologram. The words were lifted above the pages. Ego and devil popped out from the pages of my book."

I prayed for clearing and aligning of her ego and devil within. As I was praying, Cathy saw devil busted into pieces and smoke went up to heaven. Then Cathy felt her pain begin to ease off and a warm loving energy was flowing in her back, neck, shoulders, and feet where there had been pain before. Cathy said, "I hope I will sleep at night, as I haven't been sleeping well for past few months."

January 26, 2010—HOLLY'S PARENTAL IMPRINTING SESSION:

I began with prayer requesting Angel to bring her little girl and parents. Her whole family came—her step-father, brothers, sisters, and cousins. They all had wings, but when Holly approached her mother, she opens her mouth and hissed. I told her she was possessed in many lifetimes including the present one. Through prayer, I requested Jesus and Angels to bubble (create a circle of light), remove and cleanse all of her lifetimes in all dimensions. We both saw bubble, after bubble, after bubble; a very long line of lifetimes were cleansed. She looked normal and took the garbage bag from Holly that was filled with anger, dependency, approval, guilt, fear, laziness, control, indecisiveness, money issue, fighting, etc. Then she went to her stepfather and her little girl said, "I feel sad because I know he is suffering with cancer."

I told her that every soul makes his/her choices when to exit and I suggest you get your own answers from him. Holly said, "He is saying, it is part of my path, but she is still sad because she loves him." I said, "Give him a hug and all your love. He will always be with you in spirit. This way, you will allow him to move forward because soul makes this choice prior to coming in this life." Holly saw her step-father was very peaceful, had wings and took the bag. Then Holly moved to her biological father and gave him his bag. I finished the prayer, requesting healing and clearing for everyone. Holly asked for forgiveness. After this, her little girl felt very comfortable and very eager to learn and grow. "Give her a hug," I said, "and bring her to your heart." I closed the session, thanking Jesus and His team of Light Beings.

January 30, 2010—LISA'S PAST LIVES HEALING SESSION # 1

Lisa had attended Emotional Healing Workshop in October 2009 and saw two past lives with her mother. In one, her mother was a queen and she was a young servant girl. The queen suspected her of having affair with king and treated her exactly how she treats her now, by keeping her away from her father, yet she wasn't having an affair. Prior to this life, they were sisters and she stole her boyfriend.

Lisa wrote: I am having issues with my current relationship and I asked my Angel to help me with these issues. Next morning, first thing that came to my mind was your name, as if someone had put your name in my mind. I was very clear about my Angel's message to come and see you.

I asked Lisa's permission to write her sessions in this book. She wrote: I am sure these experiences will help many others to understand how emotional healing through Angels works, and how important it is to find out about our past lives and heal them, otherwise the same emotions continue life after life.

During consultation, Lisa said, "I am having health, communication, and other emotional issues since I met my boyfriend four months ago. I knew there had to be a spiritual explanation for this because I am having flashbacks of being a nun in a place that looked like a convent."

I mentioned that she had lost a lot of weight. She replied, "My mother was visiting and I am almost allergic to her." I told her, you will have to make peace with your mother and then see where Angels will lead us to clear these issues.

I began the session with prayer. Angel brought Lisa to meet her little girl and parents. As she was filling trash bags, she saw and described, "I am dressed as nun, praying and walking in long, dark hallway of a convent. I feel like my heart is being squeezed. I'm feeling lonely, suppressed, and confused." I told her, she was in love with the priest and it was a lifetime in England. She wasn't sure, so Angel showed her. She saw all nuns were listening to a priest and he was teaching from fear; it was much suppressed teachings. I prayed to free all nuns from this old fear-based belief system in all dimensions. Lisa then saw she was left alone with the priest in a room. I told Lisa to talk to the priest, as she talked, she realized that they were in love and said, "I was fearful and did not want to leave the room. I wanted to stay with him. I could see that this priest is my boyfriend now."

After that, Lisa saw herself naked, locked in a tower somewhere and said, "I am handcuffed, hungry, skin and bones, and left alone as a prisoner. It is made of stones. I was sitting on the floor. It was very cold and she begins to cry profusely saying, "I never knew when my next meal and water is going to arrive." I told her things happen for a reason and this could have been your karmic debts meeting within.

Then Lisa said, "I see that I was exposed to the public in some sort of public area, naked, as someone who did something very wrong by falling in love with priest. People threw stones at me and the priest was transferred to another town. In the tower, where I was left to die alone, I could feel how cold, and hungry I was. They were feeding me sporadically. It looks like this happened somewhere in England, may be in 1700's. This helped me to understand why I am so reserved, so afraid to talk about my private life or share stories about my past relationships with my boyfriend. I am also afraid of other's judgment. I believe this is also related to this life."

I asked Lisa to approach this girl, hold her hand and tell her that you and her are same soul and Angels are healing us to make peace with this life by asking forgiveness from everyone, knowing that we must have planted a seed to create this experience. Then I prayed for healing and clearing of this life's trauma. Lisa saw the girl was no longer cold, naked, or hungry, but beautifully dressed and integrated in Lisa's higher Self. I told her that she will be processing this healing for a while.

Then we began to release parental imprinting. The bags were ready. Her mother's bag was almost completely full; Lisa adds the issue of being secretive. When she proceeded to give the bag, her mother said, "You treated me the same way."

Lisa saw a lifetime with her mother as sister. Lisa was very mean, jealous, and extremely negative to her because she was less attractive and stole her boyfriend who is her father now. Lisa said, "No wonder she kept me away from my father in this life so far." I sensed Lisa was possessed in that life. I requested Jesus to remove her possession through prayer, so she could return her sister's boyfriend and make peace with her sister. After that, her mother took the bag. Then I requested healing, clearing in all dimensions, with gratitude.

ALICE'S HEALING SESSION:

Alice is Cathy's eleven-year-old daughter. Like her mother, she was in much pain in her neck, back, and shoulders. When I began her session, she saw a beautiful play of rainbow color lights in motion, making beautiful designs. Then Angels brought her little girl and she said, "I am seeing a past life where people are praying to Jesus secretively, fearful of being caught. We gather together and pray, but my father got caught and they killed us all.

Cathy saw they were all hanged (I knew hanging causes a lot of neck and back pain that remains in cellular memory creating pain in following lives). I explained to Alice that it was a karmic life, so ask everyone's forgiveness. Then I requested healing for everyone, releasing them from their pain and karma.

She continued to see colors and told me that she has a lot of stress from school and homework. I said, "You start drawing these wonderful patterns in between your homework. It will relax you because "creativity in children is a meditation in adults."

Alice said, "I see Jesus smiling." I told her, these are his words and he is healing you. Alice said, "It seems like you were his mother." Angels continue to heal with her parental imprinting from fetus to eleven years of age because when Cathy was pregnant she had an accident with bad whiplash and another one when Alice was in a baby seat. Cathy has been in pain for past twelve years. So the Angels cleared Alice from all that. Alice began to feel less pain and her muscles loosened up. I closed the session thanking Angels.

February 1, 2010—My sister called and said, "My grandson (2 year old) had a very difficult seizure in his sleep because his parents forgot to give him medication. He was not looking good, as if he had lost all his energy."

I said, "Angel had told me how to do his healing by asking permission from his higher-Self. And clear his past life. I will do it now."

Next morning, after my prayer, I requested the Angels to bring his higher Self and I saw him come running. He held my fingers with his little hands and said, "Let's go."

I explained that Angels are taking him to heal his past life of Napoleon Bonaparte and he will face much devastation of human life done by his hands. You had no Self-esteem and used your anger and hate to control and destroy others. You paid this karmic debt in life, after life. Then I saw Napoleon. As we approached him, he didn't feel right. I requested Jesus to remove his possession through prayer. Then the Angel showed him his karmic destructive actions. I requested to bring in all souls from every dimension to hear his prayer of forgiveness, as I instructed him to kneel and pray. They forgave him and he made peace with this life. I requested healing and cleansing for everyone, thanking God, Jesus, and Angels.

My sister called and said, "I noticed instant change in him, the very same day. His color came back; he is smiling a lot and full of energy." Three weeks later, she gave me update on his health. His doctor took a brain scan with all kinds of wires attached to his head and he did not even cry as he did previously. His doctor found everything normal, reduced his medicine by one third and in six weeks he will take him off the medication. My niece was amazed to see day and night change in his personality. He doesn't cry and willingly goes to nursery school. He is a much happier and healthier child. My sister asked, "Will his seizures will return?" I told her, "It all depends on what level Angels had allowed this healing to take place."

February 5, 2010—Holly was telling me about her struggles in life. Jesus came through and said, *"If you believe in struggle, you struggle to believe."* Holly saw her parents struggling in all aspects of their lives. We released parental imprinting through Angels' process of healing and prayer. Holly said, "How am I going to accomplish what I have to do in this life?" I saw Hitler with his drive and determination to accomplish his goals and told her you have the same drive, but in the light, bringing hope and healing to many.

February 10, 2010—Holly: a message from Jesus: *Rekha, your spouse/husband is good, but from events of the past, it is not good for the commune of your two souls' pure energy. When you release him physically, removing the security and need, you, as an individual, will fly. Lessons/challenges will lead you to your answers. You cannot meet those who will carry our message if you do not reposition yourself.*

February 11, 2010—Lorna was apologizing for complaining about a lady who lived in her house without paying rent for over a year. She said, "I shouldn't be so angry about it and I feel bad expressing those feeling to you." I told her, "There must be a reason for this and maybe you need help to release these feelings. Do you want to know why this happened to you and what you did to her in your past life, so you can heal?" She agreed.

I did prayer and requested the Angels to show her why Lorna created this experience. Lorna said, "I am her mother and totally neglecting my daughter (four years old). Finally, I left her at this tender age with her grandmother." I told her, "Ask forgiveness from your daughter and forgive yourself, as you have paid your karmic debts to her." They made peace with each other by hugging and accepting. Then I requested for healing and clearing with gratitude. She felt good and less angry with this situation.

February 19, 2010—DAVID'S SESSION:

Nine year-old David came with severe depression. He didn't talk much, so I explained him about his parental imprinting and how he can clear it to feel better. He understood. I was telling him his behavior mirrors his parents' issues and asked his mother if she had been depressed. She told me about her childhood trauma that caused her a great deal of pain and depression. His father's issues were lack of communication, fear, and did not like to study. I could also see that he did not came willingly to see me, so I asked his mother if she was forced by her parents to do things that she did not want to do. She agreed, so we worked on these imprinting.

Through prayer, Angel brought him back to age five to release these issues. At first he wasn't able to see his little Self. I said, "What do you like—a dog, cat or what?"

He replied, "I like a Red Lamborghini." I told him to imagine you are in your car and driving it. Once he saw that, I told him to imagine his little boy, and he was able to see. "Talk to him and tell him what Angels are doing to heal him."

After his healing, he felt much better and began talking. His mother was relieved. I told them, it will take more than one session for his depression to heal.

February 23, 2010—David's mom called and booked his next appointment, stating he was fine for two days, but on third day he began feeling depressed again. This time I found a big change in him. He came willingly and he was talking to me. Angel showed me because of his depressed energies he attracted a depressed soul who had committed suicide in their house. This 40-year-old man possesses him with his depression. I needed to confirm this with his mother and she told me that David hears footsteps and voices.

I told David, "The Angels are going to bring this depressed soul to the light and free both of you."

I began the session with prayer and Angel brought David to meet his five year old. I told him to go to his house with his little boy and tell me what Angel is showing him. David replied, "He is sitting on his bed and there is a man about forty years of age."

I told this man. "Your life on earth is completed and the Angels are helping you to move into light." He left. I thanked the Angels. Then we did the parental imprinting that David didn't want to do in his first session. He was more willing this time.

Next, I prepared him and his mother as to what to expect in next session. I told them that depression is an inverted anger, and he will have a hard time with his anger because it comes from a past life. His mother replied, "He is already very angry and he is having nightmares of jumping off the building." I told her this is his past life of how he committed suicide in anger and frustration. And we will work to heal both these issues.

February 22, 2010—I received an email from my client in Canada. She wanted a session on the phone telling me that she had been feeling very tired, unable to sleep, and had pain all over her body, almost like Fibromyalgia. She goes to bed at 8 p.m., exhausted after putting her children to bed.

I told her that it sounded like a possession and asked if her neck, shoulders, and ankles are in pain. She replied, "Yes, but I did healing to clear it and felt better after that."

"It was temporarily removed, but came back, holding you from your neck and ankles." She wanted it removed.

I prayed, asking Jesus and the Angel for clearing and finished praying with gratitude. Right away, she started to feel very cold and tingling on her neck and shoulders and asked what exactly I did. I explained again and asked if she was feeling anything on her ankles. She replied, "No." We left it there.

Next morning she wrote: Dear Rekha,
Last night after talking to you, I brushed my teeth, pulled my cover, wrap around me, and got into bed to read, my arms were still very chilly.

About ten minutes later, my duvet-covered ankles did indeed start the same sensation, tingling and cold. It went on for about 15 minutes. My first six hours of sleep were blissfully dreamless.

Today, I have been aware all day of being in a state of grace; it is like an Angelic afterglow. I do feel so much lighter, unburdened, but also, everything today was effortless. All of my concerns melted away as the day arranged itself around me. Everything flowed on its own and resolved. And best of all, my two beautiful girls were SO light and happy. They played, danced, and giggled themselves all the way to sleepy time. Thank you for your generous spirit. I feel there is a golden thread I can pick up and hold onto. A warm hug!

April 8, 2010—HOLLY'S SESSION:

Holly wanted to work on her eating issue. Angels brought her five year old and I asked, "Why she is hiding behind food and using it as comfort? She can give it back to her mother so both can be free."

She did not want to listen and replied, "I like food; it makes me feel good." Her little girl wasn't even listening to Holly. She was controlling her parents by placing them in chairs and keeping them quiet, but no one was listening. I asked Angels, "What's going on?" and heard, "All of them are possessed."

I requested Jesus and Angels to remove everyone's possession and clear the whole family. Holly saw Amber sitting on top of the stairs. Behind her, hung their great grandfather's picture in their current house, indicating the cause of possession. When the energy got cleared, her little girl settled down and began to listen. Her parents stood up and all was quiet. She filled up garbage bags with tons of parental imprinting, including impulse eating. I requested healing and clearing. We thanked Jesus and his Angels.

Next day, Holly said, "We removed great grandfather's picture from frame and burned it then we sage the house, clearing residual energies."

April 9, 2010—I asked Holly to channel information about healing **Autistic children:**

Jesus: *Holly is filled with fear of failing these children. She is concerned with liability issues and offering false hopes unintentionally. Rekha is equipped to be guided to heal these children. Healing will take place quietly. Do not verbally offer bigger than what can humanly be accomplished. Allow them to be placed in our hands and us to do the unearthly healing.*

Rekha: Do many people bring possession at birth from previous lives?

Jesus: *Possession in itself is lesson. It requires a removal from one's Self to gain awareness of loss of "Self." Then soul entity must begin the fight for surviving as one "Self," as opposed to multiple selves. This is just another way of gaining authenticity and the Self. Shifting to next step then would require removing the unauthentic selves; hence, the word exorcism, hence the miracle happening through people, hence the community and unity. Only through humanity do true miracles happen. Anything that you allow as a hold on your authentic selves is a possession. One must lose ego to create connection.*

[This was new information to me that all negative emotions are possessions as they block our authentic Self.]

CHAPTER 11

CONTINUATION
OF HEALING SESSIONS

March 31, 2010—HEALING EXCHANGE WITH DORIS USING CRYSTALS:

I went to Doris' house. She had many crystals and I was guided to use them. I placed them where the crystals wanted to be. Doris looked at brown Granite placed on her third eye and said, "This one is for the root chakra." I said, "No, this one wants to stay on your third eye."

I began with prayer. Doris instantly saw a spiral energy expanding infinitely. I requested the Angel bring her little girl and I asked, "What were Angels showing you?" She saw a lot of children with frozen smiles on their faces. I told her to find the one who is not smiling. Doris found an older boy trying to hide behind young children. She asked him to show her what was going on! He brought her to a tall scary man. I told Doris to talk to this man. She tried to talk to him, but he let out a hideous laugh. Doris was judgmental, reactive, telling me to get him out of there quick. He is very ugly.

I told her, "That is you, your dark spark. You can't get him out until you heal it, for he is within you." So she settled down. "He is possessed and I need to request Jesus to clear him." After that, he became calm and sat down, but trying to get up, so Doris said, "Rekha, quick, give me my crystal wand." She pointed at him and he sat down.

Crystals amplify the energies of our intensions. I told Doris, "Tell him what he has done to these children and how he treated them that they are so unhappy, scared, sad, and helpless, yet smiling out of fear. Teach him how to ask forgiveness. He said, "No one ever loved me."

I told Doris, "Place your hand on his heart and send him your love." Doris was hung up on his ugly looks. I told her, "Accept it, because he is you." Then I requested healing and clearing for the children. They got unfrozen, happy and forgave him, then lifted into the heavens.

The older boy was still standing there. He asked, "Why did she take me away from my parents?" I explained, "Because in that lifetime she did not have awareness that she has now and allowed possession to take over. That was a part of her learning, but now Angels are changing it." Then Doris made peace by hugging him and returning him to his parents.

Doris was so excited, saying, "For the first time, my vision was so clear and I can see my spiritual growth in past eight months." I told her the Granite did that.

June 21, 2010—Doris did Reiki on me. She stood at my head doing Reiki and saw energy flowing from my left brain to right brain, balancing it. She moved to my left arm and saw me with a group of women playing and having fun. Then she moved to my left upper leg. She saw me climbing a rocky mountain, but looking back as if waiting for someone to accompany me. Then she moved to my feet and saw a huge, bright, yellow butterfly, flapping her wings in a very slow motion, saying, "It is beautiful bringing you joy, love, prosperity, transformation, and Sun Shine in your life. Then on the right leg, she saw me as a leader, dressed up in a white gown with a big crowd. Upper leg, she saw me swimming peacefully—a peaceful smooth path.

In another session, Doris was complaining that she felt depressed, tired, lazy, and did not feel like doing anything. I requested the Angel to show her who was depressed in the family. She answered, "Both my parents."

Angels brought her inner child and when I questioned her little girl, she kept running away, not answering us. I said, "You'd rather not face the situation. When you don't like something, you prefer to run away. Who behaved like this?" She told me that was her mom. Angels healed and cleared this parental imprinting from her DNA and we thanked them.

To Doris' disbelief and excitement, she called in the evening saying, "I have been busy doing things non-stop since you left this afternoon. I have finished everything and still have energy to keep going." I told her to thank the Angels.

LINDA:

July 8, 2010—Doris and I went to see our friend, Pat, a psychic reader. Pat needed to cleanse her friend Linda's house, but the entity was playing with her mind, changing her personality. When I was praying to Jesus for Linda's clearing, Doris joined us and saw a possession being removed from her husband. It was trying to go back, but Doris told him to go to the Light and he left. A few hours later, Pat received a call from Linda, totally changed and positive, to her disbelief. Doris couldn't wait to see changes in her husband.

Then I went to Doris' house, Angel wanted me to do Reiki on Doris, so I began to relax her body by gently pressing on her shoulders. Doris said, "Oh it hurts. It's supposed to relax me, not hurt me." I told her that I knew why it hurts and asked, "Do you have pain in your neck and shoulders?" It almost feels as if you are carrying a monkey on your back.

Doris replied, "I always feel something on my back, but why do you ask?" I told her, "You have had a possession for a long time and are not aware of it. They are very sneaky and move in and out of different places in the body."

Doris' funny nature kicked in saying, "Not sneaky enough to hide from Rekha!" We laughed and I said, "Many people are walking around with possessions and have no clue why they are in so much pain." Then I prayed to Jesus for clearing and did Reiki, closing the session with gratitude.

Next day, Doris called and told me about the changes in her husband, saying, "His eyes are clear blue and for the first time he saw birds flying, wondering why everything is so bright."

Pat called and said, "Linda turned negative again, I was suppose to cleanse her house, but now she is telling me she will do it herself." I told Pat the possession had taken over again, so wait till she asks you to cleanse her house. Then call me an hour before, so I can request Jesus' clearing to clear the whole family. That way, you can cleanse her house and send the entity to the Light.

July 19, 2010—Pat called and told me that Linda and her mother came to see her for readings over the weekend and she was leaving in an hour to go cleanse her house. In the reading, she saw this guy, Timothy, who was the previous owner and had died, but never left. He was living in the garage. In the past week, Linda found her garage was upside down, as if a hurricane went through it. Her garage door was always breaking down. Twice, she brought in holy water bottles and, as she set them on the counter, they broke. Her glasses were flying out of the cupboards and her mother witnessed it.

As Pat was telling me all this, I heard in her voice, "Shut up!" It was totally out of the context so I ignored it. Then I heard it again. Right away, I knew that it wasn't Pat. I told Pat stop speaking, because the possession is coming through your voice and I need to clear you first.

She goes, "Oh Rekha, you are scaring me."

I said, "You can't be scared if you are to do this work. It is simple to understand when you do a reading, you get into your client's energetic field and it is very easy for a negative entity to remain in your auric field. That's why we need to clear ourselves after every client. When Jesus first cleared your friend, Timothy got mad because his cover was blown, so he began to create chaos." Then I requested Jesus' clearing for everyone in Linda's family and told Pat to go and do the physical cleansing and send him to the Light because he is ready to move on.

Pat updated that everything went very smoothly and the guy left. Thank God, for now there will be a peace in the family and in her friendship.

July 22, 2010—Jill gave me information for Doris' next healing. I met Jill in May 2010. She came to see me for her anxiety issue. She is a gifted healing facilitator, Akashic record reader, clairvoyant, and receives channeled information from Jesus and the Angels. She needed to work on her emotional body and I needed to work on my past lives, so we agreed to work together. During our sessions, Jesus began to teach us an advanced method of healing, while healing us at the same time. Jesus' advanced healing through prayer will be written in Book 2. Jesus taught us about male and female dominant genes in DNA and how to reverse it. He told me that Doris needs this reversal.

Doris called and I told her that she had male dominant genes in her DNA. That is why she couldn't conceive a child. The Angels will switch it. When we began her session, Doris told me that she remembers in her childhood people use to say what a cute boy she was. She use to say, "I am not a boy" and grew her hair longer. Her mother wasn't very feminine either. I requested the Angels to reverse these genes from her fetus' DNA, balancing right and left brain. While I was praying, Doris saw herself as a fetus gently floating, then Angel took DNA out of its stomach and when it was reversed, she saw purple, blue light with white in the middle. The fetus went through birth canal and out, full of light, and was looking at her. I told her. "Bring her to your heart" and she integrated into her heart. We thanked God, Jesus, and the Angels.

SONIA'S SESSIONS:

April 16, 2010—Sonia came for Angel's healing once a week, to work on her uncontrollable anger and rage towards her husband who cheated on her. During the first two sessions, Angels released her anger through parental imprinting. Sonia mentioned that she knows his mistress and wanted to get rid of her because she kept showing up in her dreams telling Sonia how angry she was with her. I requested Angels to bring her higher Self and told Sonia that you must have done the same to her in a past life and need to ask her for forgiveness. She did and the lady left and did not bother her again in dreams.

In her third session, she was shown a past life in Egypt—A rich and beautiful woman, but not happy with men, and having relationship with several men at the same time. One of them was her present husband. He was married to a lady who is his mistress now. But he loved Sonia the same way he loves her now. Sonia understood how she created her experience with this lady now. I told Sonia to approach the rich lady and ask her why she is so promiscuous.

The lady looked at Sonia and said, "Who are you?" Sonia felt her ignorance and sensed that she had no respect for herself or for men, and carries the same feelings now. I told the lady, "Sonia is there to heal these issues because you feel empty and angry within, but you are using control and power through wealth to feel good about yourself." The lady began to confess and was ready to heal. I requested Angels to heal and clear these issues in all dimensions, thanking them.

Sonia's anger was less explosive after every session. In the fourth session, her dark spark opened up, way back in cave age. She saw a mad man chopping something in anger and rage. She said, "I see nothing but barren land. It feels like he was outcaste from the society."

I was told he was possessed, requested Jesus to clear him. Then told him to ask for forgiveness from all the souls he was angry at, so they could free each other. Then I requested the Angels to bring all souls from every dimension. They made peace and I requested clearing with gratitude. Amen.

Sonia returned for one more session because she had a fight again with her husband. In this session, she saw herself with a team of boys who were pick pockets and the ringleader was her husband. He treated them harshly and took all their money. I told him that he was creating a lot of karma and must ask for forgiveness. When the ringleader realized that, he felt guilty and was begging for forgiveness.

Sonia said, "It is exactly how he had been asking me to forgive him now. But the young boy (Sonia) would not forgive him." I had to convince the boy why it was so important to forgive because you chose this experience to pay your karmic debts from another life. If you don't accept this and you cannot forgive, it will repeat, life after life. It took a while, but the young boy eventually forgave him and they hugged each other. Sonia felt her anger towards her husband disappear. Finally, she felt peace within. Amen.

CINDY'S SESSIONS:

May 14, 2010—Cindy came once a month for Angel's healing sessions. In first couple of sessions, Angels cleared her biological parental imprinting and adopted parents' learned behavior, making peace with them. Angel showed her why she chose this experience to learn her lessons. She understood that roles had been reversed in this life with her adopted parents. In the second session, Angels removed her possession that was causing neck and back pain for almost thirty years. She was relived.

In this particular session, she still did not feel quite peaceful. She was feeling helpless, afraid, and unable to speak her truth or stand up for herself. I requested the Angels to show Cindy where these issues began. Cindy saw a lifetime in a small village outside of Israel and said, "I am a young boy, standing by the water well where people gather to hear Jesus' stories from his disciples. There are two of them. The older one is John, who is instructing James. The boy was happily being with them, listening to stories."

I told her to move forward and see what happened next as he grew up. Cindy described, "Now he is old and in rags. He is poor, but all his needs are met. He is so happy to do God's work and he is preaching unconditionally without any concern of worldly gains. Now I see **Jesus** is here saying, *"Because you did your work with such love, total devotion, and Selflessness to uplift other souls, I am balancing out all of this life's suffering and pain. Healing every issue you mentioned earlier. The veil of sleepiness is lifting from all, and souls are becoming awakened."* Then Jesus blessed her. Amen.

May 21, 2010—Cindy told me that after her last session she was flying in clouds for the next two days, but today she wanted to know why she feels this disconnection with God. Although she feels moments of connection, she still feels disconnected. She wanted to have a continuous connection as she felt in Jesus' lifetime. She wanted to know how she could get that back.

I began with prayer and the Angels showed her a past life as 13-year old, Jewish boy. He was extremely devoted to his Jewish religion. He was in a place where many bunk beds and many people were around him. It looks like a concentration camp and he is about to go in the gas chamber the following morning. He is very confused and praying, but does not understand why God would do that to him. He is angry at God, blaming God. In blame and anger, he is disconnecting his belief, trust, and faith in himself and in God.

I told her to talk to this boy and tell him he brought this experience by his own hands. It is not created by God's hands. It is his karmic debt from another life that he is meeting within. Does he understand the law of Karma? He nodded in agreement. Then I ask the Angel to show him what he did to other souls and created this suffering. Cindy saw herself as a Roman Captain way before Jesus' era and horribly treating slaves by beating and kicking them, making fun of them. Showing them food then throwing it on the ground for animals to eat. He starved them to death. I felt he was very angry, full of rage and hate. Therefore, he allowed possession to work through him and would not listen.

I asked Cindy if she see darkness in his eyes and she nodded. I began praying to Angels for removing and clearing his possession, but it did not work because as we were talking to him he turned his back as if he was not interested in what I wanted him to do. I quickly realized that I forgot to call upon Jesus. Without his help, possession cannot be cleared. So I prayed again and Jesus cleared it. Then I told him he had created a lot of karma by hurting these helpless souls and meeting within in concentration camp. The Roman Captain fell on his knees and said, "I had no one, no family or friends or loved ones."

Upon hearing this, Cindy said, "Ironically I have the same feelings in this life."

I explained that these feelings have served you well in this life because you chose love and searched within for your answers, but as the Roman Captain, you chose from your ego, ignorance, anger, control, hate, greed and power allowing possession to take over. There is God's perfection in every experience, as negative energy propels us towards light. He understood and was ready to ask for forgiveness. I requested all souls from all dimensions be sent to hear his prayer for forgiveness.

They all came and Cindy said, "Please forgive me for I used my ego, power and ignorance, I did not know what I was doing to you. I did it to myself. And I did not know any better because my consciousness was not advanced enough to know this." Then, through prayer I asked for healing and karmic release by changing the lifetime, thanking Jesus and His Angels.

Cindy was back to the young boy; he understood why he and others created their undesirable experience and was ok with going to gas chamber. They all went through their physical death and came out in the other dimension.

Cathy said, "He is confused again!"

I said, "Now we have to ask for their healing and clearing of the entire group." After I finished praying and thanking, **Jesus spoke:** *"The healing WE just did, lifted the veil of sleep from four generations of people living on earth today. Because that has been a thread of that consciousness of anger, confusion, insecurities, condemning God, being a victim of God's wrath, and lack of anything and everything. That veil has been lifted from earth. These are all souls of my generation from that time forward have been cleansed. They will have Self and Selfless love. This is the key to freedom. They all are one; they vibrate in 'Oneness'."*

We thanked Jesus for his blessings for all souls. Amen.

May 28, 2010—Cindy returned for her monthly session and I began with prayer. Cindy described, "I see myself with Jesus, Melchizedek, and Archangel Michael. They are in a cave in Himalayas. They are telling me that I am one of them and treating me like we are buddies. Melchizedek is answering my question that I had asked in my meditation, 'Why I have chosen such a lonely, being alone, and different path in my life?'"

Melchizedek: *This is a meeting of the mind with your Sprit. The most important thing to know is that it is a singular path of going within. Outer things are illusion and reflection to understand about your deeper part. Karma is not important because Christ elevated all humanity's karma. Then more karma was created as you are birthing through your energy by your intentions and choices.*

Cindy: Why do we have an issue of not being able to meditate?

Melchizedek: *When you have intent and sit quietly, focusing on your energy to flow within, you are rebooting your energies. It is sufficient and equal to meditation.*

Cindy: Why does it have to be such a lonely journey and it is so alone that I can't connect to anyone anymore?

Melchizedek: *This is important because it is a very personal and private path to follow. Healing lifetimes of very dark sparks are very heavy energy is like carrying armor on your back, although one can get rid of them in any instant, a few sparks at a time.*

Rekha: How?

Melchizedek: *If you ask your Angel to reveal your journey through the past and the karmas that are attached to you from that past life, they will drop off like going through an electromagnetic car wash. You are almost to a point where all debt karmas and negative sparks are opening up to heal and integrate into your higher Self. Duality is at the tipping point where all negative karmic debts of all souls are showing up in their lives to be dealt with. This can be a beginning of this balanced consciousness. Every soul has to clean themselves as quickly as they can by doing personal work on the SELF. Anything that you clean in yourself, you clean in others. It is a Law of Oneness—A source of Divine Gift. Cindy, WE do a lot of work with you in the dream state, but right now you have some beliefs that are preventing your growth. You need to work and clean them:*

1. *Focusing on "Self" instead focusing on others.*
2. *Not to feel guilty about the past.*

Then they begin to walk away. I said, "Wait, aren't you going to clear her from these issues?" They smiled and said, "That is your job," and left. Then I requested the Angels to heal and clear her issues from parental imprinting and learned behavior with gratitude.

May 26, 2010—HEALING EXCHANGE WITH KIM:

Kim begins her session, saying, "There are so many Angels and they all wanted to talk, but the one coming through is so big that my arms feel so heavy by his energy."

I told her that he is **Archangel Michael**. He said, "You have helped so many and as you continue to do so, you must take care of yourself by clearing your energetic field from all debris, through intention and prayer."

ARCHANGEL MICHAEL'S ATTUNEMENT:

You are to give Angelic attunement to people who come to you in teacher's training class, by placing your hands as Angel's wings on the back of their head, requesting Michael to begin rising gold and white Divine lights as spiral energies from your root to crown chakra moving into their crown to root. Stay there for few seconds and then start with another thread of Divine love and light's color pink intertwining with white and gold from your root to crown into their crown to root. Let it flow back and forth 3 times, connecting each other with Love, Light, and Oneness. Then gently touch their Crown Star Chakra (about 1 foot above the Crown) to lock the energy in. And then finished attunement with gratitude.

Michael: *Now I have given you "Angelic Attunement." It will happen naturally. Some need this attunement when their soul is more lost and they are not connected. They will end up noticing their soul a lot more and become aware of their soul's agenda. You can use it in your healing session as well.*

Rekha: Why is Cathy still in pain?

Michael: *Cathy fell back into her old patterns. She babied her back. She needs to stretch her back by someone pulling her feet. She is giving power to her pain.*

Rekha, wear a silver scarf and place silver sheets for dark energies to reflect back into Divine light. You are walking the walk very well.

TUNING FORK THERAPY:

Begin filling the right side of the body with 'Lime Light,' then move through the left side, up to the fingertips and toes, bathing the whole body, as the Angels go through the entire body cleansing them at the DNA level. After 'Angelic Attunement,' do this to raise their vibration using a tuning fork.

You will be very busy, that is why your own clearing, cleansing, and fine-tuning through prayer or meditation is very important for your growth to be more than you are. Book your clients with a 15-minute break in-between. Take 5 minutes for yourself, for your clearing. After the New Year, keep in balance.

Then I asked if Jesus would allow me to reveal to Kim who I was. Kim said, "Wait, Jesus is here and the love He carries I have never experienced before. He is so gentle and in a soft voice He is saying, '*She is Mary.*' He is coming around behind you wrapped his arms and hands on your heart, hugging you."

All of a sudden my tears began to flow.

Jesus: *The tears are of joy and love for the work you are doing for our Father. He is very proud and saying, "In this life, finally, she got it.*

Kim: Now he is putting his hands on top of your head as an attunement and kissed your head saying, *"My sweet child, you got it."*

Rekha: I thanked Him.

Kim: I am seeing your past lives, but they went by very fast, so I couldn't read them. But now they have slowed down and the Angels are showing me your future. The Angels are placing a pink rose crown on your head. There will be total of four books with new information, new healing techniques, and new experiences. You will be speaking in front of people.

I thanked Jesus, Angels, and Kim.

KIM'S SESSION:

I asked about her issue and what she wanted to heal. Kim replied, "I had a problem in childhood and now, people I know, especially my family, have a hard time believing in my gift." I began with prayer and the Angel brought her 3-year old, inner child. She was scared. I told her not to be afraid because Angels are with her to clear her issue.

Kim saw a past life in Europe. She was doing healing work but, her ego got in her way and purity left, so she was faking and telling people things that were not true, treating people with herbs and potions that were not working. When they questioned her, she would tell them another herb will work and give them poison. These souls are her family now and they don't believe her, but now she is in the Light and doing work from her heart. The dark past had served her well. I requested the Angel to bring all these souls who suffered from her ego and ignorance. She asked everyone's forgiveness to free from karmic bond. I requested Angels heal, clear, and change this lifetime. Amen.

Then the Angel showed her another life and she saw a woman with her older son doing prayers and fire ritual. In this life, she was serving the Light and helping many to heal, but her husband did not believe in her and turned her in. Her son (he is her son now) believed in her because he had spiritual gift of inner sight as well. She saw the army burst open her door and capture her. Her son was devastated and was telling them that she was not evil, but they condemn her and killed her. The Angel healed and changed this lifetime as well. Amen.

Then the Angel showed her another life where she had inner sight, hearing, and knew things, but kept it to herself and didn't do much with the information. She learned her lesson well as she kept quiet about her gift and did much growth within, instead of diluting her truth by telling others who did not understand. The Angels healed this life, so now she can speak her truth. We closed the session with gratitude to God, Jesus and the Angels. Amen.

Kim reported instant changes in her family members. Her brother who never believed in her had a Reiki session with her and wanted to help her in her work. She was amazed to see changes in the same day.

June 19, 2010—CHANNELED READING WITH ANN:

Ann wrote: *Because you are close to me, you take care of your Sprit. Make sure you take the same care of your body with rest. The world will try to intervene, but hold your course. What you do is a Miracle and should be treated as such—a modern miracle, if you will. The time will come when more and more will need this. You will be a teacher of races, not just students alone. Take care of your physical Self to do this work. Energy work is all well and good, but the physical care is also of paramount importance. Rest, eat well, and work on your meditation. Take time to connect with nature. When was the last time you really listened to the songs of birds? Release all doubts that may be hidden, to ME. It will be washed away by the water of life that flows from ME.*

You are listening with your heart, but listen with your ears also. People speak in various tongues and WE will help you discern in truth from deception. Be vigilant at all times. In a span of time, one will appear who will add, not subtract from you. The world is preparing you both. Hold your faith. What is due will be done. Amen.

July 1, 2010 GINA'S SESSION # 10

My friend, Gina, came after a long time to catch up with our new growth and experiences. I told her that Jesus want us to have channeling session with Him. She said, "Ok." We talked for a while and then began the session with prayer. This time, it felt like Gina didn't have to leave her body at all. She was consciously aware of everything, telling me her physical body was with her where ever she is moving. She described, "I am riding in an escalator of light and it keeps going through clouds. The clouds are the interpretation of dimensions. So we are just traveling this beautiful escalator of Light that just keeps on moving from one dimension to another but very smoothly, peacefully and lovingly."

"As we continue to ascend, the clouds change colors. The colors start from dark pink, getting lighter and lighter until it blends into dark blue, making the shades and combinations of colors that have no name. When you enter a new dimension it becomes a very interesting color that I have never seen before. It continues because there are many dimensions, infinite in number. I am with my guardian Angel. She is dressed in white, satiny, flowing gown and her skin is translucent. She is very tall with huge, white wings. Her hair is blonde and she has piercing blue eyes, just like when Jesus comes, he has the same blue eyes. As they are saying, it is the same energy.

"We have stopped where there is a Violet Flame, it is fifth dimension. They took me there because violet flame is now active on the planet earth. This energy is from many masters including Jesus, Angels, Edgar Cayce, Albert Einstein, Thomas Edison, etc. (Collective Consciousness). There are many masters sitting side-by-side in a circle. In the center of this circle it is like a void, but it's really not a void because it's a direct connection to third dimension, so we can relate to what they are doing."

"They each have golden fishing rods and the hook is made of diamonds. They all have kind of hooked the entire earth so the planet is literally, being attached by their hooks and they are slowly, gently, and lovingly reeling it at the same time. They are lifting the planet with all her inhabitants and at the same time, raising vibrations. There are also imprints of the planet that stay in lower vibration because not all of the inhabitants will be able to tolerate and accept high vibration. This way, nobody gets lost. They have prepared imprints of the planet with all its conditions so these vibrations of the planet match the vibrations of people that haven't been able to tolerate the higher vibration."

"It's very interesting seeing them sitting around in circle, very relaxed, but saying to us, 'We've got you' as they are reeling in together."

"As the planet rises and goes into different positions, this is what is causing the earthquakes, snowstorms, hurricanes, volcano, tsunami and all it's breaking down things that do not support that vibration. There is a lot of shifting taking place in the planet, creating natural disasters."

"They are all sitting there and smiling, saying, '*There are only two energies that are present right now and always have been: The energy of fear with all of its emotion because fear is the core energy that creates doubt, confusion, greed, anger, anxiety, guilt, lack, and separation. And the energy of love that gives you freedom, joy, gratitude, and humility*'."

Rekha: Is it true, in order to clear emotional body, we must clear all our negative fragments of soul?

Collective Consciousness: *That is the goal: To really go into the deeper core and ultimately find how you created fear. It's like layers of onion; you peel one at a time. Then you have the next layer/level and next and so on. When you peel all layers, what you find in the deep core is LOVE. Fear manifests as anxiety, doubt, worry, confusion, greed, guilt, jealousy, envy, control, anger, and hate. The key is that all of your karma and emotions that need to be cleared are locked into your emotional body.*

Rekha: If original soul divides into 12 fragments, do half of them choose darkness and other half, light?

C.C: *There are definitely 12 fragments of one original soul and the original soul makes it number 13. You can say that and it is not entirely a false statement, but when your first fragment came to the planet, to this consciousness, to do your work; it started with very basic consciousness. So it is not really about six dark and six light. It is about the development and evolution of consciousness. So you came as a very basic, very low frequency and as you grew and evolved, your vibrations kept shifting. And when you expand your consciousness, then you have free will and make your own choices.*

You are provided with certain challenges and experiences where your soul needs to make a choice from fear/darkness or from love/light. At the same time, you have accumulated so much negativity, which is what you are clearing in this consciousness in this lifetime. You have expanded your perceptions, growth, and inventions, etc. You have become more, so there are more souls, more interaction, and more exposure to the material comforts and other choices. This is all part of learning lessons because there is nothing wrong or right. Even Hitler or Napoleon, any of those dictators who caused mass genocides, still hold a place in their heart, per say, because although that soul chose much darkness, out of darkness came a lot of awareness to other souls.

Rekha: Who is speaking through Gina?

Gina: I am in the presence of all the masters and they are from Collective Consciousness. They are all sitting in a circle, as if they are sitting at the banks of a pond and in the middle is a beautiful violet flame swirling in a very gentle and smooth speed with golden fishing roads and diamond hooks. It's not water, but a beautiful energy field.

Rekha: What is wrong with Melanie?

C.C: *Melanie's physical manifestation is the physical body bringing in awareness for what hurts. Her emotional body is congested. She has been doing a lot of work on herself for many, many years and she is like a volcano. The energy is building up, building up because she is doing a lot of work and it hasn't been totally released. Now, it is at that point of eruption period. The interesting thing is that most of this accumulation is all the lessons that she already learned.*

Rekha: She thinks that she is having food poisoning. Is it true?

C.C: *No. What is poisoning her is holding onto all of this stuff she already processed. Right now, she is at the breakdown phase so there could be a break through. Not everybody's breakdown and break-through comes in one breath.*

Rekha: Why haven't I been able to finish this book?

C.C: *Your book is not finished because there are new experiences new information and teachings that are coming to you now. You are going into a whole new place, a whole new space, and vibrations with new case stories and history of work. This is that part of integration because now you are at the closing part of this book. There is always a beginning, middle and end. Now, you are accumulating and you will be accumulating that cloth of material of people that have done a lot of work on their own and they are at this level.*

Rekha: I began this book thinking it's Archangel Michael's teachings, but it changed to Jesus' teaching.

C.C: *Well! It is Archangel Michael's work and teachings. His energies are motivating and bringing in the people and guiding you, but He doesn't have to physically manifest for you or for His book. His work* *will continue. Remember, there has been a shift in consciousness, so it doesn't necessarily mean that it depends on his presence. Dependency creates a lack of freedom. We are dealing with really shifting all of the conscious condemnation. It is not necessary for him to come at all because that is limiting you. You need to let go of that preconception and just let it flow naturally.*

You are tripping your third dimensional mind. Although you don't live in third dimension you still have your work there and you still function and are affected by third dimensional consciousness. So any thought you have that this is "dependent on" or this is "what has to happen," just creates limiting energies.

Rekha: Then I certainly have to make some changes in this book.

C.C: *No. You don't have to change anything because that was a consciousness in the timeline where you can incorporate and assist others doing this work. You started with a certain set of vibrations and perceptions that changed and grew so expansion-ally. What is happening is that it has shifted and changed the timeline.*

We are even in awe with everything that is going on because you are shifting so rapidly. More and more of you are becoming aware and when one awakens, it makes the Light stronger. Don't be fooled by the illusion because there is more Light in the planet and in your life than darkness.

The main key here is to work on your emotional body to release all of the pent-up and built-up accumulated karma through eons of time. As you clear and balance your emotional body, your physical bodies will cease to have disease. Your physical body is a physical manifestation of what is going on in your emotional body.

In Melanie's case, for example, her fatigue, her tiredness is because she is emotionally drained. She has put herself in a place where she cannot give anymore. She has neglected herself. Her physical manifestation is showing that it cannot go on anymore. Everything is totally out of alignment.

Rekha: Will Jill and I work together for a while? She is amazingly gifted.

C.C: *She is very gifted as long as ego does not get in her way. And you cannot destroy your ego; it is your personality destroying your third dimensional body. Soul is a connection with your heart, the Love source, instead of your mind (ego).*

Rekha: Do I have many dark sparks from past lives to work on?

C.C: *There is still a residual of emotional energy because you have done a lot of work and now it is about clearing residual energies of resentment and sense of loss coming from separation and devastation of the role of mother and child.*

Rekha: When did that happen to me?

C.C: *With Jesus, because you have to understand that you played the role in a very human way so you still have that residual anger of "you are destroying my child." You felt loss of your child on the cross and that loss of unfairness that do we speak truth—Fear of speaking your truth. Shift it till it is gone. Residual energy means it is not the energy of that emotion; it is the holding of energy that can create the same experience again. Remember clearing, clearing, clearing, and when you have cleared all of those emotions, then you liberate the physical body as they become lighter.*

Rekha: Is it true that Jesus didn't die and continues to live in his perfectly healed physical body!

C.C: *Jesus was the perfect example of ascension process. This is what we try to instill: that there shouldn't be any fear because he was so pure, even though his physical body was so badly damaged and hurt, his essence or his soul was able to transcend all by going to a higher plane of consciousness and reclaim his physical body. So he was able to shift energy fields in light body to have physical body when he needed to do physical body's work that required a body. This is the process of ascension. This is going to happen to you. You will be able to be in your light bodies and also claim your physical body when you need to do the work that requires physicality. It won't be diseased and it won't be damaged. It will be a perfect vehicle to accommodate your light body.*

Rekha: Mary knew who Jesus was. He came back in his physical body after crucifixion and told all of us to leave Jerusalem.

C.C: *Yes. Because at that time, humanity was not ready for such a profound message, so they needed to really exile themselves to other areas where nobody knew about them. Unfortunately, WE say, the book that you call The Bible has been so, so filtered and altered by egos that a lot of truth that was written is hardly there. There have been too many distortions.*

Rekha: When Mary knew all this then, why would she be so attached with this mother-child separation issue?

C.C: *Because she was going through the physical trauma experiencing pain, anguish, and loss. Her emotional body absorbed everything, even after the fact that her son was there. That trauma created an imprint of that experience in her cellular memory and it recorded into DNA. The anger of that entire experience is worked out, but this is the residual. As you peel the layers, this is how you are getting your physical body to be more in alignment with your light body—by getting rid of all remnants of memory, imprints, and encoding that is within your cellular memory and DNA. It is like washing and replacing all those cells with the new vibration. Same thing is happening in your DNA's strands as you heal. We activate them because your physical body can tolerate the higher vibration of DNA. That is why moving and manifesting things is becoming easier by the power of intention. You will be able to accomplish more things and remember: you have to do it in a very balanced way.*

Rekha: Why do we create money issues?

C.C: *All of your needs are abundantly supplied for you. As you continue to grow and evolve and work from your heart, the money is totally attached to that energy of love, heart, and the Light. So it will automatically just flow. It is for this consciousness for now because when you evolve to another level, your different needs are being met with different things, as the energies comes into play. Remember the higher you vibrate, the quicker you create.*

Rekha: Could you please give guidance for Gina.

C.C: *To continue on her path. She is right on track with her ideas. We will continue to support her and guide her. We are very proud of the work she has accomplished for herself and for others. There are more gifts, talents and ability that are going to be downloaded for her in the weeks and months to come.*

VIOLET FLAME MEDITATION

Bask yourself with a beautiful violet flame energy. Connect to it daily. When you go into a harsh environment before you leave your sad faces, just allow yourself to be in a beautiful column of this Violet color flame. Know that your duet energy connection to us is to the cosmic consciousness because that is what you are right now—the cosmic consciousness.

Rekha: Will I ever be able to see again as I did as a child?

C.C: *As soon as you clear the residual energies, you will be able to integrate more of that kind of energy. Not as a child, but even more. Your abilities, your information, talents, gifts, downloading information, new opportunities, new growth, new mission, and the integration of vision, wisdom is happening everyday for you. So, yes, you will see, and then you will see with different eyes and different consciousness than you did as a child. So, no, you will not see as you were a child. You will see with the new eyes of this new child that you are now.*

Rekha: Do we all have intergalactic life as negative spark, as I did?

C.C: *You are multidimensional beings of Light. Light means you can exist in any plane of consciousness. You can travel through many universes and galaxies. These lifetimes are like holograms.*

Rekha: What about space ships and alien beings experimenting on humans?

C.C: *There are other planes of consciousness with many different life forms. Just because they don't look like you, it doesn't mean they don't create and are supported by the same source. They are going through the same challenges as the Earth-dwellers. Although you have healed your intergalactic life, there is always a residual. That is what we insist on—the emotional body is clear, but there is always a residual until to the point that all residual is cleared. Then only **love and gratitude** will exist in every molecule and every atom of your body. How to do this? Continue what you are doing, it's a natural process.*

Rekha: Does it take a long time?

CC: *Not necessarily. What is time, we ask you? It is a process and you must honor the process joyfully, gratefully, lovingly because it brings you experience that you would miss otherwise. It's not about destination; it's all about the journey. As some of you say, "Stop and smell the*

roses." Don't be so concerned about arriving at the destination. Be
focused and present and enjoy each moment as a gift.

WE say to Gina that WE are working and your tumor is being
totally and absolutely dissolved. She is on the right path. Remember:
as you purify yourself and you become higher vibrating energies, you
attract all of that which vibrates at that frequency. Your power of
creativity matches that vibration. You can create whatever world and
reality you want to create for yourself. The Universe provides infinite
amounts of creative energy for your use. It will never run out; it is
ever present. Worlds, universe, galaxies, dimensions of consciousness
are continuously being created.

Rekha: People think lack of money stops them from having what they
want.

C.C: *Then people have to understand the concept of money. Money is*
energy, the consciousness of an old belief system and thought forms/
patterns that needs to be changed, adjusted, and corrected. It is that
belief and thought form of money that money is the root of all evil.
That is not a true statement. Greed is the root of all evil; see the
difference. Money is energy; greed is emotion, that's the difference.
If you go along, doing what you do with love and gratitude, the
money will manifest. It is very simple and very basic, but you create
complexity by over-analyzing and making everything so complex that
you forget what the original question was!

Rekha: How are my son and daughter doing in their spiritual
growth?

C.C: *They are evolving; going through their challenges. More karmic*
experiences will be manifesting. There are more challenges, more
emotional congestion, and it is simply because they need to address
their emotional bodies. Everything is starting to build up and growing
in the emotional body. It is interesting that your planet is doing pretty
much the same thing. Within the next few years, as you call it in your
linear time consciousness, more earthquakes, more volcanic eruption,
and more floods will occur. There is going to be more of that because
the planet is gathering those entire negative emotions and expelling
them. You, each individual, are following the same vibration, same
map, and the same guidelines. You are building up negative emotions,

creating a forever-growing mountain and then come the eruption. What happens when there is an eruption? Everything gushes out hot, lots of destruction. Then everything calms down and goes back to peace and healing and beauty takes place.

Rekha: May I have your last words of guidance for us!

Collective Consciousness: *Stay focused, stay with the joy, and always stay in Love, Light, and Gratitude. Be grateful for all that you have because when you are grateful for all that you have, the Universe will gift you and bless you with more of the same.*

Rekha: Thank you so much for all your wisdom, understanding and love to teach us. Amen!

June 27, 2010 JOY'S HEALING SESSIONS:

Joy had attended a couple of Angel's workshops and asked for a session. She had many issues with her parents, especially with her mother, such as anger, control, guilt, and abandonment. She was having such a hard time accepting her mother's unloving treatment. I requested the Angels to show her what she did to her mother in a past life. Joy saw a past life—leaving her six children without any emotions or care. I told her to look at all these children; one of them has to be your mother. She said, "The oldest girl is my mother." Joy understood why her mother treated her so harshly and abandoned her. I told Joy to ask their forgiveness and make peace with your children by loving them. Then the Angel changed her past life and cleared it. After that, we worked on her parental imprinting and she was able to release many issues with her mother, thanking the Angels. Joy cried a lot, but said, "This session lightened my heart and lifted the heavy weight that I had been caring for such a long time." Amen.

July 4, 2010—Joy returned for her second session. She said, "I had been trying to meditate to reach the state of nothingness where there are no thoughts and I get very close, but never get there because my mind won't stop. It keeps on going." She was almost crying.

I said, "First of all, know that you are already there, but your mindset is telling you that you are not, so you keep experiencing that. The Angels will release your mindset." Then she talked about some personal issues, so I told her to wait and see how the Angels will resolve all of this.

I began the session with prayer and asked Joy to breathe deeply and get in touch with her feelings and knowing, and tell me what comes to her mind. She said, "Actually, there is nothing; it's empty, no thoughts, and I feel very peaceful."

I said, "This is the state you desired to achieve; enjoy it. How hard was it to get there?" She realized that it was always there and always will be.

Then we looked at Joy's issue that she mentioned earlier: Feelings of being rejected or not belonging, cast out, insecure, lonely, and alone. I requested the Angels to show her where these feelings were coming from. Joy said, "I am a young woman in the forest looking for food. I had no family, but a boyfriend who I loved and trusted. I am very gifted with healing and inner sight, but people in the village do not understand me and wanted to kill me. My boyfriend turned me in out of fear, so I was cast out and ended up in the forest to save my life. It's Europe and I will not survive in the winter.

I told her to talk to this young lady and tell her that you are her future incarnation and the Angels want us to heal this life. So turn around and ask forgiveness from all villagers and your boyfriend because it is karmic. She saw them all and they forgave her. As she did that, Joy saw this lady walk across the forest and end up in another village, working to support herself and keeping quiet about her gifts. She learned her lesson. We thanked Angels for healing and changing the lifetime.

Joy was so amazed that the Angels changed the experience because it was new to her. She said, "Otherwise, I would have died in the forest."

August 7, 2010—Joy called and said, "So many changes and much growth had taken place in a month." During consultation, I asked what she needed to heal. She replied "fear." I explained, "Fear is a very deep and often, the root of all negative emotions. It will clear in layers. So let's see what Angels want to show you to release layers of fear.

I began with prayer and requested the Angels to show Joy a life when her fear began. Her little girl didn't want to see. I told Joy, "The little girl has to trust that the Angels are with her and you must take total responsibility of her. Besides, there is nothing to fear because fear is an illusion.

She agreed and said, "Somewhere in Middle East; I see a woman buried in sand up to her neck and people are throwing rocks at her." I told her to talk to her and ask why she had been punished. Joy said, "She was a poor servant to a rich man and they loved each other, but it was a taboo in that society and she had to pay for it with her life." Joy wasn't sure if she was really seeing or making this up. I told her to believe in herself by feeling this woman's fear, guilt, anger, and hate. "If it resonates with you, then you are not making this up." She agreed.

I requested the Angels to show her why she created this experience. In another lifetime, Joy saw she was a daughter of rich parents with status in Europe's Renaissance time, dressed up with fancy clothes and hats. She was very arrogant, judgmental and insecure. A poor man without status loved her, but she couldn't care less and treated him like a dog, putting him down and being very mean to him.

I told Joy to look in her eyes and tell me what you see. Joy replied, "They are cold and black." I told her that I am going to request Jesus to clear her possession. She was shocked to learn about possession. I said, "Many people have it and do not know, but possessions are lessons for growth. They are agreements prior to birth." It began to make sense to her because she feels a negative sprit in her apartment.

After Jesus' clearing, I told her, "Accept his love because he is the same soul whom you loved in your Middle East lifetime. The Angels are going to change this life by you accepting him and giving him a hug." She was full of fear and was not able to give him a hug. I told her she can make a different choice by choosing love over fear. "Why so much fear?" I asked.

Joy said, "If I choose love, my parents will kill me."

I said, "It is your mindset, but you can change it all in this moment and face your fear." She got encouraged and told me "I am hugging him now, but my parents are screaming, telling me 'NO!' But we are happy and moving on to live our life together." We thanked the Angels.

Then we came back to buried woman and I requested the Angels to show Joy what she did to all these people who are punishing her. Joy saw a lifetime in Greece when she was the person in charge to sentence people to death by throwing them into the lion's den to be eaten alive. I told her to look in his eyes. She saw darkness and emptiness.

I requested Jesus to clear him from his possession. Then I told him that he is creating a lot of karma by hurting souls. He did not want to let go of his position because of his status, lifestyle and ego. Then I requested the Angels to show him the buried woman's life as his karmic consequences. He decided not to choose from his ego, ignorance, and, instead, live a humble life. He was ready to ask for forgiveness.

I requested that all souls come forward from all dimensions to hear his prayer. I requested the Angels to heal and clear them all. He then took a different position as a servant. Then we return to buried woman. She was very peaceful and in total acceptance. I requested healing, clearing, and changing all lives, thanking Angels.

September 4, 2010—Joy came for her fourth session. Initially, her purpose was to resolve karmic bonds with three women Laura, Cathy, and Erin. She experienced a lot of fear, helplessness, and anger with them. But during consultation, she was telling me her different needs, saying, "During meditation I still can't seem to quiet my mind. I am supposed to be an observer living in soul, not in my mind, and I almost achieve that state, but fear gets in my way and I would choke, gasping for air, abandoning my meditation."

I told her fear might be in her childhood or in a past life. Joy remembered. "When I was six years old, my family was on vacation at a swimming park. It had a large water slide. I climbed up to the slide with my dad and sat in front. Then we both went down the slide together. In the water he let go of me, as I watched him walking away because the pool was not very deep for him, while I was struggling to swim. I had been taking swimming lessons, but was still a novice. It was terrifying. I swallowed water and started coughing. Somehow I managed to dog paddle to the shallow end.

"Another experience in junior high gym class, I was hit in the chest with a volley ball. It knocked the wind out of me. I stood there for what seemed like forever before I could relax my throat enough to gulp some air."

I began her session with prayer and heard the Angel saying, something happened when she was four years old. So I requested the Angels to bring her four-year-old and asked what was going on? Joy replied, "Mom and dad are fighting and she didn't understand why. It was usually after kids had been put to bed. They would go in their room and start arguing, usually about money. This would have been about the time dad thought mom had an affair because my youngest brother was born with five years gap." I requested the Angels to clear her pattern of fighting and her fear as mother's imprinting, making peace with her mother. They were hugging each other.

Then she went to the waterslide incident and I asked to describe her feelings about her dad. Joy said, "I was very angry and felt it is dangerous to have fun or enjoy life or that experiencing joy always ends up badly. Until now, I always thought that it was my mom who tried to kill my natural happiness. Not deliberately, but she did not understand her own joy. My dad did not realize how it would undermine my trust in him and men in general."

I said, "Can you forgive your father to bring trust and joy back in your life. Tell him how much it hurt you and how afraid you were."

Joy: Yes. I am sitting safe on his lap with my arms around his neck, telling him not to do this again.

Rekha: But the Angel told me it was karmic, so I said, "Angel wants you to go back to a life before and see when you did something similar to your dad."

Joy was fearful and said, "No. I don't want to go there." So I told her that we wouldn't be able to peal another layer of fear.

Joy: No, no, we have to do this. I am seeing there is a swimming hole like a quarry filled with water and a tire swing hanging from a tree. There is a little boy (father) on the swing. I am a man standing on the bank watching my son. He is swinging out over the water, he let go and falls in water. I asked if he can swim to the edge.

Joy: No. Something is wrong. He isn't swimming, but splashing around and I can't go because I don't know how to swim either. [A feeling of despair, anguish, helplessness, fear and guilt came over her saying no man wants to see his son drown.]

I requested the Angels to change this situation by Joy knowing that she can swim and jumped in the water to save his son.

Joy: He jumped in and his son was hanging on to his neck as he was moving towards the edge of the quarry. Now we are hugging each other.

We thanked the Angels. Amen.

Joy returned for another session because she really wanted to clear the energy between Cathy and herself and wanted to know why Cathy treated her so badly when she was under her care. I requested the Angels to show Joy what she did to Cathy in a past life.

Joy said, "I am a warden of this old dark, damp dungeon with many prisoners, mainly women, walking up and down a row of cells carved from rock with bar gates. The women were crowded at the back of the cell because they were terrified of me as I torture them."

I told Joy that he was possessed and requested Jesus' clearing. I told him, "You must ask for forgiveness from all these souls you are hurting."

As I prayed, Joy saw a Divine Light rush in, opening every cell and freeing all prisoners. They were all hugging each other. Joy recognized one of them was Cathy. All women were leaving and he was standing there, thinking of his consequences of being beaten to death.

I said, "You leave with them." Joy replied, "It's not easy because I have a family."

I told her to go and get them. Joy saw him leaving in a boat with his family.

Next, the Angels showed her a past life with Laura as Joy wondered why she was so angry with her. Joy said, "We were sisters and I mistreated her and she was also there in the jailer's life with Cathy. I am apologizing and asking for forgiveness, but Laura is still reluctant to let her anger go." I told Joy that it is you who are not taking the responsibility for your own actions of what you did to her in the past, but only seeing what she did to you now. You are not accepting it and still blaming her. Joy understood and they hugged each other, making peace with both lives.

With Erin, she had competition issues. Joy saw that in a past life they were tribe leaders fighting with each other, killing to take over other tribe. Much bloodshed took place.

I explained that her soul is not in competition. Only their ego's control creates this illusion. Both of you look within and see Divine connection with all as 'ONE' energy and ask for forgiveness from each other and from all souls who perished during your fights. They all came and Angels cleared them in all dimensions. Joy and Erin put their swords and knives down, making peace. The Angels changed this life, as they continue living in peace side-by-side. We thanked God, Jesus, and the Angels. Amen.

Joy wrote: I understand now that I am responsible for all experiences I draw to me. They are based on my past life's personalities mirroring back to me. The body may change lifetime to lifetime, but the soul involved does not. If I am having a hard time in this life with someone, I may well have been giving them the hard time in a past life.

★   ★   ★

These are some of Jesus and His Angels' healing sessions. The Angels teach us to look at life's experiences from soul's agenda and the lesson that experience is teaching us for our soul's growth, instead of looking at it negatively. Life's lessons are learned within the "Self." Life moves you because you are the lesson in your life. Angels' interactive healing leads you on a Journey back to your "Self." Asking for forgiveness is the key to find "Self Love." Love is the core essence of the Self and connects us in Jesus' heart. Every day is a new beginning with new learning, creating more Love and more joy, as Jesus and His Angels continue to teach and heal on deeper levels for all of us.

Jesus: *Every end has a beginning. This is a must because every beginning has an end, only to begin again. This is a cycle of LIFE, from the largest being to the smallest circumstances. It all changes and shifts, but humanity holds on tightly, trying to understand it all. In the end, you must understand that you are here to learn to just BE. From here you begin.*

"In Jesus' holy name I request protection, clearing, and blessings for knowledge, wisdom, teaching, and healing provided in the entire book. Amen."